D0848045

The Shape of Hawthorne's Career

The Shape of Hawthorne's Career

NINA BAYM

813
H
c.1

Cornell University Press | Ithaca and London

First published 1976 by Cornell University Press.
Published in the United Kingdom by Cornell University Press Ltd., 2–4 Brook Street, London W1Y 1AA.

International Standard Book Number 0-8014-0996-9
Library of Congress Catalog Card Number 75-36994
Printed in the United States of America by York Composition Co.
Librarians: Library of Congress cataloging information appears on the last page of the book.

Contents

Preface

This book examines Hawthorne's development from *Fanshawe* through the unfinished romances. That Hawthorne's literary career *was* a development, in the sense of a series of consecutive changes, is its chief finding. The author is regularly read, studied, and taught as though throughout a writing life of almost forty years he did not change. Our knowledge of human nature suggests that such stasis is improbable, and common sense argues that such an inelastic and unimpressionable character could not produce writings of the first rank.

In the colleges and universities, where most of those who read and think and write about Hawthorne reside, it has been the custom for some decades to teach a literature consisting of the major works of major authors. An "English major" may graduate having read nothing more of Hawthorne than *The Scarlet Letter* and a handful of tales. He can put this small sample together in a number of interesting ways. He goes on to graduate school, perhaps, and reads a larger selection of tales and romances, which, again, he manipulates into various abstract designs in his term papers. The scholarly journals are full of such artificial exercises. This student may even write a dissertation on Hawthorne without knowing of—or if knowing of, not having read—the sketches, the children's works, the life of Franklin Pierce, or the twelve essays on

7

England. For such a student, "Hawthorne" signifies an arbitrary collection of works rather than a human sensibility.

My assumption is that Hawthorne's writings reflect a single and actual literary sensibility. In order to discover this sensibility it is necessary to study everything he wrote that had a literary purpose—that is, was designed to be published—and to study these works in chronological order, in the context they provide for each other. I give emphasis to major works that Hawthorne seems to have considered major; but I touch only lightly on some much-discussed stories that evidently carried little weight with the author. I try to encompass the whole of Hawthorne's production, and to distribute emphasis among the parts according to the author's own emphasis.

I find a controlling preoccupation, throughout all of Hawthorne's career, with defining a way of writing that could embody the imagination and justify it to a skeptical, practical-minded audience. In the greatly prolonged early period (1825–1849) and in the brief major phase (1850–1859), each work or group of works proceeds from this impulse but takes a different route toward fulfillment. As the weaknesses and shortcomings of a formulation manifested themselves in practice, Hawthorne shed it and tried another; or he corrected it; or he revised it.

For the first twenty-five years he worked under the influence of a commonsense attitude about imagination and the artist's place in society; he put forward very modest claims for literature and for himself as a literary man. With *The Scarlet Letter* he broke through to a much more aggressive position, one clearly linked to American and English romanticism; he describes his "conversion" in "The Custom-House." This romantic synthesis functioned throughout the 1850s and enabled him to write his major works; then it began to disintegrate. In his last phase he wavered between a return to earlier modes of conceptualizing and a push on toward another new formulation, literary realism. In the movement from common sense to romanticism to—potentially—realism, Hawthorne epitomized the history of fiction in nineteenth-century America.

In a sense I began to work on this study more than ten years ago, when Hawthorne's work presented me with a teacher's dilemma. I found it impossible to teach *The Scarlet Letter* to undergraduate students according to interpretations of that work then current. Under the powerful influence of Randall Stewart, whose biography of Hawthorne, published in 1949, still has not been superseded, a number of major studies of Hawthorne had been produced in the 1950s, viewing the author anachronistically as a neo-orthodox writer controlled by a vision at once Christian and tragic. Among such works I think particularly of Richard Harter Fogle's *Hawthorne's Fiction: The Light and the Dark* (Norman: University of Oklahoma Press, 1952), Roy R. Male's *Hawthorne's Tragic Vision* (Austin: University of Texas Press, 1957), and Hyatt Waggoner's *Hawthorne, a Critical Study* (Cambridge: Harvard University Press, 1955). Sensitive and thorough as these studies are (and their role in re-establishing Hawthorne as a serious artist must never be forgotten, even by those who, like myself, disagree with them), they did not seem right to me. Try as I might, I could not present Hawthorne convincingly as a Christian author; his concerns were too evidently secular, his distrust of all doctrine too obvious, his language too patently untheological. I could not resist my students' absolute certainty that Hester was meant for an admirable character in *The Scarlet Letter*, while of course in Christian terms she is from first to last an unredeemed sinner.

In 1965 Frederick C. Crews published *The Sins of the Fathers* (New York: Oxford University Press), outlining a psychoanalytic interpretation of Hawthorne's work. Although I did not, and do not, accept most of his analysis, I

was encouraged by his first chapter—a declaration of independence from then-standard readings of Hawthorne—to
embark on the task of making sense of Hawthorne for myself.
Early in my researches I was much influenced by Rudolph
Von Abele's unjustly neglected *The Death of the Artist*
(The Hague: Martinus Nijhoff, 1957), even though I dis-
agreed strongly with its key idea that the 1850s was a decade
of artistic decline for Hawthorne. After many false starts, I
finally decided that the great romances (as Hawthorne always
called them) of the 1850s were all built on the foundation of
a romantic vision. The romance form Hawthorne imitated
from eighteenth-century works, but the romantic vision was
allied to that of Coleridge, Wordsworth, and particularly the
American transcendentalists. Since such romanticism was a
phenomenon of Hawthorne's own time, while neo-orthodoxy
was not, this view of Hawthorne's writings made more sense
to me than the neo-orthodox.

But when, after having worked out interpretations of the
major romances according to the underlying romantic vision,
I turned to Hawthorne's earlier works, I found that such a
reading was not possible for them. The point of view in the
short fiction written before 1850 is distinctly commonsensical,
even antiromantic. Evidently, Hawthorne had changed. It
began to seem necessary to know his whole career, and so I
went on to look at all his writings, trying to follow the movement of his literary changes. To chronicle these changes from
first to last is the aim of this study.

My logic requires that proportionately less space be devoted to individual tales than to the long romances of the
1850s; I treat the tales in chronological groupings, looking
for their shared characteristics and their developmental trends.
The reader may thus be surprised to find "Young Goodman
Brown" or "The Minister's Black Veil," for example, figuring
as one of a group rather than receiving the full-scale reading
that the contemporary reputation of these works might seem

to require for them. For my purposes, the short works demanding individual attention are those that are most representative of a particular period in Hawthorne's career and those that foreshadow change. On the other hand, each of the long romances represents in itself a major effort and a discrete stage in Hawthorne's development, and thus each calls for a full reading. Although this method may dissatisfy some who prefer the tales to the romances, I believe that it gives a truer representation of the shape of Hawthorne's career as it developed through time than would a series of full readings of those stories singled out in our own day for particular approbation.

In the past ten years many scholars have made important contributions to our knowledge of Hawthorne, and I am much in their debt: William Charvat, C. E. Frazer Clark, Jr., J. Donald Crowley, Neal Frank Doubleday, Terence Martin, Roy Harvey Pearce, and Claude M. Simpson, especially.

Some of my readings of individual Hawthorne works have previously been published in different form. For permission to draw on my essays I thank the editors of: *The Centennial Review*, Vol. 15 (1971), for "Hawthorne's Women: The Tyranny of Social Myths"; *ESQ*, Vol. 19 (1973), for "The Romantic Malgré Lui: Hawthorne in the Custom-House"; *JEGP*, Vols. 67 (1968) and 69 (1970), for "The Blithedale Romance: A Radical Reading" and "Hawthorne's Holgrave: The Failure of the Artist-Hero" respectively; *Nathaniel Hawthorne Journal 1974* for "Hawthorne's Gothic Discards: *Fanshawe* and 'Alice Doane' "; *The New England Quarterly*, Vols. 43 (1970) and 44 (1971), for "Passion and Authority in *The Scarlet Letter*" and "*The Marble Faun*: Hawthorne's Elegy for Art" respectively; and *Studies in Short Fiction*, Vol. 10 (1973), for "Hawthorne's Myths for Children: The Author versus His Audience."

Whenever they are available, I have used the volumes from the Centenary Edition of Hawthorne's work, published by

the Ohio State University Press, for my texts. These include:
Vol. I, *The Scarlet Letter*, with an introduction by William
Charvat; Vol. II, *The House of the Seven Gables*, with an
introduction by William Charvat; Vol. III, *The Blithedale
Romance* and *Fanshawe*, with an introduction by Roy
Harvey Pearce; Vol. IV, *The Marble Faun*, with an intro-
duction by Claude M. Simpson; Vol. V, *Our Old Home*, with
an introduction by Claude M. Simpson; Vols. VI and VII,
Writings for Children, with an introduction by Roy Harvey
Pearce; Vol. VIII, *The American Notebooks*, edited by
Claude M. Simpson; Vol. IX, *Twice-told Tales*, with an in-
troduction by J. Donald Crowley: Vol. X, *Mosses from an
Old Manse*, with an introduction by J. Donald Crowley; and
Vol. XI, *The Snow-Image and Uncollected Tales*, with an
introduction by J. Donald Crowley.

For a thorough reading of my manuscript, and for encouragement and support while I was writing it, I am indebted
to my colleague and husband, Jack Stillinger.

NINA BAYM

Urbana, Illinois

The Shape of Hawthorne's Career

❧ 1 ❧

Beginnings
1825–1834

As a student at Bowdoin College between 1821 and 1825, Nathaniel Hawthorne, like other young men from moderately circumstanced families, had to choose a career. His decision to become a professional author rose in large part from a distaste for the conventional choices of the educated—doctor, lawyer, and minister. Even before going to college he had resisted these and played with the idea of authorship as an alternative. In a letter to his mother dated March 13, 1821, he wrote:

I have not yet concluded what profession I shall have. The being a minister is of course out of the question. I should not think that even you could desire me to choose so dull a way of life. . . . As to lawyers, there are so many of them already that one half of them (upon a moderate calculation) are in a state of actual starvation. A physician, then, seems to be "Hobson's choice;" but yet I should not like to live by the diseases and infirmities of my fellow-creatures. . . . Oh that I was rich enough to live without a profession! What do you think of my becoming an author, and relying for support upon my pen? Indeed, I think the illegibility of my hand-writing is very author-like. How proud you would feel to see my works praised by the reviewers, as equal to the proudest productions of the scribbling sons of John Bull.[1]

1. Julian Hawthorne, *Nathaniel Hawthorne and His Wife* (Boston and New York: Houghton, Mifflin, 1884), I, 107–8. Hereafter cited as Julian Hawthorne.

15

If he elected writing because it seemed less like drudgery than other careers, he also felt a positive enthusiasm for his choice. An avid reader from boyhood, he particularly loved the books that were popular successes in the early decades of the nineteenth century. The efforts of his sister and later academic critics to insist that Hawthorne was influenced chiefly by authors in the great tradition—Shakespeare, Spenser, Milton, and Bunyan—have obscured the evidence of his adolescent reading lists, which shows that he was captivated by fiction of the previous century, especially gothic, and that his favorite author was Sir Walter Scott.[2] And it is precisely an admiration for Scott that might be expected to stimulate literary ambition in the 1820s. For this writer was enjoying, along with Lord Byron, an unprecedented popular success that established professional authorship—in its modern sense

2. These lists are reprinted in Randall Stewart, *Nathaniel Hawthorne: A Biography* (New Haven: Yale University Press, 1948), p. 8, and Neal Frank Doubleday, *Hawthorne's Early Tales: A Critical Study* (Durham: Duke University Press, 1972), pp. 34–35. They first appeared in Julian Hawthorne, I, 105; George Parsons Lathrop, *A Study of Hawthorne* (Boston: James R. Osgood, 1876), p. 108; and Jane Lundblad, *Nathaniel Hawthorne and the European Literary Tradition* (Upsala: *Essays and Studies in Language and Literature*, No. 6, 1947), p. 35. The list in Julian Hawthorne from a letter dated September 28, 1819, includes *Waverley, The Mysteries of Udolpho, The Adventures of Ferdinand Count Fathom, Roderick Random,* and the first volume of *The Arabian Nights.* Lathrop quotes a letter dated October 1820, which lists Hogg's *Tales, Caleb Williams, St. Leon,* and *Mandeville.* Hawthorne writes, "I admire Godwin's novels, and intend to read them all. I shall read the 'Abbott' by the author of 'Waverley' as soon as I can hire it. I have read all Scott's novels except that. I wish I had not, that I might have the pleasure of reading them again. Next to these I like 'Caleb Williams'." Lundblad's list is from an undated scrap of paper in the Huntington Library: it includes *Melmoth, Tom Jones, Amelia, Eloisa, Memoirs of R. L. Edgeworth, The Abbott,* and "Romantick Tales by M. G. Lewis." Since Hawthorne had by this time read *The Abbott,* this list must have been made fairly soon after that of October 1820.

of a writer making a living by sales of his books—as a contemporary reality.[3]

Scott's career, like those of all modern authors, was made possible by many new cultural and economic circumstances: wide literacy, aggregated populations enjoying leisure and cash, improved publishing and publicizing techniques, more rapid and efficient means of transporting and marketing books. Modern authorship is a product of a mercantile, technological, middle-class society and is therefore dependent on that society. The writer offers his work as an article for consumption to be selected first by a publisher who manufactures and advertises it, then by reviewers who evaluate it, and finally by an audience that buys it. The implications of this dependency, however, were not evident to the young Americans—mostly men—inspired by Scott's example and emboldened even further by the successes of Irving and Cooper. Indeed, as middle-class, democratic youths they found this model of authorship superior to the patronage model it had supplanted. What they saw—at least what Hawthorne seems to have seen—was that a person might spend his life inventing literature of the sort he liked to read.

Far from assuming feelings of hostility, distrust, or superiority on the part of the writer toward his readers, this idea of authorship implies shared values. Since he liked books that were popular, Hawthorne could assume that he was one with the audience he would write for. He had no way yet of understanding the precarious economic situation of the infant publishing houses in the United States and the consequent difficulties for American writers, no matter how gifted. He could not possibly foresee the evolution of both popular and critical taste away from the gothic, romantic, and historical toward the domestic, realistic, and contemporary. Nor could he realize that the American readership as it grew and ac-

3. See William Charvat, *The Profession of Authorship in America* (Columbus: Ohio State University Press, 1968), p. 20.

quired character between 1830 and 1850 would come to be composed chiefly of women, and therefore responsive to concerns different from his.

As he did become aware of these obstacles in the way of the great success he hoped for, Hawthorne felt irritation, frustration, and anger, which was expressed in letters and conversations. But such difficulties did not really alter the core of his fiction. On the other hand, his fiction was marked, even shaped, throughout his career by his perception of one problem that already existed in 1825: the general American indifference to the arts, based on their supposed uselessness. The American pragmatic character early manifested itself in the idea that because art had no use the new nation had no use for art. Benjamin Franklin had written that the arts would not be required in America for some time to come. This pragmatism merged in New England with residual Puritan hostility toward art as feigning, and with the distrust of imagination implicit in Scottish commonsense philosophy, which was at that time widely taught in American colleges and universities.[4] Hawthorne's writings show that he agreed to some extent with this adverse and condescending characterization of his enterprise. Yet there were reasons why even these accepted objections might have seemed at first possible to overcome.

To begin with, despite the many pronouncements against fiction from various sources, fiction was clearly holding its own. Moreover, the new doctrine of literary nationalism was attributing to literature precisely that usefulness its detractors denied it. Literary nationalism conceived of authorship as public service; by expressing the special virtues of the American mind in literary form, American authors would bring their country into the community of civilized nations and

4. See Terence Martin, *The Instructed Vision: Scottish Common Sense Philosophy and the Origins of American Fiction* (Bloomington: Indiana University Press, 1961).

establish her pre-eminence there. Most theorists of literary nationalism thought of the verse epic when they spoke of a major literature; yet they were more exhortative than prescriptive in their essays, especially in the early years of the movement, between 1815 and 1830. A young person like Hawthorne might be heartened by their doctrine to believe that any well-executed and well-received work, by virtue of its demonstration of skill and feeling, would be a contribution to his country's reputation and therefore useful. In addition, the literary nationalists assumed the existence of an enlightened popular audience that would be responsive to their ideals of literary excellence. Their writings consequently encouraged the neophyte to take a readership for granted.

As a result of this convergence of theories and circumstances, reinforced no doubt by his temperament, Hawthorne would all his life long blame himself for his failure to achieve the massive popular success he wished for. Many years later he might express bafflement and outrage at the vogue of a work like Maria Cummins's *The Lamplighter* but he found no refuge in a facile contempt for popular opinion. His training was all against it, and there was always the example of his Bowdoin classmate Longfellow to prove that a writer could reach the public heart without lying or lowering his standards. His failure to become a popular author quickly meant to Hawthorne that something was wrong with his work. Popular success would have justified his commitment. After the first few unself-conscious forays into publication, his early writing developed a characteristic atmosphere of ambivalence and caution. In a typical early work Hawthorne appears to try to discover the nature and value of his enterprise even while presenting it, despite his doubts, in the most favorable manner he can. The narrator explores, expresses, and conceals his doubts all at once. Significantly, this apologetic stance disappears in "The Custom-House" and *The Scarlet Letter*, and does not return until the final years of his career.

Another kind of person, experiencing disappointments where he had expected an easy success (and without the compensation of a living wage), might have given up the profession. In fact, economic necessity forced Hawthorne into other kinds of work more than once, but each episode reconvinced him that despite its trials and doubts authorship was more right for him than any other human labor. This was partly because of his temperamental distaste for routine, and a balkiness as profound as Thoreau's against modes of life not truly self-expressive. But it was also because of an unshakable certainty that, for him at least, imaginative writing was more real than any actuality, and because as an author he could both live in his imagination and embody that conviction. As a matter of fact, he never felt this conviction more strongly than when he was deprived of the opportunity to write. Each period of separation from authorship brought him back to his profession with renewed energy. But the return to writing meant the inevitable resurgence of doubt.

After his graduation from Bowdoin in 1825, Hawthorne returned to his native Salem and lived with his family for more than twelve years. The financial situation—precise details of which have not been recovered—was apparently such that so long as he remained at home Hawthorne might live without an income. His mother, widowed when Hawthorne was four, had taken up residence with her own family, the Mannings. Through some combination of her own assets and the liberality of her siblings, she was able to live quietly but comfortably with her children for the rest of her life. Horatio Bridge, Hawthorne's companion at Bowdoin and afterward his closest friend, wrote in his *Personal Recollections:* "In two or three flying visits, made him by invitation after our graduation, I saw no evidence of narrow circumstances in their environment."[5] There is no sign that any of his relations,

5. Horatio Bridge, *Personal Recollections of Nathaniel Hawthorne* (New York: Harper, 1893), p. 38.

including Uncle Robert Manning, who had paid for his college education, pressured him to go out into the world and earn a living. If this lack of pressure permitted him to dedicate himself to writing without worrying about money, it also tempted him to indulge his indolent and self-doubting nature. Many theories have been put forth by analytic biographers and critics to explain why Hawthorne stayed so long in Salem and made so little effort to impress himself on the literary scene. Later, when he had become a famous author and a man of the world, Hawthorne often whimsically exaggerated his situation in Salem in a manner that some literal-minded readers have accepted as factually accurate. "I sat down by the wayside of life," he wrote in the preface to *The Snow-Image* in 1851,[6] "like a man under enchantment, and a shrubbery sprung up around me, and the bushes grew to be saplings, and the saplings became trees, until no exit appeared possible, through the entangling depths of my obscurity." Yet in other writings he probably comes closer to the reality, as for example in the self-portrait of the children's sketch, "Little Daffydowndilly," written probably in April 1843:[7] "Daffydowndilly was so called because in his nature he resembled a flower, and loved to do only what was beautiful and agreeable, and took no delight in labor of any kind."[8] And in 1853 he wrote an autobiographical account in which he says, "It was my fortune or misfortune, just as you please, to have some slender means of supporting myself; and so, on leaving college, in 1825, instead of immediately studying a profession, I sat myself down to consider what pursuit in life I was best fit for.

6. *The Centenary Edition of the Works of Nathaniel Hawthorne,* ed. William Charvat et al., Vol. XI, *The Snow-Image* (Columbus: Ohio State University Press, 1974), p. 5.
7. See John J. McDonald, "The Old Manse Period Canon," *Nathaniel Hawthorne Journal 1972* (Washington, D.C.: NCR/Microcard Editions, 1973), pp. 13–39.
8. *The Snow-Image,* p. 200.

. . . And year after year I kept on considering what I was fit for, and time and my destiny decided that I was to be the writer that I am."[9] The years at Salem were both a deprivation and an indulgence. Hawthorne's wish to have no profession and his doubts about authorship as a career kept him from a full commitment. At the same time his certainty that he did not want to be anything *but* an author kept him writing.

The self-immurement in Salem has also been explained by critics as Hawthorne's response to bad treatment by editors and publishers. There is evidence that he encountered setbacks in his initial attempts to publish, and that when he published he was not well paid. But such experiences are common at the beginning of a career, and might well have inspired him to more strenuous efforts. But after *Fanshawe*, Hawthorne abandoned all attempts to write what Bridge called "a work of magnitude"[10] for many years, even though such a work would have been far more likely to bring him the reputation he wanted than the short stories and sketches he wrote instead. Indeed, since his short pieces were published anonymously, it is difficult to see how they could have brought him any reputation at all. Some critics believe that Hawthorne withdrew into a deliberate twelve-year anonymity in order to perfect his craft. But such an exalted idea is inconsistent with the continual fretting that Hawthorne confided to Bridge, who responded with infallible support and encouragement.

"There is more honor and emolument in store for you, from your writings, than you imagine," Bridge wrote to him late in 1836. "The bane of your life has been self-distrust. This has kept you back for many years; which, if you had improved by publishing, would long ago have given you what you must now wait a short time for."[11] And again early

9. Julian Hawthorne, I, 96.
10. Bridge, p. 71.
11. Bridge, p. 73.

in 1837: "I wish to God that I could impart to you a little of my own brass. You would then dash into the contest of literary men, and do honor to yourself and to your country in a short time. But you never will have confidence enough in yourself, though you will have fame."[12] Had not this good friend secretly advanced the money to guarantee publication of *Twice-told Tales*, Hawthorne's reputation might have been delayed still longer. The inner man and the outer circumstances reinforced each other in this long dalliance, and Hawthorne's writings reflected his self-awareness and self-distrust.

In the nine years after his graduation Hawthorne undertook four literary projects, although not all were completed. He wrote a short novel in the manner of Scott—*Fanshawe*, probably composed late in 1825; and he prepared a collection of stories called *Seven Tales of My Native Land* at about the same time. These writings, as first attempts, testify to Hawthorne's initial self-confidence and the unexamined nature of his literary premises at the outset of his career. In different ways, both are experiments within the gothic mode. That is, they are fictions striving for emotional effect by sensational devices, including terror, mystery, hints of the supernatural, and extremes of good and evil.

Toward the end of the decade (about 1829) he planned and at least partially completed a collection entitled *Provincial Tales*, which, like the *Seven Tales*, seems to have been a group of loosely associated gothic fictions. In the early years of the next decade—perhaps in 1832 and 1833—he worked on a much more ambitious project, a framed narrative combining a variety of literary genres. Like the other works, *The Story Teller* (as it is now called) had an American setting. None of these collections appeared as Hawthorne intended them to. Stories from all of them were separately published, and it is a difficult task to re-establish their original designs.

12. Bridge, p. 74.

Nothing remains of the *Seven Tales of My Native Land* except "Alice Doane" (as it can be extracted from the revised version called "Alice Doane's Appeal") and probably "The Hollow of the Three Hills" and "An Old Woman's Tale." What we know today about this group derives from two slightly differing accounts, written many years later by Hawthorne's sister Elizabeth.[13] She recalled that Hawthorne wrote the stories either while in college or immediately after graduating, that he submitted them to a publisher who agreed to bring them out but then delayed until Hawthorne, in a rage, called them back and burned them. The legend of the destroyed manuscript has been very appealing to Hawthorne scholars, and it is supported by the mordant fiction "The Devil in Manuscript," as well as by the revised "Alice Doane's Appeal" and a letter from 1845 in which Hawthorne expressed regrets that he had burned fictions that might have been useful after all.[14]

Nevertheless, no direct evidence proves that a complete and integrated collection of tales was burned. On the contrary, the narrator of "Alice Doane's Appeal" observes that this story and one other escaped the flames because they happened to be in the possession of a friend at the time. If this is true, then the idea of Hawthorne throwing the whole manuscript into the fire after demanding it back from the publisher is necessarily false, unless he had copies. And if he had copies, there is no way of knowing what was irrecoverably lost and what survived. There are no extant descriptions of missing tales; although we may extrapolate from the surviving tales what the whole collection might have been like, we cannot begin to conjecture about the interrelations among the stories.

13. Julian Hawthorne, I, 123; Randall Stewart, "Recollections of Hawthorne by His Sister Elizabeth," *American Literature*, 16 (1945), 316–31, especially p. 323.
14. The letter is quoted in the "Historical Commentary" to *Mosses from an Old Manse*, Centenary Edition, Vol. X (1974), p. 515.

Elizabeth wrote that the tales were all about witchcraft, and the three surviving tales loosely fit this description. But it is not at all evident what relation this motif was to have to the nationalism implicit in the collection's title. Although each of the tales is set in America, there is no attempt to Americanize the material by developing local setting, native manners, or historical detail.[15]

"Alice Doane" no longer exists, and to analyze it we must assume that the extracts reproduced in "Alice Doane's Appeal," as well as the narrator's summaries of the remainder, accurately represent the original. The hero, Leonard Doane, is a typical figure of gothic excess, "characterized by a diseased imagination and morbid feelings." His sister Alice, the heroine, is also representative, "beautiful and virtuous, and instilling something of her own excellence into the wild heart of her brother." Neither character seems to have been developed beyond these generic attributes. The story is plotted around the triangle of Leonard, Alice, and a youth named Walter Brome, who appears to have designs on Alice's virtue. It climaxes in a gothic medley of murder, incest, and fratricide, as the jealous Leonard kills Walter only to discover that he has murdered his long-lost brother. The final scene, a kind of nightmare carnival, takes place in a cemetery.[16]

Later, we learn that the whole plot issued from the machina-

15. The most important scholarly study of the early collections, drawn on by all later scholars, is by Nelson F. Adkins, "The Early Projected Works of Nathaniel Hawthorne," *Papers of the Bibliographical Society of America*, 39 (1945), 119–55. Adkins assumes that the stories were connected by likeness of subject matter. A recent work by Alfred Weber speculates that the unity of the collection lay in its mode. All the tales, he believes, were fireside tales narrated by an old man or woman and attributed by this narrator to a New England locale (Alfred Weber, *Die Entwicklung der Rahmenerzählungen Nathaniel Hawthornes: "The Story Teller" und andere frühe Werke* [Berlin: Erich Schmidt, 1973], p. 49).

16. "Alice Doane's Appeal," in *The Snow-Image*, pp. 270, 275–77.

tions of a vicious wizard; the unfortunate Leonard was only a puppet. This story is uncharacteristic of Hawthorne both in the declamatory rant of its style and its attribution of the protagonist's errors to outside agency. Before the decade was out Hawthorne was to master a psychological gothic in which aberrant or destructive behavior always stems from a diseased imagination. Supernatural agents will function only in response to, or as projections of, the psyche's wishes. Later still, Hawthorne came to feel that *all* behavior, diseased or not, proceeds from a person's perception of events, and therefore from his imagination.

Except for the casual placement of Walter Brome's corpse on the old Boston road, "Alice Doane" is American only in Leonard's sudden vision (as he kills Brome) of the death of his father in an Indian raid. Indian raids are American gothic events, and this isolated motif anticipates Hawthorne's mining of history for gothic incidents. He did not make much subsequent use of Indian material, however. "An Old Woman's Tale" and "The Hollow of the Three Hills" have even more cursory native reference. The former is simply set in "a village in the Valley of the Connecticut." In the latter, the heroine says that she is a stranger in the land—therefore presumably a recent immigrant to America.[17] These stories differ in mood and mode, showing that within the loose classification of the witchcraft tale Hawthorne was trying to achieve variety of effect. "The Hollow of the Three Hills" is a domestic melodrama of grief and terror, while "An Old Woman's Tale" is quaintly fantastic and written in the language of oral delivery.

These three earliest surviving stories[18] share a preoccupation

17. "The Hollow of the Three Hills," *Twice-told Tales*, Centenary Edition, Vol. IX (1974), p. 200; "An Old Woman's Tale," *The Snow-Image*, p. 241.

18. I omit from my discussion the several apocryphal works that date from this earliest period.

with visions, and are technical exercises in creating a fictional world where vision and actual event are equally real. Leonard Doane acts on the strength of his visions; the lady in "The Hollow of the Three Hills" is killed by hers. The lovers in "An Old Woman's Tale" fall asleep and dream of something that really happens. The first sentence of "The Hollow of the Three Hills" places the tale in the old times when "fantastic dreams and madmen's reveries were realized among the actual circumstances of life." This casual observation takes for granted what, in much of Hawthorne's later writing, will become central preoccupations: the intermingling of fantasy and actuality in a convincing fictional structure, and the interpenetration of fantasy and reality in the real world. The fragments from *Seven Tales of My Native Land*, however, do not suggest that Hawthorne was exploring ideas. He seems to have been trying to create successful examples of recognizable literary types and to achieve a range of emotional effects.

The title *Seven Tales of My Native Land* embodies his wish to write identifiably American fiction, although the surviving stories have no particularly American characteristics. In the short novel *Fanshawe*, which he published anonymously at his own expense in 1828, nationalist and gothic intentions work at cross-purposes. Although Hawthorne set the story at a college modeled after Bowdoin, he developed his characters and landscapes in a conventional rhetoric blending Scott and gothicism, and he failed to reproduce a convincing local reality. The gothicisms of the plot, however, were sharply restricted by an apparent sense of the unlikelihood of gothic events actually occurring in America. William Charvat has pointed out that even in the very earliest examples of American gothic the villains were always European; Americans did not think themselves vicious.[19] Hawthorne himself was to write many years later, in words repeated and en-

19. Charvat, pp. 22–23.

dorsed by Henry James, that "no author, without a trial, can conceive the difficulty of writing a Romance about a country where there is no shadow, no antiquity, no mystery, no picturesque and gloomy wrong, nor anything but a commonplace prosperity, in broad and simple daylight, as is happily the case with my dear native land."[20] Of course, by the time he wrote that, Hawthorne had surmounted the difficulty in many works, but in *Fanshawe* he did not. He presented a slight story with weak characters and directed the reader through description and allusion to interpret the work as high gothic drama.

In itself the idea of enriching the thin American atmosphere indirectly by allusion seems reasonable. But without some true evil, gloom, or wrong at its core the gothic mode will not work. The smiling gothic that Hawthorne attempted in *Fanshawe* is an impossibility, and he lost the gothic effect without a compensating gain. He soon knew the work to be a failure, although whether his recognition was a perception of its artistic defects or arose from its poor sales we cannot say. Roy Harvey Pearce has disproved the legend, recorded in many biographies, that Hawthorne recalled and burned all the copies he could find.[21] But he never acknowledged having written it—even his wife was unaware of his authorship of the work—and he never repeated its method.

Besides trying, and failing, to present the commonplace as gothic, Hawthorne made his first attempt in *Fanshawe* to create an effective protagonist. He set his hero apart from the common herd, but just as he could not or would not find a picturesque and gloomy wrong to motivate the action, he could not give Fanshawe that fascinating mixture of good and evil qualities at the core of the gothic hero. Fanshawe

20. Preface to *The Marble Faun*, Centenary Edition, Vol. IV (1968), p. 3.

21. Introduction to *Fanshawe*, Centenary Edition, Vol. III (1964), pp. 308–12.

embodies pure goodness and spiritual refinement; he is no more suited than the gothic hero to the broad and simple daylight of American life. His heroism is remarkably passive; in two scenes of confrontation with the "villain" in the work, he achieves victory by staring the bad man down. The bad man feels and acts while Fanshawe simply holds his ground and exists. Apparently, Hawthorne could invent no action by which his hero could bridge the gap between himself and his environment. The logical outcome of his situation, fore-shadowed in his wasting pallor, is an early death.

Critics who think of Hawthorne as an alienated, reclusive man take Fanshawe as self-portrait, despite the accumulation of biographical evidence suggesting that Hawthorne enjoyed a range of deep human ties during his life. Others argue, more plausibly, that Fanshawe is an adolescent's vision of himself as special, set apart, mysteriously doomed. But as a student and a dreamer, Fanshawe can be understood to represent a literary type who embodies a certain conception of imagination. In this type, imagination and insight disqualify one for participation in human affairs. A character embodying so negative a view of imagination certainly cannot serve as a literary pro-tagonist; more than that, he cannot demonstrate the inter-relation between imagination and living by which fiction implicitly justifies itself.

After *Seven Tales of My Native Land* and *Fanshawe* there is a two-year gap in Hawthorne's writings, during which he may have produced and destroyed manuscripts. It is certain that in these years he read a great deal, much of it in American history. The record is in the Salem Athenaeum and in his subsequent fiction.[22] The first products of that reading were a group of tales set in the American past and a number of bio-graphical sketches of historical personages and events. These

22. See Marion L. Kesselring, "Hawthorne's Reading, 1828–1850," *Bulletin of the New York Public Library,* 53 (1949), 55–71, 121–38, 173–94.

are two distinct treatments of historical material, which imply that at this stage of his career Hawthorne separated historical from imaginative writing quite sharply. He planned to collect his historical fictions under the title *Provincial Tales*. We know that this group included "My Kinsman, Major Molineux," "Roger Malvin's Burial," "The Gentle Boy," and "The Wives of the Dead," and perhaps the original version of "Alice Doane" as well. We do not know precisely what Hawthorne meant to imply by his title, nor how the tales were to be arranged and interrelated. If Hawthorne had a unifying scheme in mind, it is not implicit in the known stories. Critics' attempts to identify a thematic focus in *Provincial Tales* have often involved assigning additional fictions to the group or removing one or more stories from it.[23] Two of the stories are generally thought to be among Hawthorne's finest work, but critics dismiss "The Gentle Boy" as overly sentimental and ignore "The Wives of the Dead" entirely.

It is possible that the known fictions in *Provincial Tales* do not as a group suggest a thematic center because they were

23. Elizabeth Lathrop Chandler, in "A Study of the Sources of the Tales and Romances Written by Nathaniel Hawthorne Before 1853," *Smith College Studies in Modern Languages*, 7 (1925–1926), 1–63, proposes adding "Dr. Bullivant," "The Gray Champion," "The May-Pole of Merry Mount," and "Young Goodman Brown," making a total of nine stories in the collection. Adkins proposes "The Gray Champion," "Young Goodman Brown," "The May-Pole of Merry Mount," and "The Minister's Black Veil." Richard P. Adams, in "Hawthorne's *Provincial Tales*," *New England Quarterly*, 30 (1957), 39–57, rejects "The Wives of the Dead" and "Alice Doane," but adds "The Gray Champion," "The May-Pole of Merry Mount," and "Young Goodman Brown" in order to arrive at a unity through the theme of initiation. Weber, who believes that the *Provincial Tales* investigated the Puritan spirit, adds "The May-Pole of Merry Mount" and "The Gray Champion" and suggests that the seven stories were chronologically arranged (pp. 83, 96, 98). My own conservative inclination is to stick with the known group, and reject the others because they were all written later than the original four or five.

not primarily written for theme. Taken as a unity, the stories seem to be concerned with evoking feeling and atmosphere and to seek an effect, whether of beauty, melancholy, mystery, or terror. These effects would accord with an aesthetic current in Hawthorne's time and are typical of gothic and sentimental fiction. But in the *Provincial Tales* Hawthorne achieved them in fictions that are relatively free of gothic or sentimental devices, and in distinctly American settings. Thus, after two different kinds of failure, he succeeded in making a connection between his idea of fiction and his country. In a past which by virtue of its distance may be conceived of as shadowy and indistinct, America and the imagination may meet. The American past is thus Hawthorne's first—and in the opinion of many critics, his most successfully created— "neutral territory, somewhere between the real world and fairy-land, where the Actual and Imaginary may meet, and each imbue itself with the nature of the other."[24]

Yet it is important to note that the past itself must be "imagined" as shadowy and remote before it can be an effective ground for fictions. In these four tales no actual historical personages appear, no actual historical events are represented. Both "The Gentle Boy" and "Roger Malvin's Burial" begin with the conclusion of a historical event; "My Kinsman, Major Molineux" is modeled on actual events but its own episode is fictional; "The Wives of the Dead" uses no more than a historical probability as its occasion. As we shall see when we look at the "Biographical Sketches," at this point Hawthorne seems to have experienced recorded history— actual historical facts—as a constraint on his imagination rather than a stimulus to it. Recorded history demands fidelity to its outlines and thus precludes imaginative free play. It follows that at this time Hawthorne was not interested in making history the subject of his fiction or in

24. "The Custom-House," *The Scarlet Letter*, Centenary Edition, Vol. I (1962), p. 36.

creating fictions for the purpose of commenting on the American past. (It is indeed arguable whether these were ever his purposes in fiction.) Some years later when he revised "The Gentle Boy" for *Twice-told Tales* he further reduced the historical denotativeness of the tale by cutting down the few longish passages of historical generalization and realistic detail.[25] The other stories in *Provincial Tales* devote no more than a few paragraphs, usually introductory, to lodging their actions in a remote historical atmosphere.

Underlying all the stories is the view of reality as a mingling of vision and actuality implicit in "The Hollow of the Three Hills" and "An Old Woman's Tale." If the nature of reality is not a theme in these stories, it is central to the action. In "The Wives of the Dead" Hawthorne's effects are all achieved by manipulating the interrelations of dreams, dreamlike states, falsehoods "realized" (the women's husbands are not dead, but are believed to be so) and "unrealizable" truths (after each woman learns that her husband is alive, she is unable to comprehend or adjust to this truth). The story is most effective in describing ordinary household furnishings as perceived through the estranged vision of these grieving women. Hawthorne builds from the fact that perceptions of even the most trivial and everyday objects change with changing emotional states of the perceiver. The disruption of the normal course of life results in a radically alienated vision.

This psychological fact underlies the other stories in the *Provincial Tales* group. "Roger Malvin's Burial" presents an example of simple pathology, where an inner, secret preoccupation drives the protagonist to an increasingly subjective perception and interpretation of outer events. Reuben Bourne

25. Hawthorne's revisions are included in the apparatus to the Centenary Edition *Twice-told Tales*, pp. 613–19. A different view from mine concerning Hawthorne's intentions in these revisions may be seen in Seymour L. Gross, "Hawthorne's Revisions of 'The Gentle Boy,'" *American Literature*, 26 (1954), 196–208.

is the first in a long line of Hawthorne protagonists whose extreme behavior demonstrates that the imagination controls what people do and hence is inseparable from actuality. Hawthorne emphasizes this point here, as he does in many of his later stories, by switching at a crucial moment from within the protagonist's mind, with its wholly integrated but seriously distorted version of reality, to the outside world. In the penultimate segment of the story Hawthorne moves from Reuben's point of view to that of Dorcas, the wife whose son will be killed in Reuben's act of "expiation." Doing so, Hawthorne makes us see Reuben's act through the eyes of another character and reminds us of the delusion that distorts the protagonist's vision.

In "My Kinsman, Major Molineux" Robin has no inner compulsion, but he misperceives reality because he lacks the necessary knowledge to interpret what he sees. Unable to interpret, in fact he cannot see. Consequently, events appear threatening and mysterious, but these qualities are simply aspects that the incomprehensible wears. In themselves the events have no such character, and to make sure that they will not appear strange and threatening to the reader Hawthorne carefully explains in his introductory paragraphs exactly what is going on. As Neal Frank Doubleday has written, "The reader who knows something of the history of the period before the Revolution and of the activities of the Sons of Liberty will be ahead of Robin at every moment, and watch him act in ignorance of conditions that are historically clear enough."[26] Psychologically, Robin's adventure depends on the fact that every perception involves an act of interpretation, and that without knowledge and experience there can be no interpretation, hence no perception. Actuality conditions the imagination, and imagination interprets actuality. Reality is a composite.

One would think Hawthorne had developed here that

26. Doubleday, p. 233.

satisfyingly aggressive conception of imagination so strikingly absent from *Fanshawe*. Demonstrations of the active participation of imagination in the real world might appease the skepticism of pragmatic readers. But much evidence suggests that he was not pleased with this work. When he made his first selection of works for a volume published in 1837, he used only "The Gentle Boy" from this group, and then with significant revisions. "Roger Malvin's Burial" appeared in *Mosses from an Old Manse* in 1846; "The Wives of the Dead" and "My Kinsman, Major Molineux" remained uncollected until 1851. The writings of the 1830s and 1840s clearly attempt to modify the type of story he created in the *Provincial Tales* group, as well as to develop genres that would balance his vision. For when the stories of the *Provincial Tales* show imagination in action, it is a destructive or alienating force. Could the imagination be shown as a power for good? The only character in the group whose vision encompasses love and harmony, little Ilbrahim in "The Gentle Boy," is passively crushed between the opposing energies of the Quaker and Puritan imaginations. If Hawthorne could express the imagination active only in disease, how could he justify his own activity? In fact, Hawthorne did not answer this question to his own satisfaction until he wrote *The Scarlet Letter*.

At the same time that he worked on the *Provincial Tales* Hawthorne also wrote four biographical sketches of historical personages: "Mrs. Hutchinson," "Sir William Phips," "Sir William Pepperell," and "Dr. Bullivant." His choices reveal an interest in the sweep of Massachusetts history from the founding of the Bay Colony through the revolutionary era.[27] The sketches incorporate conventional historical judgments of Hawthorne's time. He observes the decline of religious in-

27. Roughly, Ann Hutchinson belongs to the first generation of Puritans, Dr. Bullivant to the second, Sir William Phips to the third, and Sir William Pepperell to the fourth.

tensity and the rise of secularity in Massachusetts; he links the military activities of Phips and Pepperell to the worldliness of the later colonists, which is in turn an effect of the loss of self-government. The sketch of Ann Hutchinson argues that women should keep their place; his portrait of her is unsympathetic as are, curiously enough, the other three.

Technically, these sketches develop an entirely different approach to historical material from that in the *Provincial Tales*. As I have suggested, Hawthorne seems to have been careful to keep history, in the sense of representing actual events from the past, out of those fictions. Actual events are the concern of the sketches, and thus it appears that Hawthorne saw history and fiction as two different genres because fiction is invented and history is not. The storyteller who attempts to write history must understand that, although he might have a special service to perform for history, he has to restrain his imagination. Here is how Hawthorne describes his duties in "Sir William Phips":

The knowledge communicated by the historian and biographer is analogous to that which we acquire of a country by the map,— minute, perhaps, and accurate, and available for all necessary purposes, but cold and naked, and wholly destitute of the mimic charm produced by landscape painting. These defects are partly remediable, and even without an absolute violation of literal truth, although by methods rightfully interdicted to professors of biographical exactness. A license must be assumed in brightening the materials which time has rusted, and in tracing out half-obliterated inscriptions of the columns of antiquity; Fancy must throw her reviving light on the faded incidents that indicate character, whence a ray will be reflected, more or less vividly, on the person to be described.[28]

28. "Sir William Phips," *The Complete Works of Nathaniel Hawthorne*, Vol. XII (Riverside Edition; Boston: Houghton, Mifflin, 1884), p. 227. The other biographical sketches are also printed in this volume.

This passage justifies the imaginative writer of history over against the proper historian. In each of two images Hawthorne indicates that the imaginative writer brings something necessary to history forbidden the other. To the accurate and cold map of history he adds warmth and life; where the historian must stop for lack of fact, the imaginative writer can leap to an intuition of the truth. But in both images the writer is dependent on the prior activity of the historian; he is limited to refining and illustrating what the historian has already discovered. Moreover, he has only a few functions. He cannot alter or invent. He is restricted to throwing light on faded incidents: he is the restorer, not the creator, of the painting.

In the sketches Hawthorne observes these self-imposed restrictions so scrupulously that he does not enter the mind of any historical character or even provide dialogue. He makes no attempt to establish the illusion of reality. Whereas the stories written earlier were relatively unmediated—that is, were mostly free of a strongly defined authorial presence—in these sketches a speaker calls attention to his artifice at every turn: "We shall here resume the more picturesque style of analysis"; "a part of the peculiarities of the affair may be grouped in one picture, by selecting the moment of General Pepperell's embarkation"; "And now, having arranged these preliminaries, we shall attempt to picture forth a day of Sir William's life."[29] We are located at such a distance from these "pictures" that they seem like pantomime: "The affair grows hot, and the clergymen endeavor to interfere in the blessed capacity of peacemakers. The governor lifts his cane; and the captain lays his hand upon his sword, but is prevented from drawing by the zealous exertions of Dr. Mather."[30]

In this depiction history is a succession of tableaux. Animating them, Hawthorne is as much interested in his own func-

29. "Mrs. Hutchinson," p. 222; "Sir William Pepperell," p. 237; "Sir William Phips," p. 229.
30. "Sir William Phips," p. 232.

tion as in the pictures themselves. But so long as the showman's presence is evident, the pictures cannot assume an independent life. The biographical sketches thus indirectly provide evidence that at this point in his career Hawthorne had not yet found a fictional use for actual historical event. The *Provincial Tales*, scrupulously avoiding historical explicitness, confirm this indication.

The revision of "Alice Doane," however, achieves a unified structure wherein fiction, history, and the author are brought together. The revision inserts the original "Alice Doane" into a frame that calls attention to the original's defects and advances a different idea of fiction in its stead.[31] In this frame the author-narrator escorts two young ladies to the top of the Gallows Hill in Salem where he reads them "Alice Doane." Despite its concatenation of thrills, the story fails to move the listeners; indeed, after a moment of polite silence they begin to laugh. Chagrined, the narrator turns to the surroundings for inspiration and makes "a trial whether truth be more powerful than fiction."[32] He improvises a crowd scene like the graveyard climax of "Alice Doane" but deriving from the Salem witchcraft episode rather than the conventions of gothic witchery. For the innocently persecuted Alice Doane he substitutes the unfortunate accused of Salem, "a woman in her dotage, knowing neither the crime imputed her, nor its punishment"; another, "distracted by the universal madness, till feverish dreams were remembered as realities, and she al-

31. Seymour L. Gross sees the revisions as Hawthorne's attempt to cut out the incest motif in "Hawthorne's 'Alice Doane's Appeal,'" *Nineteenth-Century Fiction*, 10 (1955), 232–36. Robert H. Fossum, "The Summons of the Past: Hawthorne's 'Alice Doane's Appeal,'" *Nineteenth-Century Fiction*, 23 (1965), 294–303, and Roy Harvey Pearce, "Hawthorne and the Sense of the Past," *Historicism Once More* (Princeton: Princeton University Press, 1969), pp. 150–52, see continuity rather than contrast in the early story and the revisions.

32. "Alice Doane's Appeal," p. 278. Subsequent references are given parenthetically in the text.

most believed her guilt"; a proud man so broken "that he seemed to hasten his steps, eager to hide himself in the grave" (pp. 278–79).

Leonard Doane, the gothic hero-villain, has been replaced by Cotton Mather, "darkly conspicuous" and "sternly triumphant," and instead of the causative machinations of the wizard, Hawthorne gives us "vices of spirit and errors of opinion that sufficed to madden the whole surrounding multitude" (p. 279). These substitutions do not abandon the gothic, but rejuvenate it. By their means the narrator accomplishes the aim of gothic fiction: "But here my companions seized an arm on each side; their nerves were trembling; and, sweeter victory still, I had reached the seldom trodden places of their hearts, and found the well-spring of their tears" (pp. 279–80). "Alice Doane's Appeal" thus chronicles the narrator's discovery of how to write American gothic. Compared to the *Provincial Tales* and the biographical sketches, it takes a much bolder attitude toward the handling of historical material, since Hawthorne manipulates actual events and characters for fictional purposes. Nor are those purposes moral or didactic: the author is seeking to move his audience.

If Hawthorne was not writing about history for the purpose of interpreting it, his use of the past nonetheless implies an interpretation. The images of Cotton Mather and the delusion-maddened crowd suggest once more the danger of the diseased imagination. Charles W. Upham's seminal lectures on Salem witchcraft, delivered in Salem at just the time Hawthorne was working on this fiction, explained the persecution as the result of unregulated imagination. Upham wrote near the conclusion of the published version of his lectures:

Man is never safe while either his fancy or his feeling is the guiding principle of his nature. There is a strong and constant attraction between his imagination and his passions, and if either is permitted to exercise unlimited sway, the other will most certainly be drawn into cooperation with it, and when they are allowed to react without restraint upon each other and with each other, they lead to the derangement and convulsion of his whole system. . . . Reason, enlightened by revelation and guided by conscience, is the great conservative principle; while that exercises the sovereign power over the fancy and the passions, we are safe; if it is dethroned, no limit can be assigned to the ruin that may follow.[33]

The confluence of imagination and passion, so heartily deplored by Upham, is of course the ground of this early writing by Hawthorne. Upham's commonsense point is that imagination, like a wild beast, is inherently dangerous.

Whether he absorbed it from Upham or some other source, apparently Hawthorne took this lesson to heart, for his work after 1830 shows one attempt after another to write more rational and conservative fiction. From 1830 through 1833 he experimented with a variety of short literary forms, evidently trying to expand his technical range. Late in June 1832 he wrote to Franklin Pierce, a college friend, that he was going to write a volume of tales built around his summer excursions, deriving unity from "a travelling story-teller, whose shiftings of fortune were to form the interlude and links between the separate stories."[34] Early in 1834 Hawthorne sent a bulky manuscript to Samuel Goodrich, who had published individual stories from the *Provincial Tales* in his annual, *The Token*. Goodrich sent it on to the *New England Magazine*, which began to serialize it in November 1834. After the second installment, however, a change of editorship (the magazine merged with the *American Monthly Magazine* within a year) led to a change in the handling of this work. Throughout 1835 and on into 1836 tales and sketches from *The Story Teller* appeared regularly, but without the interludes and

33. Charles W. Upham, *Lectures on Witchcraft* (Boston: Carter, Hendee and Babcock, 1831), p. 274.
34. Quoted in Adkins, p. 132.

links, and apparently in an order bearing no relation to the original. Possibly some of the manuscript was scrapped by the editor of the *American Monthly Magazine*.[35]

Although we know something of Hawthorne's intentions in *The Story Teller*, and although a good proportion of its contents survives, it is impossible to tell whether Hawthorne succeeded in carrying through his design or to know what the finished whole was actually like. A reader today finds additional difficulties in theorizing about *The Story Teller* because Hawthorne seems to have used its material in later collections without any attention to his original unifying plan. He selected five pieces for the 1837 *Twice-told Tales*, two more for the 1842 *Twice-told Tales*, one for *Mosses from an Old Manse* in 1846, five for *The Snow-Image* in 1851, and two more in the expanded reissue of *Mosses* in 1854. Still another four (the count is somewhat arbitrary, since some of the pieces are composites) he never collected at all.[36] Evidently, he ceased to regard the collection as a unity. According to

35. Besides Adkins, a good recent study of these events is Lillian B. Gilkes, "Hawthorne, Park Benjamin, S. G. Goodrich: A Three-Cornered Imbroglio," *Nathaniel Hawthorne Journal 1971* (Washington, D.C.: NCR/Microcard Editions, 1971), pp. 83–112.

36. *Story Teller* works in the 1837 *Twice-told Tales* were: "Mr. Higgenbotham's Catastrophe," "The Gray Champion," "Wakefield," "A Rill from the Town-Pump," "The Vision of the Fountain." In the 1842 volume: "The Ambitious Guest" and "The White Old Maid" (published originally as "The Old Maid in the Winding-Sheet"). In *Mosses* he included "Young Goodman Brown." In *The Snow-Image*: "Old News" (originally published in three separate installments), "Old Ticonderoga," "The Devil in Manuscript." In the 1854 *Mosses*: "Passages from a Relinquished Work" and "Sketches from Memory." Left uncollected was a second sequence of "Sketches from Memory" as well as "My Visit to Niagara," "Graves and Goblins," and "Fragments from the Journal of a Solitary Man." I do not accept in *The Story Teller* any material published in other magazines than the *New England/American Monthly Magazine*, or even published there after 1836.

twentieth-century tastes, the quality of the work in *The Story Teller* varies wildly, ranging from some of his weakest pieces, such as "The Vision of the Fountain," to some of the most powerful, such as "Young Goodman Brown."[37] It is quite possible that Hawthorne invented the frame after having written a substantial quantity of unrelated matter, and that he never achieved coherence in the first place. The frame itself, in its surviving fragments, is internally inconsistent since it begins in the first person and concludes in the third. And when his work was being reissued in the early 1850s (to capitalize on the success of *The Scarlet Letter*) and he could have brought out *The Story Teller* in its original form, he made no attempt to do so.

Still, the framing idea is so intriguing, and the included material so various, that it is tempting to speculate on the accomplishment of *The Story Teller*. Fortunately for the speculator, the opening section survives along with the storyteller's first tale, so that we do have a statement of the work's intentions as well as an example of its operation. Hawthorne planned to follow the progress of a young man who had run away from home and was supporting himself as a storyteller while wandering around the country. He meant to blend three distinct kinds of material: a characterization along with a kind of major fiction concerning this narrator; a series of descriptions "of the circumstances in which the story was told. . . . Frames, perhaps more valuable than the pictures themselves, since they will be embossed with groups of characteristic figures, amid the lake and mountain scenery, the villages and fertile fields, of our native land";[38] and finally, a

37. Seymour Gross has argued that "The Vision of the Fountain" would be a satiric story if we had the missing frame, and that therefore it is not so weak as it appears ("Hawthorne's 'Vision of the Fountain' as a Parody," *American Literature*, 27 [1955], 101–5).

38. "Passages from a Relinquished Work," in *Mosses from an Old Manse*, pp. 408–9. Hereafter cited parenthetically in text as "Passages."

variety of tales fitting the character of the speaker and the circumstances.

The two critics who have attempted to reconstruct the arrangement of *The Story Teller*—Adkins and Weber—have mapped the teller's journeys and strung the tales along a geographical route following that taken by Hawthorne on various summer excursions. But it is clear from the opening section that the unifying movement of the work was intended to be psychological, following the defiant flight and chastened return of the narrator-protagonist, Oberon. At the outset, Oberon is a young man "of gay and happy temperament, with an incorrigible levity of spirit, of not vicious propensities, sensible enough, but wayward and fanciful" ("Passages," p. 407). An orphan, he has been reared by Parson Thumpcushion, a stern and severe, though not unloving, guardian. For all his good intentions toward his ward, the Parson has not the right kind of nature to deal with Oberon: "He could neither change the nature that God had given me, nor adapt his own inflexible mind to my peculiar character" (p. 406). Among their many disagreements, the most serious concerns the youth's unwillingness to choose a profession.

Oberon has no taste for the solemn drudgery of the work ethic. He wants to keep "aloof from the regular business of life," and, as he says,

This would have been a dangerous resolution any where in the world; it was fatal, in New-England. There is a grossness in the conceptions of my countrymen; they will not be convinced that any good thing may consist with what they call idleness; they can anticipate nothing but evil of a young man who neither studies physic, law, nor gospel, nor opens a store, nor takes to farming, but manifests an incomprehensible disposition to be satisfied with what his father left him. The principle is excellent, in its general influence, but most miserable in its effect on the few that violate it. I had a quick sensitiveness to public opinion, and felt as if it ranked me with the tavern-haunters and town-paupers

—with the drunken poet, who hawked his own Fourth of July Odes, and the broken soldier who had been good for nothing since last war. The consequence of all this, was a piece of light-hearted desperation. [P. 407]

Motivated by "discontent with home and a bitter grudge against Parson Thumpcushion," he resolves to run away and become a wandering storyteller (p. 408). One naturally interprets this character as a refraction of Hawthorne himself, not as he was in 1825 when he cheerfully determined on the profession of authorship, but as he had become after seven years of vacillation and disappointment. His life had no Parson Thumpcushion in it—indeed, his situation was the reverse of this orphan's, surrounded as he was by indulgent and undemanding relatives—but the Parson is clearly a generic representation of the New England spirit. He represents the ideological combination of faith and toil, and as such is an inescapable pressure on the psyche of any young New Englander following an unconventional mode of life. Hawthorne's literary commitment lacked the bitterness of Oberon's and involved no running away from home; but it shared Oberon's wish to escape the charted, tedious futures of the conventional professions. It seems legitimate to theorize that Oberon expresses a part of Hawthorne's character and feelings, though certainly not the whole.

What fate has Hawthorne in store for this rebellious aesthete, who expresses some segment of his own more complex literary awareness? "I write the book for the sake of its moral," says Oberon in "Passages from a Relinquished Work," "which many a dreaming youth may profit by" (p. 409). And in the conclusion ("Fragments from the Journal of a Solitary Man") Oberon, now dead, his words conveyed to us by an unnamed friend through passages in his journal, advises the dreaming youth to "adopt some great and serious aim . . . [and] not to follow an eccentric path, nor, by stepping aside from the highway of human affairs, to relinquish his claim upon human sympathy" and to remember "that he is an American."[39] We must conclude, then, that Oberon's adventures teach him the folly and futility of his intentions, causing him to reject his original premises and to embrace the principles of Parson Thumpcushion.

The opening section foreshadows this misfortune and expresses Oberon's self-doubt. Leaving town at daybreak, he observes a kind of rainbow in the west, "Bestriding my intended road like a gigantic portal. . . . It had no brilliancy, no perceptible hues; but was a mere unpainted framework, as white and ghost-like as the lunar rainbow, which is deemed ominous of evil. But, with a light heart, to which all omens were propitious, I advanced beneath the misty archway of futurity" ("Passages," p. 411). Oberon's first venture, the recital of "Mr. Higgenbotham's Catastrophe," is very successful, but chiefly because someone pinned a horse's tail to his collar; the tail jerks up and down as the narrator speaks and occasions most of the laughter Oberon fatuously attributes to his comical narrative. "In after times," he comments, "when I had grown a bitter moralizer, I took this scene for an example, how much of fame is humbug; how much the meed of what our better nature blushes at; how much an accident; how much bestowed on mistaken principles; and how small and poor the remnant" ("Passages," p. 420).

Immediately after the performance, a letter arrives from Parson Thumpcushion. In a scene anticipating "The May-Pole of Merry Mount" Oberon writes: "I seemed to see the puritanic figure of my guardian, standing among the fripperies of the theatre, and pointing to the players,—the fantastic and effeminate men, the painted women, the giddy girl in boy's clothes, merrier than modest,—pointing to these with solemn ridicule, and eyeing me with stern rebuke. His image

39. "Fragments from the Journal of a Solitary Man," in *The Snow-Image*, pp. 326–27.

was a type of the austere duty, and they of the vanities of life" (p. 421). After a mental struggle, Oberon burns the letter unopened. "It is fixed in my mind, and was so at the time, that he had addressed me in a style of paternal wisdom, and love, and reconciliation, which I could not have resisted, had I but risked the trial. . . . The thought still haunts me, that then I made my irrevocable choice between good and evil fate" (p. 421).

From the beginning of *The Story Teller*, then, we know that Oberon was wrong to run away and that he will pay for it. We know it because the Oberon who is telling *The Story Teller* is not the young man himself, but the older and wiser Oberon who has returned from his travels and is looking back to judge his early self.[40] He has learned a hard realism. The wish to avoid the unavoidable cannot be realized; to act in defiance of reality is to invite disillusionment and destruction. So far as the artist is concerned, to produce a literature that is founded on an evasion of life's serious truths is to produce trivia and to make oneself a trivial person.

Almost as soon as he sets out on his journey, Oberon meets and joins with a young man named Eliakim Abbott. Eliakim is also an itinerant, but his trade is preaching rather than storytelling. As Oberon narrates "Mr. Higgenbotham's Catastrophe" in the theater, Eliakim addresses "sinners on the welfare of their immortal souls" in the schoolhouse ("Passages," p. 418). Although Eliakim is a ridiculous figure, he is also Oberon's alter ego; his appearance so early in Oberon's travels signifies that the New England heritage is not cast off simply by running away. Oberon is, whether he likes it or not, himself a product of the New England heritage and cannot but feel a self-reproach that will invite the sad destiny that so quickly overtakes him. But although Hawthorne had a plan for the general development of *The Story Teller* as a moral and psychological tale about authorship, there is no evidence

40. This point is made by Weber, p. 257.

that he had worked out the details of Oberon's darkening progress. From the surviving material it appears that he was inconsistent in his plotting. Some passages suggest that Oberon wandered for years, others imply a catastrophic journey of only several months. Oberon describes himself at one point as notorious, but elsewhere as obscure and unknown. The switch from first-person to third-person narration, and the place of "The Devil in Manuscript," which is a story about Oberon and not a framing episode, are inexplicable.

Possibly the frame could not function both as a story in itself and as an umbrella for the great variety of narratives Hawthorne wished to include in *The Story Teller*. In fewer than a dozen fictions Hawthorne covered a range including the comic, serious, sentimental, gothic, historical, contemporary, folksy, broad, subtle, and literary. If they reflected the psychological development of their narrator, they did so in a way that continually demonstrated his prowess as an artist. Indeed, the "Passages from a Relinquished Work" show how seriously even the disillusioned Oberon takes the matter of his craft: "I had immensely underrated the difficulties of my idle trade; now I recognized, that it demanded nothing short of my whole powers, cultivated to the utmost. . . . No talent or attainment could come amiss; every thing, indeed, was requisite; wide observation, varied knowledge, deep thoughts, and sparkling ones; pathos and levity, and a mixture of both, like sunshine in a rain-drop; lofty imagination, veiling itself in the garb of common life; and the practised art which alone could render these gifts, and more than these, available." Is not this view of the narrative art as a noble calling at variance with Oberon's rejection of ambition? "It is one of my few sources of pride, that, ridiculous as the object was, I followed it up with the firmness and energy of a man" (p. 416). The task for Hawthorne the storyteller, after he had expressed and discarded the Germanic or Byronic romanticism of

Oberon, was to find a way of carrying on this noble trade in a social rather than an antisocial context.

Throughout all the narratives from *The Story Teller* we find Hawthorne's underlying preoccupation with the intermingling of actuality and dream—dreams so vivid that they seem real, actuality so odd that it seems dreamlike—and the compelling power of fantasy. In humorous fashion, "Mr. Higgenbotham's Catastrophe" treats a fantasy that realizes itself; without humor, "Young Goodman Brown" does the same. In "The Gray Champion" a communal legend takes actual shape, impelled by the collective power of a people's imagination; in "The Vision of the Fountain" an actual shape is perceived by the cliché-stuffed mind of the speaker as a vision. In "Old News" the narrator tries to make the past come alive; the speaker in "Graves and Goblins" is an actualized ghost. Wakefield, acting out a fantasy, becomes its victim; the town that ignores Oberon's fantasies learns their actual power all too vividly when the burning manuscripts start a tremendous fire. Only in "The Ambitious Guest" are the two worlds kept rigidly separate, and this is precisely to emphasize the point that lives, for the people who live them, take their shape not from grim and gratuitous actuality but from their private fantasies.

If Hawthorne arranged these narratives in relation to Oberon's psychological evolution, they would reflect his darkening mood and change of heart. It is more than likely that he did not do this, but it is possible to arrange the stories according to the progression of Oberon's moods. The order, beginning with the known first tale (it appeared as such in the first installment), is: "Mr. Higgenbotham's Catastrophe," "A Rill from the Town-Pump," "The Vision of the Fountain," "Old News,"[41] "The Gray Champion," "Graves and Gob-

41. Of all the works published in the *New England Magazine* and the *American Monthly Magazine* within the *Story Teller* time span,

lins," "The White Old Maid," "The Devil in Manuscript," "The Ambitious Guest," "Wakefield," and "Young Goodman Brown." The first three are comic tales composed from different narrative standpoints. "Old News" re-creates history through old newspapers, while "The Gray Champion" is a historical legend. "Graves and Goblins" and "The White Old Maid" are standard gothic exercises, one mordantly humorous, one melodramatic. The tone darkens progressively through the sequence, but all operate within standard fictional modes. At the point dramatized in "The Devil in Manuscript," Oberon burns his fictions in disgust; the three tales that follow, different though they are from one another, are all somber exploratory studies of human folly. From the jocularity of "Mr. Higgenbotham's Catastrophe" to the oppressive gloom of "Young Goodman Brown" is a progress indeed.

The *Story Teller* material least tractable under analysis, and least readable today, is that deriving from Hawthorne's summer excursions and intended as setting for Oberon's recitations. Scholars assume that much of this descriptive material was scrapped by the journal editors, and the remaining published fragments appear to be travel sketches without any sign of Oberon's sensibility in the narration or of Oberon's audience in the circumstances. It is difficult to avoid the conclusion —even when allowance is made for the fragmentary state of these sketches—that Hawthorne had simply transferred material from his journals without revising it to suit the supposed intentions of *The Story Teller*. To make matters worse, the travel sketches are not particularly interesting; evidently, dense external material had the effect of paralyzing rather

---

"Old News" is the most difficult to understand in context, because it is not in any sense of the word a "tale" that might have been narrated. Either it was not, in fact, part of *The Story Teller*, but was a separate work that unaccountably got mixed up in the larger work, or else it is an indication of Hawthorne's failure to integrate his works into a whole.

than stimulating Hawthorne's creativity. Unlike Henry James, whose imagination warmed to the task of reproducing a rich actuality in a complex verbal structure, Hawthorne's sensibilities simply froze before a wealth of external impression. In fact, the chief interest of the travel material in *The Story Teller* is its continuous testimony to this imaginative failure accompanied by a defensive assertion of the superiority of the inner vision.

In "My Visit to Niagara," for example, the speaker has delayed his visit to the falls after arriving in town, fearful that his imagination will fail him, as indeed it does: "I had come thither, haunted with a vision of foam and fury, and dizzy cliffs, and an ocean tumbling down out of the sky—a scene, in short, which Nature had too much good taste and calm simplicity to realize. My mind had struggled to adapt these false conceptions to the reality, and finding the effort vain, a wretched sense of disappointment weighed me down."[42] At "Old Ticonderoga" Oberon (or whoever is speaking) feels himself superior to an engineer for whom the fort is only "an affair of brick and mortar and hewn stone, arranged on certain regular principles, having a good deal to do with mathematics but nothing at all with poetry," but his method of poeticizing Ticonderoga to his own satisfaction involves closing his eyes to shut out the Ticonderoga of today, and casting "a dreamlike glance over pictures of the past, and scenes of which this spot had been the theatre."[43] In other sketches the speaker strives self-consciously toward an appropriate response: "To my mind there was a sort of poetry in such an incident"; "I was inclined to be poetical about the Grand Canal"; "my fancy found another emblem"; "perhaps there was an emblem"; "how stern a moral may be drawn!" and so on. From an artistic point of view, Hawthorne experienced the pressure of the imagination on the actual as liberation, the

42. *The Snow-Image*, p. 284.
43. *The Snow-Image*, pp. 187, 189.

pressure of the actual on the imagination as constraint. This feeling he represented most effectively in "The Ambitious Guest."

The three pieces written during the *Story Teller* years that were not worked into the collection had either been published or were in press when Hawthorne conceived of the framing idea. One of them, "The Seven Vagabonds," anticipates the frame of *The Story Teller* and is identified in "Passages from a Relinquished Work" as the germ of Oberon's idea. A young man on a business trip meets a group of traveling show people and toys with the idea of joining them as an itinerant story-teller, thereby escaping both life's boring routines and its troubles. But, after the summer shower (which has brought him into company with these people) subsides, he continues on his way, relegating his wish to the limbo of unrealizable fancies. At much greater length, *The Story Teller* was to work out a different but related idea—that it is better not to try to realize such fantasies.

The two other pieces—"Sights from a Steeple" and "The Canterbury Pilgrims"—might certainly have been incorporated into *The Story Teller*, given the flexibility of its theoretical structure. Coincidentally, however, they represent something different from anything in that collection, and are peculiarly characteristic of Hawthorne's work for the rest of the decade of the 1830s. As we see, Hawthorne's writing was moving toward one of two final positions: either to an assertion of the dangerous power of the imagination or to a counterassertion of its triviality. In neither of these positions could a New Englander like Hawthorne rest content. He longed to do socially legitimate work that would bring him public esteem. Therefore, he strove throughout the rest of the 1830s to make his dangerous works less dangerous, his trivial works less trivial. "The Canterbury Pilgrims" is a good example of the techniques he employed for the former goal, "Sights from a Steeple" a good example of those for the latter.

"The Canterbury Pilgrims" is a fiction with a heavy over-lay of allegory and moralizing. It justifies the literary product and hence literary activity by displaying fiction as the vehicle for conservative wisdom. Arranging the story for the purposes of a moral, Hawthorne creates a space between its events and the readers; within that space all strong emotional effects will dissipate. "The Shaker youth and maiden looked mournfully into each other's eyes. They had but stepped across the threshold of their homes, when lo! the dark array of cares and sorrows that rose up to warn them back. The varied narratives of the strangers had arranged themselves into a parable."[44]

"Sights from a Steeple" is an impressionistic sketch, the first of a type that was to become his dominant mode for the rest of the decade. Ostensibly about some aspect of the every-day, it is really the occasion for an exercise of the narrator's fancy. In "Sights from a Steeple" the narrator pretends that he is perched on the steeple of the town church; from this central raised vantage point he can observe the life around him, describe it, comment on it. The sketch progresses as an alternation of description and associative reverie; it is delicately fanciful. The speaker's activity of mind transforms life into something beautiful and pleasurable; the sketch is re-creative in the sense of making new.

The narrator's ability to embellish the reality he transcribes with pleasing and cogent fanciful touches obviously depends on the quality of his fancy, but also on his position of detachment and withdrawal. Free from the pressure of immediate events, he can contemplate them. Such detachment is the undefiant equivalent, or the social modification, of Oberon's flight, which in turn was the active equivalent of Fanshawe's passive superiority. Now it is justified because it represents a social impulse—not the desire to be aloof from life or avoid it, but the wish to enrich it.

44. *The Snow-Image*, p. 130.

Implicit in both forms, which, new to Hawthorne's repertoire, quickly come to dominate his practice, is a greatly expanded authorial presence. In both the moralized fiction and the sketch, a sensibility—now wise, now fanciful—must be visibly at work. Thus Hawthorne must develop a persona. This persona is a modest man who makes a modest claim for literature as a reinforcer of social values and an enhancer of our perceptions of life. He is no more the author's self than were the discarded protagonists, Fanshawe and Oberon. Later in his career, from a position of literary eminence, Hawthorne deplored the readership that confused the persona with the author. But in all probability, during the years he used this persona, he intended the confusion.

The *Twice-told Tales* Period
1834–1839

Oberon's story demonstrated that estrangement from society
destroys an author. It also raised the possibility that authorship
in its very nature might be an antisocial profession. Hawthorne's work for the next several years was designed to
demonstrate that this possibility was false by showing writing
to be a social activity. If the author was not a man of society
in the fullest sense of the phrase, he nevertheless wrote with
society's interests rather than his own in mind and wrote in
full awareness of, and compliance with, society's values. Both
the sketch and the moralized fiction—the two kinds of work
Hawthorne mostly produced in this period—show the writer
projecting back onto society what he assumes to be society's
values.

When Hawthorne put together his first published volume
of tales in 1837, and when he expanded that collection to two
volumes in 1842, he drew heavily on recently written material
and lightly on works dating from *The Story Teller* and
earlier. In the 1837 volume, eight of the eighteen short pieces
came from the early period, and in 1842 he added three more:
in all, he used eleven early pieces in a collection of thirty-nine,
roughly one-third of the material he had to draw on. Examined
in the light of Hawthorne's wish to connect with society
through his writing, the rationale of his selection from the
early works is quite understandable. Those that he used sup-

port the depiction of a social persona. All are tightly and rationally controlled, which is why twentieth-century readers tend to prefer some of the stories he left out: "My Kinsman, Major Molineux," "Young Goodman Brown," and "Roger Malvin's Burial."

The moralized fiction and the sketch are, to some extent, literary opposites, since the material of one is invented (or, to use Hawthorne's term, "ideal") and that of the other, actual. Yet both tend to the same end. The invented stories are shaped to illustrate a social moral, and in the sketch, the play of fancy on the actual shows that faculty to have a moral and social character. Both literary types accept a very limited place for literature in America, resigning themselves to an auxiliary and supportive social role. By making itself useful in an uncontroversial way, this literature appears to beg for audience tolerance. Hawthorne's tone is appropriately modest and even self-deprecating. His argument seems to be less that literature is capable of great good than that it is not productive of harm. His stance is appeasing. He makes no revolutionary claims, asserts no avant-garde pretensions.

Later in his career Hawthorne consigned the speaker in these works—with the gentlest irony—to the realm of discarded personae along with Fanshawe and Oberon. In 1851, when he wrote a preface for a reissue of the *Twice-told Tales,* he found this work to have "the pale tint of flowers that blossomed in too retired a shade. . . . Instead of passion, there is sentiment. . . . Whether from lack of power, or an unconquerable reserve, the Author's touches have often an effect of tameness. . . . They are not the talk of a secluded man with his own mind and heart, (had it been so, they could hardly have failed to be more deeply and permanently valuable), but his attempts, and very imperfectly successful ones, to open an intercourse with the world."[1] The bolder

1. *Twice-told Tales*, pp. 5–6. Subsequent references are given parenthetically in text.

author reproaches his younger self for timidity and lack of force, recognizing how these qualities follow from the wish to show friendly feelings toward the world. "On the internal evidence of his sketches," Hawthorne continues, the author "came to be regarded as a mild, shy, gentle, melancholic, exceedingly sensitive, and not very forcible man. . . . He is by no means certain, that some of his subsequent productions have not been influenced and modified by a natural desire to fill up so amiable an outline, and to act in consonance with the character assigned to him; nor, even now, could he forfeit it without a few tears of tender sensibility" (p. 7). With this last phrase Hawthorne bids a mocking farewell to the ideas of decorum that controlled his work during the period of the *Twice-told Tales*.

Between 1834 and 1837 Hawthorne wrote eight moralized fictions: "The Wedding-Knell," "The Minister's Black Veil," "The May-Pole of Merry Mount," "The Great Carbuncle," "Dr. Heidegger's Experiment," "The Man of Adamant," "David Swan," and "The Prophetic Pictures." Between 1837 and 1840 he wrote another five: "Peter Goldthwaite's Treasure," "Sylph Etherege," "The Lily's Quest," "Edward Fane's Rosebud," and "The Threefold Destiny." (Of this number, probably only "The Minister's Black Veil" and "The May-Pole of Merry Mount" arouse the enthusiasm of twentieth-century readers.) As a group the fictions celebrate the common highway of life and deplore all attempts to step aside from it. Whether ambition, reforming zeal, eccentricity, or accident causes the protagonist to step aside, they are all the same in effect, and the appropriate subject for authorial criticism. The moral truth in these fictions is normative—that is, it assumes that the way most men and women do live is the way all men and women ought to live. It appears that the moral lesson behind all this fiction could be reduced to the tautology that he who is not like his fellows is not normal. "The May-Pole of Merry Mount" and "The Minister's Black

Veil" are probably popular today because their themes are not so easily reduced to this moral triviality. The Puritans in "The May-Pole of Merry Mount" are too gloomy to represent a convincing normality; Parson Hooper in "The Minister's Black Veil" seems too good a man for the severe judgment that the structure of the story makes on him. Yet in the context of the other fictions written at the time, their fit to the larger pattern is clear.

In this group of narratives Hawthorne shows the inevitable consequence of an act of separation to be an increasing subjectivity leading ultimately to insanity. The inherent drift of the mind toward madness must be constantly opposed by bringing oneself into contact with other minds and with everyday actuality. Unremitting effort is required to stay sane, because the mind naturally tends toward total self-enclosure. Thus, a single isolating act can have extreme consequences. There is, then, in these fictions a regular tension between the uncorrected and the corrected, or the unregulated and regulated, imagination. Here is a representative passage from "Peter Goldthwaite's Treasure": "His brief glimpse into the street had given him a forcible impression of the manner in which the world kept itself cheerful and prosperous, by social pleasures and an intercourse of business, while he, in seclusion, was pursuing an object that might possibly be a phantasm, by a method which most people would call madness. It is one great advantage of a gregarious mode of life, that each person rectifies his mind by other minds, and squares his conduct to that of his neighbours, so as seldom to be lost in eccentricity" (p. 400).

And here is another, from "Old Esther Dudley": "Living so continually in her own circle of ideas, and never regulating her mind by a proper reference to present things, Esther Dudley appears to have grown partially crazed" (p. 298). In the moralized fiction of this period Hawthorne does not show the crazed imagination inflicting harm on others, as he had in

"Roger Malvin's Burial," and would again in "Rappaccini's Daughter" and "The Birth-mark." Here the unregulated imagination is not dangerous to society, only to the self. Moreover, as the narrator adroitly distinguishes himself from his various protagonists, he demonstrates how the imagination as *he* exercises its function can be used to rectify rather than indulge itself. His imaginative fiction counteracts the natural bent of imagination.

Within the constraint of their overt moral purpose, these stories display a variety of tones and moods, exemplify different fictional types, and in general show a considerable range. If one thinks of the work of the *Twice-told Tales* period as performance rather than creation, one will perhaps better grasp its aesthetic assumptions. The author is doing what he is expected to do, and doing it well. Each piece is further evidence of his versatility and technical skill. His achievement is pleasing; it satisfies the assumptions that the audience brings to the reading of his work. This aesthetic also underlies the nine sketches of this period, which I shall examine below in greater detail.

Besides moral fictions and sketches Hawthorne also composed, during this period, one broadly comic story, "Mrs. Bullfrog," and two gothic studies of the mind, "Fancy's Show Box" and "The Haunted Mind." "Mrs. Bullfrog" fits into the normative pattern of the other writings because it tells of the disillusionment of Mr. Bullfrog, and his chastisement for imagining that he could marry a creature of fantasy and not a real woman. The gothic mental sketches, however, are quite different from the bulk of material Hawthorne produced in these years. Additionally, there are two unmoralized fictions—"The Shaker Bridal" and "John Inglefield's Thanksgiving." The former is a somber story in the mode of "Roger Malvin's Burial" and "Young Goodman Brown," wherein the obsession of the male protagonist is judged by the damage it does to the trusting female partner. The latter is a gothic fantasy like "The

Hollow of the Three Hills" and "The White Old Maid." Hawthorne did not use it in either volume of *Twice-told Tales*.

After the *Provincial Tales* Hawthorne's engagement in historical fiction had somewhat slackened. In *The Story Teller* only "Young Goodman Brown" and "The Gray Champion" have historical reference, and in the first years of the *Twice-told Tales* period (1834–1837) he wrote only one historical fiction, "The May-Pole of Merry Mount."[2] But after 1837 he wrote the four "Legends of the Province-House" as well as "Endicott and the Red Cross" and the uncollected historical sketch "A Bell's Biography." The resuscitation of interest in history culminated in his history of Massachusetts for children, which he wrote in 1840 and 1841. This culmination also marked a virtual end to the historical concern in his writing— a concern that has been blown far out of proportion by the amount of critical attention it has received—for after 1840 only "Main-street" and *The Scarlet Letter* were cast in the historical mode.

If the historical emphasis in Hawthorne's writing has been much exaggerated, the great quantity of sketch material in the canon has been largely ignored; anthologies and critical studies alike have presented a part of Hawthorne's writings for the whole. During the dozen years between *The Story Teller* and *Mosses from an Old Manse* more than half of Hawthorne's literary output may be classified as sketches. As I have already suggested, this genre embodies a way of subjecting actuality to the operations of the imagination—or more precisely, of the fancy, since fancy is the term Hawthorne uses.[3] His chief metaphor for fanciful activity is the flight of the butterfly,

2. In some discussions of Hawthorne's historical writing "The Minister's Black Veil" is counted as a historical fiction, but it contains less than half a sentence devoted to historical localization.

3. If he had read Coleridge by this time, he would be deliberately selecting the lesser over the greater creative power for his domain in the sketch.

whose image appears in many of his works. The butterfly implies a light, airy, playful, evanescent beauty; its flight stands for the free, erratic leaps of association, the pauses and new starts, the airborne and yet earth-hugging nature of the faculty. In another characteristic image Hawthorne describes his fancies as gleaming softly like "stars at twilight, or like violets in May—perhaps to fade as soon" (p. 344). Shining, subdued, and transient—this is the fancy, and these are Hawthorne's sketches.

Obviously, Hawthorne cannot make a weighty claim for the faculty or the literature it creates. He praises it, cautiously, as a kind of refreshment for the moral and intellectual system of the socialized adult. In "Little Annie's Ramble" he identifies fancy specifically with the child's perceptions, "those fountains of still fresh existence." To associate with children is to feel one's "moral nature revived" and to experience within oneself a "kinder and purer heart, and a spirit more lightly wise" (p. 129). The moralized fictions suppose that the imagination needs to be regulated by a continual submersion of the individual mind in the social mainstream; but the sketches argue that an exclusively social existence can destroy spiritual vitality and resiliency. To correct this, one withdraws temporarily—but not into one's private fantasies. One takes up briefly the attitude of observer rather than participant; literally, one gets a new perception of things. The circle of observation is confined to the speaker's native town and the surrounding countryside; he is always close to home. Some sketches, like "Sights from a Steeple," "Sunday at Home," and "Little Annie's Ramble," follow the ordinary activities of the townspeople; others like "Snow-flakes," "Foot-prints on the Seashore" and "Night Sketches," chronicle the shifting face of nature. They assume that the audience believes in the salutary effect of a connection with nature. In some sketches the speaker occupies a stationary position and observes the movement of life around him; in others he rambles about, and invariably these sketches conclude with his return. It is made clear that the purpose of withdrawal is not hedonistic or self-indulgent, and that there is no danger of solipsism. The speaker withdraws to fortify himself for the business of life. Then he rejoins the procession better able to carry on, ready "to struggle onward and do our part in life . . . as fervently as ever" (p. 129). So the fancy has no excuse for being if it is simply exercised in and for itself, but when incorporated into the Puritan ethic it can be justified. The reader will presumably experience a similarly clarified vision through reading the sketch that the speaker attained in his ramble. In the act of writing the sketch, the speaker offers the fruits of his fancy to the reader in the hope that they will be tonic.

Behind the technique of these sketches is a basically pictorial aesthetic. All the sketches abound and excel in visual descriptions, some minutely detailed like a Dutch genre painting, and others more impressionistically depicting the appearance of landscape and sky under changing conditions of light and weather. The descriptions of morning and evening, of snowstorm and rainfall, distinctly remind one of the interests and accomplishments of English and American romantic painters. Such visual representation may not interest a reader in the age of the photograph, but evidently Hawthorne expected his sketches to make an impression through their skillful pictorialism.

At the same time, he goes beyond picture into poetry when he shows the narrator's perceptions merging with his fancies: "Turn we again to the fireside, and sit musing there, lending our ears to the wind, till perhaps it shall seem like an articulate voice, and dictate wild and airy matter for the pen. Would it might inspire me to sketch out the personification of a New-England winter! And that idea, if I can seize the snow-wreathed figures that flit before my fancy, shall be the theme of the next page" (p. 346). Here Hawthorne shows a paradigmatic interaction between the mind and the actual. The wind summons up a personified image of winter in the narrator's mind, which he then realizes in his prose and thus projects back out again as part of his description of the snowstorm. The aesthetic task here is to depict these fancies or ideas with the same vividness as his sketches of the actual, so that within the texture of the written work both appear equally real. The sketches thus indicate Hawthorne's continuing absorption in what he later came to define as the pre-eminent aesthetic requirement for a romancer: the ability to merge actual and ideal in a successful literary structure.

There inheres in some of these sketches a sort of romantic pastoralism, where the value of the fancy lies in its ability to perceive the simpler and purer values of life. Such pastoralism is implicit in "Little Annie's Ramble," where the fancy is childlike; it is also found in "The Toll-Gatherer's Day," where the narrator imagines himself into the simpler existence of a toll-gatherer, whose position alongside the highway of life enables him to observe the concourse of traffic going by and who reflects on all he sees with a humble, uncomplicated vision. Similarly, in "The Village Uncle" (originally entitled "The Mermaid") the narrator projects his own fancy into the simpler sensibility of the poetic fisherman. Other sketches, however, present fancy as a faculty that adds complexity and depth to the coarse superficial texture of the everyday. In either case, the fancy performs a kind of compensatory activity that enriches the whole life of the organism.

Yet this defense of fancy is set round with limitations. At one end of the scale, Hawthorne is ever mindful that the dream world is no substitute for real living: "And now for a moral to my reverie. Shall it be, that, since fancy can create so bright a dream of happiness, it were better to dream on from youth to age, than to awake and strive doubtfully for something real? Oh! the slight tissue of a dream can no more preserve us from the stern reality of misfortune, than a robe of cobweb could repel the wintry blast. Be this the moral, then. In chaste and warm affections, humble wishes, and honest toil for some useful end, there is health for the mind, and quiet for the heart, the prospect of a happy life, and the fairest hope of Heaven" (p. 323).

At the other end of the scale are the great truths preserved in religion, which the fancy may approach but may not dwell upon. Hawthorne seems much concerned to present fancy as a sort of handmaid to religion, which he defines not as a body of doctrine or a set of observances but as an emotion of faith. In his sketch called "Sunday at Home" he builds on the assertion that he is more truly religious staying away from church than most of those who routinely attend services. His inner man, he says, goes constantly to church, and his inner flights of fancy bring him constantly to the gate of heaven. In "Chippings with a Chisel" he opposes the faith attainable through fancy to the puritanic gloom implicit in tombstone carvings. "Every grave-stone that you ever made is the visible symbol of a mistaken system," he tells the stonecutter. "Our thoughts should soar upward with the butterfly—not linger with the exuviae that confined him" (p. 418). The rejuvenated speaker's return to society at the conclusion of every sketch symbolizes both the contribution that fancy can make to the general welfare and the necessary limits of the faculty. The proper exercise of fancy leads inevitably to the recognition of its proper bounds.

In only one sketch from these years does Hawthorne drop his mask of affability and return to the self-indulgent expressionism of Oberon. The narcissistic sketch "Monsieur du Miroir" is the narrator's meditation on his own image in the looking glass. Beginning his reverie as a little mental game, he permits his thoughts to lead him on into the future, and his projected image acquires a Byronic gloom:

I involuntarily peruse him as a record of my heavy youth, which has been wasted in sluggishness, for lack of hope and impulse, or equally thrown away in toil, that had no wise motive, and has accomplished no good end. I perceive that the tranquil gloom of a disappointed soul has darkened through his countenance, where the blackness of the future seems to mingle with the shadows of the past, giving him the aspect of a fated man. Is it too wild a thought, that my fate may have assumed this image of myself, and therefore haunts me with such inevitable pertinacity, originating every act which it appears to imitate, while it deludes me by pretending to share the events of which it is merely the emblem and the prophecy? I must banish this idea, or it will throw too deep an awe around my companion.[4]

Words like "involuntarily," "wild," "blackness," "fated," and finally "awe" indicate the surrender of reason and the impulsion of imagination past the limits of the decorous and sane. And what does Hawthorne mean by "too deep an awe"? Here is the most significant of all limitations on the fancy and the sketch that embodies it. The world of gripping images and strong emotions—its own proper domain—is denied to fancy except on the most superficial levels. How small a space Hawthorne has allowed himself for displaying his artistic powers! Fancy is bound to stop short of religious speculations about man's place in the universe—these are out of its reach. It is obligated to reinforce the everyday morality of domestic affection and honest toil—otherwise it might be interpreted as subversive. And it is prohibited from investigating the psychological depths, for such an investigation may unseat the controlling reason. Hawthorne's sketches represent a voluntary repression of a powerful talent that is astonishing in its apparent perversity. No audience would have demanded from him the concessions that he made in advance.

No doubt his rueful preface in 1851 recognizes this fact, and probably it explains how the situation came about. Working in solitude, his pieces published anonymously, Hawthorne developed no real understanding of that audience whose favor he was soliciting; he was attempting to open an intercourse

4. *Mosses from an Old Manse*, p. 168.

with a world he did not know. The audience he tried to please is one he invented, evidently composed of rational teachers and stern ministers—a readership of Parson Thumpcushions! Ought he not to have spoken as he felt and let the audience judge rather than anticipate its responses and adjust his work accordingly? Evidently, such a procedure was out of the question for Hawthorne. His two strongest literary convictions were at variance with each other: that we live in our imaginations, and that an author measures his achievement by the audience's approbation. We cannot wonder that he always wrote with an audience in mind; but we have to wonder at the severity of his conception of that audience.

Besides "Monsieur du Miroir," which stops at the point where its material transgresses the limits the sketch sets for itself, and which contains its rebellious imaginative gestures within a Byronic cliché, Hawthorne wrote two other works in the *Twice-told Tales* period that approach the world of the wild, fated, and awful. These are the two allegories of the mind, "Fancy's Show Box" and "The Haunted Mind." The subject matter of both is the fantasizing mind as it creates or gives way to images ordinarily suppressed by reason or morality. Only when rational or moral controls relax can these images be apprehended. Even if the content of these images was innocuous, the fact that the mind must relax its grip to receive them means that they would be dangerous in effect. They testify to a continuous undercurrent of forbidden thought. Perhaps because he wished to neutralize the dangerous charge of these images, or perhaps because he was not prepared to run the risk himself of dealing extensively with this material, Hawthorne filtered it through a severely inhibiting allegorical form.

"The Haunted Mind"—unique in Hawthorne's canon because it is written in the second person ("your" mind is its subject)—begins at an hour when, "starting from midnight slumber," the mind hovers in "an intermediate space" between yesterday and tomorrow, sleeping and waking.[5] "In the depths of every heart, there is a tomb or dungeon, though the lights, the music, and revelry above may cause us to forget their existence, and the buried ones, or prisoners whom they hide. But sometimes, and oftenest at midnight, those dark receptacles are flung wide open. In an hour like this, when the mind has a passive sensibility, but no active strength; when the imagination is a mirror, imparting vividness to all ideas, without the power of selecting or controlling them; then pray that your griefs may slumber, and the brotherhood of remorse not break their chain" (p. 306). This pre-Freudian model of the subconscious mind, like Poe's, uses gothic elements for its symbolism: the midnight hour, the castle with its tombs and dungeons.

And the allegorized specters that manage to cross the threshold of the entranced vision also appear in gothic guises. First comes Sorrow, "sadly beautiful, with a hallowed sweetness in her melancholy features, and grace in the flow of her sable robe," then Disappointment, "a shade of ruined loveliness," and Fatality, "with a brow of wrinkles, a look and gesture of iron authority." After this stock group comes one more awesome: "The devils of a guilty heart," including one "in woman's garments, with a pale beauty amid sin and desolation" and another in male form that stands "at your bed's foot, in the likeness of a corpse, with a bloody stain upon the shroud" (p. 307). Although this band of specters is supposed to refer to the dreamer's private experiences, they imply, in conventional images, the conventional gothic crimes of seduction and murder. With these generalities Hawthorne actually severs his representation of the secret mental life from con-

5. Barton Levi St. Armand, impressed by the emphasis in this sketch on the threshold between the conscious and dreaming mind, takes it as a central document of Hawthorne's aesthetic and psychological intentions ("Hawthorne's 'Haunted Mind': A Subterranean Drama of the Self," *Criticism*, 13 [1971], 1–25).

nections with any private reality. Thus this material, though out of the control of the passive mind that is represented as envisioning it, is in fact very much under the control of the author, who has forced it into the shapes of literary stereotypes.

As the reveries of "you," the dreamer in "The Haunted Mind," become increasingly anxiety-producing, "you" join the author in the process of exerting authority over your fantasies. Through conscious effort you wake from the hypnagogic state and return the control of your mental life to the higher faculties. You sink back to sleep now with your fancy at the helm to assure that you will have pleasant dreams: "Your thoughts rise before you in pictures, all disconnected, yet all assimilated by a pervading gladsomeness and beauty. . . . You stand in the sunny rain of a summer shower, and wander among the sunny trees of an autumnal wood. . . . Your mind struggles pleasantly between the dancing radiance round the hearth of a young man and his recent bride, and the twittering flight of birds in spring, about their new-made nest" (p. 308). The gothic horrors are returned to the dungeon. Hawthorne's intentions seem contradictory: forbidden material surfaces in hackneyed shapes. If there is an element of personal release in this sketch, it is presented in most impersonal terms.

"Fancy's Show Box" also takes "the secret soul" for its subject. The venerable protagonist Mr. Smith, alone with his Madeira, sees the imagined though uncommitted misdeeds of his youth pictured forth by Fancy, who is personified as an itinerant showman with a box of pictures. As Mr. Smith, with the help of Memory, who stands next to him and reads from a book, recognizes each of these crimes for his own fantasy, his personified Conscience stabs him in the heart. This allegory is mechanical and awkward, perhaps deliberately quaint like the moving figures in an old clock-tower. The crimes are predictable: a young girl seduced and abandoned, a close friend murdered, some helpless orphans swindled out of their inheritance. As in "The Haunted Mind" Hawthorne has muffled an unconventional assertion about the mind in conventional language.

It is important to observe that Hawthorne's subject is not the human capacity to do evil deeds, but the human capacity to think evil thoughts. This is what we should expect from a writer who perceives action as dependent on, and subsequent to, the imagination. The question posed by "Fancy's Show Box" is: to what extent are we guilty of committing a crime if we merely imagine it? This is a question of special significance to the imaginative writer, because he imagines guilty deeds all the time:

> A scheme of guilt, till it be put in execution, greatly resembles a train of incidents in a projected tale. . . . A novel-writer . . . in creating a villain of romance, and fitting him with evil deeds, and the villain of actual life, in projecting crimes that will be perpetrated, may almost meet each other, half-way between reality and fancy. It is not until the crime is accomplished, that guilt clenches its gripe upon the guilty heart and claims it for its own. Then, and not before, sin is actually felt and acknowledged, and, if unaccompanied by repentance, grows a thousand fold more virulent by its self-consciousness. [Pp. 225–226]

Apparently exonerating the fantasizer of evil by comparing him to the romancer, Hawthorne in fact implicates the romancer in guilt. For, if there is no guilt in the crime until it is committed, why does Conscience stab Mr. Smith in the heart every time Fancy shows him a picture? Here is a dilemma indeed. Hawthorne refrains from resolving it, and he fails to pursue the obvious next question: in what circumstances is the mind propelled beyond dream into action? Instead, he brings his sketch to a sonorous, if equivocal, conclusion, with a resounding moral: "Yet, with the slight fancy-work which we have framed, some sad and awful truths are interwoven. Man must not disclaim his brotherhood, even with the guiltiest, since, though his hand be clean, his heart has surely been polluted by the flitting phantoms of iniquity" (p. 226). To call evil thoughts "flitting phantoms of iniquity" is inconsistently to remove responsibility for them from the imagining mind—they seem rather to be transient and independent agents. And observe how, by the pun in the word "fancy-work," Hawthorne has belittled his own writing. By stitching a moral into this fancy-work, he says, he gives it whatever significance it has; save for that moral, it is a creation of the same order as embroidered handkerchiefs, or lace doilies. The reader's attention is diverted from the fact that Hawthorne, in this very sketch, has been guilty of imagining crimes. The respectability of the persona has been preserved, at the price of deliberate self-deprecation.

The question as originally posed appeared to be theological: "Must the fleshly hand, and visible frame of man, set its seal to the evil designs of the soul, in order to give them their entire validity against the sinner?" (p. 220). But by the end of the allegory Hawthorne shows that his interests are purely psychological—he wants to know when guilt clenches its hold on the soul, when "sin is actually felt and acknowledged." Although critical studies of Hawthorne for years have noted that Hawthorne's interests in "sin" were exclusively psychological, they have all too often deviated from that fundamental perception and considered Hawthorne to be concerned with the status of a thought or action in the absolute judgment of God. To approach Hawthorne thus, as a theological writer, is to violate one of the boundaries he himself established in his works and rigorously observed. Whatever his own religious convictions might have been, and however much he might have speculated on theological questions, these have no place in his writing. A character feels guilty if he believes that he has done something sinful. Reuben Bourne felt guilty for failing to stay with Roger Malvin until he died and for failing to return to bury him; he felt no guilt at all when he murdered his son. Which of these acts, according to what theological doctrine, was more truly sinful? The question has no pertinence to Hawthorne, except in so far as the character's deviation from normal morality shows madness.

When Hawthorne put together a collection of published material for *Twice-told Tales*, which appeared in 1837, he had available fifteen pieces that postdated *The Story Teller*, and about thirty from the earlier years. He used ten of the recent fifteen, omitting "Mrs. Bullfrog," "Monsieur du Miroir," "The Man of Adamant," "The Haunted Mind," and "The Village Uncle." He chose eight from the early thirty: "The Hollow of the Three Hills," "The Gentle Boy," "Sights from a Steeple," "The Vision of the Fountain," "The Gray Champion," "Mr. Higgenbotham's Catastrophe," "Wakefield," and "A Rill from the Town-Pump." In all probability a critic of today, given the same opportunity, would choose almost none of the works that Hawthorne selected. It is not difficult to see that although ideas of balance, variety, and reader appeal surely played their part in Hawthorne's decisions, the overriding criterion was the presentation of the author.[6] The whole of *Twice-told Tales* would naturally be greater than its individual parts, and each tale and sketch would figure in the illumination of the teller's capacity and reach. Each tale and sketch needed to be tested against the final impression of himself that Hawthorne wanted his readers to receive. In most cases, he was attaching his name to a work for the first time. As J. Donald Crowley has brilliantly demonstrated, he revised these formerly anonymous pieces with an idea of public appropriateness uppermost in his mind.[7]

6. I take these criteria from Doubleday, p. 80, who also maintains that he left out ambiguous stories because he wanted clarity. Clarity, it seems to me, is an aspect of author presence and author control of the narrative.

7. See J. Donald Crowley, "The Artist as Mediator: The Rationale of Hawthorne's Large-Scale Revisions in his Collected Tales and

The impression of the author develops gradually, through an accumulation of details. The collection has boundaries. Within these boundaries, different types of writing are allotted different amounts of space. For example, the inclusion of two comic pieces in *Twice-told Tales*—"Mr. Higgenbotham's Catastrophe" and "A Rill from the Town-Pump"—indicates a light side to the author without typing him as a humorist. Hawthorne avoided using works that were almost identical in tone or structure or plot-line, but he arranged stories and sketches to bring out similarities that would give the collection unity as the product of a faceted but single mind. He left out all the works that carried the stamp of Oberon's persona as well as all his travel material and most of the unmoralized fiction. The omissions cut away the two extremes of Hawthorne's work: the most purely factual sketches and the most purely fantastical fictions. The writer we meet in *Twice-told Tales* is an abbreviation of the author we have been following from the outset of his career, but he is very much the same self-presentation that Hawthorne had been working on after *The Story Teller*, the author who could be admired for his skill, appreciated for his sentiment, and assented to for his moral views.[8] If Hawthorne hoped for greater excitement

Sketches," *Melville and Hawthorne in the Berkshires* (Kent, Ohio: Kent State University Press, 1966), pp. 79–88, 156–57. "Hawthorne's strategy of mediation," Crowley writes, "his transformation of a private style into a public style—was almost a necessary one. . . . It was also, for Hawthorne at least, a deeply personal and honest one" (p. 88).

8. I disagree here with Crowley, who, in "The Unity of Hawthorne's *Twice-Told Tales*," *Studies in American Fiction*, 1 (1973), 35–61, has written that the work is controlled by Hawthorne's sense of "the necessity to awaken an audience virtually maimed in its capacity to feel or imagine." Indeed, it seems to me that this hypothesis is in conflict with Crowley's study of the intentions in Hawthorne's revisions. Whether he believed it or not, Hawthorne assumes in

among his audience than *Twice-told Tales* actually elicited, it is hard to understand why.

Nothing is known about how carefully or with what rhetorical assumptions Hawthorne worked on the order of pieces in *Twice-told Tales*. He may have arranged them intuitively, with little or no conscious formulation of rhetorical or thematic intention. One can observe a clear, loose movement of association abruptly broken here and there by radical changes in mood or by contrasting effects, so that *Twice-told Tales* has the design of a sketch writ large. Some associations are thematic, others follow settings or subjects. The first six works in *Twice-told Tales* are, in order, "The Gray Champion," "Sunday at Home," "The Wedding-Knell," "The Minister's Black Veil," "The May-Pole of Merry Mount," and "The Gentle Boy," and they have a rough continuity and coherence. All of them pretend to be true accounts, all are set in New England, take place in the past, and focus on Puritans, ministers, or churches.[9] From one work to the next the mood grows more intense and the tone darker. There is a gradual movement from a communal to a private center. "The Gentle Boy," the most emotional and private of the stories, ends this associative train. "Mr. Higgenbotham's Catastrophe," which follows, breaks the train and changes the pace.

The middle section of the volume contains "Mr. Higgenbotham's Catastrophe," "Little Annie's Ramble," "Wakefield," and "A Rill from the Town-Pump." Together these present the greatest variety of authorial strategies in the collection. The author delivers a folk narrative, identifies with a child's viewpoint, moralizes somberly about human egotism, and finally personifies himself as the town pump to deliver a

---

Twice-told Tales that the author is obligated to comply with reader expectations.

9. See Crowley, "The Unity of Hawthorne's *Twice-Told Tales*," for a much more complicated interpretation of the order based on dialectic principles.

facetious temperance lecture. After this intermezzo, a second train of associated works is initiated with "The Great Carbuncle." These, in contrast to the first group of tales, are more frankly fantastic and artificial. This segment includes, in order, "The Great Carbuncle," "The Prophetic Pictures," "David Swan," "Sights from a Steeple," "The Hollow of the Three Hills,"[10] "The Vision of the Fountain," "Fancy's Show Box," and "Dr. Heidegger's Experiment." The volume opens ("The Gray Champion") and closes ("Dr. Heidegger's Experiment") with stories that share a strong, direct linear action, a firm authorial presence, and a sort of authoritarian father figure as their chief character. The works of delicate fancy are thus subsumed within a basic impression of decisiveness.

From a rhetorical point of view the first few stories probably make the greatest impression on the reader. All subsequent works must be defined against the impression of the opening works. Thus it is quite important that *Twice-told Tales* begins with "The Gray Champion," for this story not only sets the strong tone referred to above, it also asserts an attitude toward history and establishes the volume as an American work. "The Gray Champion" is unambiguously patriotic and its attitude toward the Puritans entirely affirmative. Thereafter, stories with more complex historical implications—the ambivalent "May-Pole of Merry Mount" and the hostile "Gentle Boy"—must be seen only as qualifications of the fervent admiration expressed in "The Gray Champion": "But should domestic tyranny oppress us, or the invader's step pollute our soil, still may the Gray Champion come; for he is the type of New-England's hereditary spirit; and his shadowy march, on the eve of danger, must ever be the pledge, that New-England's sons will vindicate their ancestry" (p. 18).

10. In 1842 Hawthorne added "The Toll-Gatherer's Day" to the first volume at this point. The sketch fits in well enough, and it makes the first volume of tales roughly equal to the second in length.

"Sunday at Home" is the second piece in the collection, the first sketch. Subsequent sketches in *Twice-told Tales* must be referred back to it as later historical fiction must look back to "The Gray Champion." It is the most pietistic work Hawthorne had written to that time, quite possibly the most pietistic he ever wrote. The speaker defends himself for not being in church: "Though my form be absent, my inner man goes constantly to church, while many, whose bodily presence fills the accustomed seats, have left their souls at home." He demonstrates the truth of this assertion by pious thoughts: "Doubts may flit around me, or seem to close their evil wings, and settle down; but, so long as I imagine that the earth is hallowed, and the light of heaven retains its sanctity, on the Sabbath—while that blessed sunshine lives within me—never can my soul have lost the instinct of its faith" (p. 21). As I have observed above, Hawthorne makes the fancy the self-effacing handmaiden of religious certainty. The first story in *Twice-told Tales* emphasizes that the author is a true American in his political and nationalist sentiments; "Sunday at Home" vouches for his religious sentiments. Together they present the author's credentials. Artist though he may be, he is one of the group, not a radical, alienated, rebellious visionary.

Third in sequence comes "The Wedding-Knell," the first sample of a moralized fiction in *Twice-told Tales*. It is a fine example of Hawthorne's manipulation of the gothic in order to make an antigothic moral. Hawthorne represents himself as one who has heard, rather than invented, the tale he recounts. He attributes the perverse wedding ceremony (which he portrays, of course, in quite colorful detail) to the crazed imagination of a madman whose "caprices had their origin in a mind that lacked the support of an engrossing purpose, and in feelings that preyed upon themselves, for want of other food" (p. 28). Hawthorne is not the madman, but the diagnostician. He disclaims responsibility for originating any part of this story except its moral. Finally, the insane wedding-funeral masque teaches the aging bride a lesson about her folly and vanity. Her sincere grief cures the madness of the groom, and the marriage of this regenerated pair provides a moral for everybody: "Amid the tears of many, and a swell of exalted sentiment, in those who felt aright, was solemnized the union of two immortal souls. . . . And when the awful rite was finished, and, with cold hand in cold hand, the Married of Eternity withdrew, the organ's peal of solemn triumph drowned the Wedding-Knell" (p. 36). Hawthorne's capitalizations are rhetorical equivalents to the organ's peal.

The cumulative point should, by now, be quite obvious. In these three works the chosen genres—the patriotic legend, the sketch, the gothic tale—are managed with technical finesse and show real mastery of verbal techniques of visual representation. Additionally, they are all sententious, and affirm the author's concurrence in the presumed values of the group for which he is writing. Whether Hawthorne held these values or not, he clearly believed that a writer must seem to hold them. He did not write in order to set out his moral beliefs; he set out moral beliefs in order to write. As part of the effort to make himself and his work respectable, the persona had forgone all claims to his or its importance. He elected conventionality at the price of creative excitement. The compromise behind *Twice-told Tales* gave Hawthorne several productive years, but it eventually ceased to satisfy because it assigned, after all, a relatively low value to imaginative activity. Practically speaking, it ceased to satisfy because it did not bring Hawthorne as much success as he wanted. *Twice-told Tales* received a favorable, but restrained, reception.[11]

Hawthorne continued to write pieces like those in the 1837 *Twice-told Tales* for two more years. By the end of 1839 he had fallen in love with Sophia Peabody and needed, urgently, to achieve financial independence. Continuing to write short

11. See the "Historical Commentary" in the Centenary *Twice-told Tales*, pp. 507–12.

pieces for magazines and eventual collection would not bring him a living. He remained unwilling, or unable, to throw himself into the production of a long work. Therefore, he looked for work outside the literary profession. He found employment as a measurer at the Boston Custom House. This was a political appointment, as were his surveyorship in the Salem Custom House and his consulship at Liverpool. He was not so unfit for the business of daily living as his persona seemed to imply and as his own personal reserve might have suggested.

Nothing collected in the 1842 volume of *Twice-told Tales* was written after 1839. He composed twenty-one short pieces in the years 1837–1839. The best of this group is probably "Peter Goldthwaite's Treasure," which brings to Hawthorne's predictable mix of gothicism and moralizing an unusually tolerant, even affectionate portrayal of its delusionary protagonist. Incontestably, however, the work of most interest from this latter part of the *Twice-told Tales* epoch is the framed narrative, "The Legends of the Province-House." Although the four stories in the group are still widely read today, and at least one of them ("Lady Eleanore's Mantle") frequently anthologized, the fictions in sequences and within their frame are a unit with a meaning and impression different from that of any one story taken singly and apart from its frame. "The Legends of the Province-House" is in fact Hawthorne's first completely achieved framed narrative. Like that of *The Story Teller*, its frame tells its own story. The "I" of "The Legends of the Province-House" is shown first as courting, but eventually as renouncing, the quest for historical legends. Taken together, the stories imply an interpretation of history; they also conduct an inquiry into the use of history in the present and into the place of fancy in the representation of historical events.

The action of the frame takes place in the old Boston Province House, which stands, the sole remaining structure of its era, in a contemporary urban landscape of warehouses and offices. Within the building, now an inn, the persona listens to various legends of the provincial epoch (the years when Massachusetts was administered by royal governors) and records them for publication. The legends are gothic; each focuses on a quasi-supernatural event, and each presents an interaction of fancy and fact to create an imaginative version of history. Three of the four legends—"Howe's Masquerade," "Edward Randolph's Portrait," and "Lady Eleanore's Mantle" —tell about individuals within the royalist power structure who are separated from the democratic life around them by the fallacies of aristocratic belief. In an odd and interesting way, Hawthorne's pattern of the protagonist isolated by false perception is applied to the historical situation. These rulers deludedly believe that their power is solid and their elite position justified. But over all of them hangs the shadow of the approaching Revolution.

Each of the aristocratic protagonists receives a chastening lesson. Though perhaps Eleanore's is more severe than her situation calls for, the purport of her story is identical to that of the others: these aristocrats and their ways have no place in the new nation and they will not last. The final story in the group, "Old Esther Dudley," carries the pattern beyond the fall of the royalist regime. Esther Dudley is obviously crazy because she is clinging to images of the past, which exist only in the tarnished mirror of her imagination. She has no contact with actuality. But in fact all the political rulers of the province are shown to have been as deluded as she, clinging to false images and unaware of their surroundings. The story sequence concludes with a blunt and unironic moral when Governor Hancock leads old Esther Dudley respectfully, but firmly, out of the Province House and lectures her on the nature of the present age.

"Your life," he says, "has been prolonged until the world has changed around you. You have treasured up all that time has rendered worthless—the principles, feelings, manners, modes of being and acting, which another generation has flung aside—and you are a symbol of the past. And I, and those around me—we represent a new race of men, living no longer in the past, scarcely in the present—but projecting our lives forward into the future. Ceasing to model ourselves on ancestral superstitions, it is our faith and principle to press onward, onward!" (p. 301).[12] The royal governors and their households represented, even in their own time, an alien and outmoded way of thinking and acting, and the Revolution eliminated them from the American scene.

This means that the events of "history" show a complete break with the "past." The Province House, standing amidst the bustle of Washington Street, is not a symbol (as the house of the seven gables will be, more than ten years later) of the past persisting into the present and continuing to influence it. Like Esther Dudley, it is a reminder of what was but is no more—of what has gone rather than what remains. By virtue of the exercise of the gothic imagination, the fabulator can breathe some life into this reminder, but that brief life is essentially a sort of delusion. What then of those in the present who, like the speaker, deliberately attempt to immerse themselves in the past? Are they not even more foolish than Esther Dudley in that their denial of reality is willful? It is always better to live in the present than in the past. The American democracy is superior to the British monarchy. To

12. Readers who have accepted the critical truism that Hawthorne's historical interest was limited to the Puritans should observe that the Puritans have no place in "The Legends of the Province-House," which is set in a later period. I have observed above that Hawthorne devoted much less of his writing to historical material than the emphasis of the criticism would suggest. I would refine that statement further now to point out that, within his historical writing, the Puritans represent only part of his interest. If Hawthorne is the great romancer of the Puritan era in our history, he is so by virtue of a small fraction of his literary output. Evidently, he would not have understood his own intentions in such a formulation.

seek out a dead aristocratic age is to elect inferior over superior values. Are not the quest for this defunct past and the wish to bring it to life again perverse or eccentric goals?

The answer of "The Legends of the Province-House" to these questions is an unambiguous yes. That is why, after hearing the story of old Esther Dudley, the speaker, as he says, "retired . . . being resolved not to show [his] face in the Province-House for a good while hence—if ever" (p. 303). Awakened to the parallels between his own attraction to the Province House and that of the historical figures who have preceded him, he makes a hasty exit. Once again Hawthorne built a literary structure only, at the end, to withdraw his support from it. The activity of fantasizing about the past, creating four legends about the Province House, turns out to be at best idle self-indulgence, at worst the manifestation of a pull toward a way of life that the American democratic spirit has rejected. If one would be a writer for democratic people in a new historical era, one must not present them with stories from a superseded past nor in literary forms appropriate to that past. Tales of the supernatural are unsuitable for the American pragmatic and rational character, just as tales of aristocrats are unfit for their democratic politics. Governor Hancock's exhortation, "Onward, onward!" speaks to the writer as much as to the anachronistic characters in his fiction. The writer who does not heed this injunction comes before the public like old Esther Dudley, antiquated, eccentric, and absurd.

In contrast, "Endicott and the Red Cross," which dates from about the same time, shows the proper way to use history for the purposes of an American fiction. Like "The Gray Champion," this is the telling of a heroic story, but unlike the earlier story it adds no supernatural business to its essential probability. Hawthorne could have found the incident of Endicott's defacement of the British flag in several early histories. His purpose in telling the story is to vindicate the

Puritan character by showing that it is the root of American resistance to tyranny. The emphasis of the story indicates that Hawthorne is writing in awareness of a contemporary interpretation of the Puritans as harsh and repressive people. At the beginning of the episode Endicott is clearly, even crudely, presented as a villain. Unfortunate and evidently decent people are undergoing all sorts of cruel and humiliating harassment. The saintly Roger Williams arrives on the scene, his mildness and gentleness an invidious contrast to the unamiable, unbending Endicott. We discover, however—perhaps to our surprise—that Endicott's aggressive response rather than Williams's conciliatory one is the right answer to British authority. We may not like Endicott, but we must greet him across the centuries as a true ancestor of the American character: "With a cry of triumph, the people gave their sanction to one of the boldest exploits which our history records. And, for ever honored be the name of Endicott! We look back through the mist of ages, and recognize, in the rending of the Red Cross from New England's banner, the first omen of that deliverance which our fathers consummated, after the bones of the stern Puritan had lain more than a century in the dust" (p. 441).

Hawthorne based "The Gentle Boy" on a stereotype of the merciless and intolerant Puritan, and exploited that stereotype to create sympathy for Ilbrahim and Tobias Pearson. In "The May-Pole of Merry Mount" he utilized the convention at first but then softened his portrait of the Puritan by showing him capable of tenderness and by equating his sternness with a sagacious realism. Again in "Endicott and the Red Cross" Hawthorne builds from an initial view of the Puritan as an evil man and then brings the story around to a defense of the Puritan character by reminding the reader of its typical virtues. In this story Hawthorne's interest in Puritan history is political and the historical vision coincides with that in "The Legends of the Province-House." The crucial event in American history, in both stories, is the establishment of independence from England and the supplanting of an aristocratic form of government by a democratic one. The royal governors are rejected and the Puritans assimilated into the main line of American historical development. In contrast to "The Legends of the Province-House," however, "Endicott and the Red Cross" contains no apology for fiction-making, because its fiction is patriotic and social and hence appropriate to the spirit of a democratic republic.

Readers familiar with Hawthorne criticism will be aware that the interpretation offered in these pages conflicts in several ways with the standard reading of Hawthorne's intentions in "Endicott and the Red Cross" and indeed his purposes with historical fiction altogether. Generally, it is assumed that "Endicott and the Red Cross" offers an ambiguous criticism of Puritanism from behind a facade of open praise. Some critics even appear to believe that Hawthorne invented the image of the intolerant and repressive Puritan![13] Therefore, it is worth repeating these important points: Hawthorne uses and modifies a stereotype of Puritan bigotry rather than creating it. He approaches American history as a secular democrat rather than a religious person. Far from concealing hostility against Endicott, he relies on it for his effects.

Underlying these fictions is an unqualified nationalism that strikes many critics, when they recognize it, as unpleasant and inconsistent with what they take to be Hawthorne's true feelings. Thus, a very fine critic complains of Hancock's exhortation that it "is hardly consonant with Hawthorne's essential attitudes. For of all our early nineteenth-century writers, it is

13. But see John Caldwell Stubbs, *The Pursuit of Form: A Study of Hawthorne and the Romance* (Urbana: University of Illinois Press, 1970), pp. 36–42, and Michael Davitt Bell, *Hawthorne and the Historical Romance of New England* (Princeton: Princeton University Press, 1971), pp. 85–104, for many examples of this stereotype in other fiction of Hawthorne's time and before.

Hawthorne, as 'Earth's Holocaust' shows us, who is at bottom the most thoroughly skeptical of the idea of progress. And of all our writers it is he who, in *The House of the Seven Gables*, has taught us most about the ways in which we are inevitable children of the past."[14] Like most readings of Hawthorne, this one ignores the dates of composition of individual works, apparently assuming that Hawthorne underwent no development whatsoever in his literary career and that works written in 1838, 1844, and 1851 would necessarily agree with one another unless one or two of them contained lies. Even were we to accept the assumption of no development, we would have to wonder about the grounds on which the critic has determined "Earth's Holocaust" to be true Hawthorne, and "The Legends of the Province-House" false. All too often critics appear to base their assertions on simple preferences for one world view over another.

The interpretation cited above—cited because it represents so many trends in Hawthorne criticism—expresses by such a word as "taught" its conviction that Hawthorne wrote in order to put forward his own personal view, for the purpose of enlightening and correcting the opinions of his readers. But as we have seen, it was Hawthorne's strategy through this part of his career to accede to the presumed view of his readers, and never assert either his superiority or his disagreement. By such a strategy he hoped to gain the goodwill of those on whom his success as an author depended. Not until "The Custom-House," and then only imperfectly, did Hawthorne declare his independence of other people's expectations.

The weakness in Hawthorne's strategy is its failure to demonstrate any real importance in the work he was doing, any serious purpose worth absorbing his better energies for the whole of his adult life. In work after work he had defined his task by its limits. The appearance of "The Legends of the

14. Doubleday, *Hawthorne's Early Tales*, p. 133.

Province-House" as the first work in the *Twice-told Tales* of
1842 indicates a choice of the self-deprecating note as the key
to the collection. And *Twice-told Tales* of 1842 does seem
even more modest in its claims for the author than the collection of 1837. The volume has twenty works, of which fifteen
date from the period after 1837; clearly then, the impression
must rise from these latest works. Of the twenty-one recent
pieces he omitted only six, and of these six only one was a
fiction ("John Inglefield's Thanksgiving"). He left out a
historical sketch ("A Bell's Biography") but included all the
sketches of the actual that he wrote in this period. He left out
one of two newsboy's addresses that he had written for the
Salem Gazette and two lengthy obituary notices that would
clearly be inappropriate in the context of a volume of tales
and sketches. It is fair to say, then, that the 1842 volume contains the bulk of his most recent writings, and that the omissions do not distort the nature of that writing.

From the period between 1834 and 1837 he chose "The
Haunted Mind" and "The Village Uncle"; from *The Story
Teller* era he incorporated "The Ambitious Guest," "The Seven
Vagabonds," and "The White Old Maid." He used nothing
from the *Provincial Tales* or *Seven Tales of My Native
Land*.[15] This selection blends into the more recent material
without distorting it. Divided about equally between sketches
and fictions, the more recent material includes such fictions as
"The Lily's Quest," "Edward Fane's Rosebud," and "The
Threefold Destiny." These are weak efforts, and it seems
legitimate at least to wonder whether Hawthorne had not
fenced his imagination in with so many restrictions as effectively to block his own creative powers. A common motif in

15. Apparently, Hawthorne's sister Elizabeth played some role in
assembling the material for this volume, but one must assume that the
final word about the selections rested with Hawthorne. See C. E.
Frazer Clark, Jr., "New Light on the Editing of the 1842 Edition of
Twice-Told Tales," *Nathaniel Hawthorne Journal 1972*, pp. 91–103.

several of these stories—both recent and early—is the folly of ambition. The special destiny that awaits ambitious people is to discover their own insanity. This idea is directly asserted in "The Ambitious Guest," "Peter Goldthwaite's Treasure," and "The Threefold Destiny," while it is implied in "The Village Uncle" and "The Seven Vagabonds." When fiction of this character is interspersed among sketches which are presented as one or another form of "fancy-work," the final impression is of a self-effacement so greatly overstated that it counteracts itself.

One begins to wonder whether behind the display of authorial modesty there may not be a frustrated and embittered imagination. Does this precipitate compliance with an imagined public opinion express Hawthorne's own sense of little worth, or does it mask an anger that the audience continues indifferent to his talent? Or do these works imply an excuse for Hawthorne's failure to achieve a significant work, his preference for remaining at home, his reluctance to commit himself to a large-scale literary achievement? For all its mildness of tone— perhaps because of that very mildness—there is a false note in the 1842 volume, a sign that the compromise that produced the *Twice-told Tales* was breaking down. The persona of these years had ceased to mediate between Hawthorne's sense of himself and his sense of an audience. It was time to change.

⋙ 3 ⋘

The Manse Decade
1840–1849

In the opinion of many critics Hawthorne's writings in the Salem period, with their alienated protagonists, embody the author's own personal isolation. An autobiographical element in his work cannot be entirely discounted. However, as I have tried to show, Hawthorne's literary intention was to develop a mode of authorship that would pacify an audience thought to be distrustful of imaginative activity. His writings reveal the imagination supporting society's conventional moral wisdom, enriching the texture of everyday life with pleasurable perceptions, and acting as the monitor of its own excesses.

The author's solitude does manifest itself in this work, however, in its almost total imperviousness to outside influence. All of this writing developed according to the inherent logic of the assumptions with which Hawthorne had begun his career. He was locked into the implications of a turn-of-the-century view of the imagination, using forms that Hazlitt had criticized as outdated, in Irving's work, in 1819. While Hawthorne's fictions solemnly asserted the necessity of exposing oneself to the regulating and corrective influences of other minds and social activity, his own work appeared hermetically sealed and responsive only to its own internal tensions.

In January 1839 Hawthorne took up work at the Boston Custom House, where he remained until December 1840. In the spring of 1841 he went to Brook Farm and lived as part of the community until the end of the summer. He had felt the need for a change, and made one. Thereby he opened himself to many new stimuli. His relationship with Sophia Peabody, which commenced late in 1838, greatly expanded and deepened his emotional range. His job in the Boston Custom House, tedious as he found it, gave him experience of the working world and the satisfaction of supporting himself by his own exertion. As a political appointment, it involved him in the affairs of the Democratic Party. Because he had published a well-received volume of tales and sketches, he had access in Boston to intellectual circles. Although he was never a gregarious man, he did develop a social life that brought him into contact with contemporary issues and ideas. His writing in the decade of the 1840s shows him trying to expand in order to accommodate these various new experiences.

Hawthorne had met Sophia Peabody through her sister Elizabeth. Elizabeth was an active and intellectual woman who sought him out, after reading *Twice-told Tales*, as a fellow Salemite. Her recommendations were among those that secured him the Custom House appointment.[1] Through her, Hawthorne became acquainted with the transcendentalists and their ideas, an acquaintanceship that was to prove the single most important stimulus to his literary development. Finally, Elizabeth played the part of literary adviser to him in these years before he married Sophia. She encouraged him to think of writing for children. Since such writing was relatively untaxing, he might be able to carry through some children's projects even while employed at the Custom House. And successful children's books made much more money than magazine publications.

In 1840 Hawthorne wrote three brief sequential volumes of Massachusetts history entitled *Grandfather's Chair*, *Famous Old People*, and *Liberty Tree*. These were separately published in 1841. He also completed the first book of what was appar-

1. Stewart, *Nathaniel Hawthorne*, p. 53.

ently intended to be another series, this time of biographies of famous people. Published in 1842, it was called *Biographical Stories for Children*. In 1851, when Hawthorne's publishers were following up the success of *The Scarlet Letter* by re-issuing his earlier works, all these books were published in a single volume called *True Stories from History and Biography*. The three historical works were collectively entitled *The Whole History of Grandfather's Chair* at that time.

Besides these four slim children's volumes, Hawthorne wrote little else from 1839 to 1841 except his love letters to Sophia. Many critics find the letters a literary achievement comparable to Hawthorne's imaginative best, but I think that in this evaluation their pleasure in Hawthorne's happiness has overcome objective judgment.[2] The letters are full of affectation and pose. Although they are deeply sincere, they are also elaborately artificial. Indeed, the writer gets sincere delight from their very artificiality. In love at last, Hawthorne was playing at being a lover, playing at being in love, and the entire correspondence is evidently a game in which both he and Sophia were participating with the greatest enthusiasm. As so often happens when deep feelings are involved, the expression is zestfully conventional. The letters are indeed so conventional that they are not even a particularly informative biographical document. They are certainly no substitute for imaginative writing.

On the other hand, *The Whole History of Grandfather's Chair* is a genuine literary achievement, which is regularly overlooked or underplayed in the critical literature. In general, Hawthorne's works for children are taken to be hackwork,

2. Until the Centenary Edition volume of Hawthorne's letters is published, this correspondence is available to the reader in the re-printed *Love Letters of Nathaniel Hawthorne, 1839–1863*, with a foreword by C. E. Frazer Clark, Jr. (Washington, D.C.: NCR/ Microcard Editions, 1972). The original text was privately printed in 1907 and contains many editorial emendations.

and even critics who allow literary merit in some of them are quite severe on *The Whole History*.[3] Many critics of Hawthorne, apparently, have not read the children's works because they do not consider them a legitimate part of the canon. It is not difficult to understand the reasoning behind such neglect. Children's writing is not accepted as a serious literary genre. A writer himself serious about children's literature is assumed to partake, somewhat, of the simple world view of the child—either that, or he is assumed to be a pedagogue rather than an artist. An author of Hawthorne's complexity, it is concluded, cannot possibly be sincere about writing for children; hence there cannot be anything "true" in these works. Given such thinking, the critic has almost no choice but to ignore Hawthorne's writings for children. But the criterion of sincerity is particularly inappropriate for Hawthorne. His deepest, and most sincere, literary feeling was the drive to be a successful author. If writing for children might accomplish that end, he could give himself wholly to such work.[4] And, again, Hawthorne's wish to characterize the author as a socially useful being might be satisfied in the production of children's literature.

A reading of *The Whole History* discloses another reason why critics who have read it might want to ignore it. Its view of American history does not accord with the generally accepted account of Hawthorne's understanding of the American experience. The critic uses the fact that these works are directed toward children to justify discounting their historical

3. Even Roy Harvey Pearce, spokesman for the children's writings as their editor in the Centenary Edition, belittles the histories in comparison with the children's myths, which he finds "incomparably more" Hawthorne's "own" than *The Whole History* (Centenary, VI, 1972, p. 287).

4. Of course, Hawthorne deprecated his children's writings in some of his correspondence, but he referred to his magazine writing in the same language.

views.[5] In writing history for children, Hawthorne was bound (it is argued) to express conventional views. But *The Whole History* should not be so discounted. It is Hawthorne's most extended historical statement; it provides a coherent view of Massachusetts history from the founding of the Bay Colony to the Revolution; it fits very well with the whole of Hawthorne's historical writing preceding it (writing which, as I have already noted, is by no means restricted to an interest in the religious dimensions of Puritanism or to the earliest settlers only). Moreover, it is a technical achievement of a very high order, marked by fluency, ease, and a successfully executed frame of considerable complexity that is organically tied to the narrative. The voice of the author is authoritatively present, but more relaxed than in any of the writing after the *Provincial Tales*.

Several elements work together in the frame of *The Whole History*. At the center are a physical object—Grandfather's chair—and a fully characterized narrator—Grandfather. As in "The Legends of the Province-House," the physical object is a relic of the past, and around it cluster historical associations. The physical presence of the chair authenticates and gives body to the imaginative reconstruction.[6] In Hawthorne's in-

5. In a brilliant study of "Young Goodman Brown," for example, Michael J. Colacurcio dismisses Hawthorne's account of the ending of the Puritan era in *The Whole History*. According to *The Whole History*, the first Puritan age concluded with the issuing of the New Charter. "Such indeed," Colacurcio writes, "are the political realities, and so indeed might the story be divided for children. But in a far more fundamental sense, 'Young Goodman Brown' shows us that witchcraft 'ended' the Puritan world." See "Visible Sanctity and Specter Evidence: The Moral World of Hawthorne's 'Young Goodman Brown,'" *Essex Institute Historical Collections*, 110 (1974), 259–99.

6. Pearce cites a letter attributing the idea of the chair to a cousin of Hawthorne's (Centenary, VI, p. 292). But Hawthorne had used such material objects as a focus in historical tales before: e.g., "The Legends of the Province-House" and "Endicott and the Red Cross."

troductory words, when one connects "the shadowy outlines of departed men and women" with the "substantial and homely reality of a fireside chair," the outlines "assume the hues of life more effectually." We "feel at once, that these characters of history had a private and familiar existence, and were not wholly contained within that cold array of outward action, which we are compelled to receive as the adequate representation of their lives."[7] Through the mediation of the chair, the imagination penetrates the concealing outward action and comes to the living heart of history. Hawthorne's words have something in common with his apology for imaginative excursions into history in "Sir William Phips,"[8] but go far beyond them.

The chair, then, represents the occasion for historical association, and Grandfather is the embodiment of the historical imagination. Beyond this, the situation is defined by the presence of Grandfather's audience of his four grandchildren, each differently characterized. Laurence is the eldest, a sensitive and thoughtful boy of twelve; Clara is a gentle, loving child of ten; Charley, an obstreperous and comical fellow of nine; and Alice, a golden-haired innocent of five. Among them Hawthorne suggests a variety of childhood temperaments and attitudes, as well as a sequence of increasing maturity. Given this audience, Grandfather's purpose in attempting to reconstruct history is certainly not to escape from the present, nor is it to indulge a taste for gothic thrills. By means of his narrative, the wisdom and knowledge of older people is transmitted to the young and gives them a background against which to view their present-day existences. Not only does Grandfather provide a way of understanding the present by interpreting it in terms of past causes, he also helps them to

7. *True Stories from History and Biography*, Centenary Edition, Vol. VI (1972), pp. 5–6. Subsequent references given parenthetically in text.

8. Quoted above in chapter 1, n. 28.

realize that their own lives are not passed in a timeless present, but transpire in a temporal framework that extends beyond the limits of their own transient existences. The learning of history is of a piece with the inevitable transition from childhood to maturity, when discrete moments become related to past and future, and unthinking experience is overlaid by reflection. History, in this view, is knowledge that we cannot help but acquire, but much depends on the method by which it is acquired. Grandfather is helping the children accept their mortality:

[Grandfather] almost regretted that it was necessary for them to know anything of the past, or to provide aught for the future. He could have wished that they might be always the happy youthful creatures, who had hitherto sported around his chair, without inquiring whether it had a history. It grieved him to think that his little Alice, who was a flower-bud fresh from paradise, must open her leaves to the rough breezes of the world, or ever open them in any clime. So sweet a child she was, that it seemed fit her infancy should be immortal! But such repinings were merely flitting shadows across the old man's heart. He had faith enough to believe, and wisdom enough to know, that the bloom of the flower would be even holier and happier than its bud. Even within himself . . . he was conscious of something, that he would not have exchanged for the best happiness of childhood. It was a bliss to which every sort of earthly experience—all that he had enjoyed or suffered, or seen, or heard, or acted, with the broodings of his soul upon the whole—had contributed somewhat.   [Pp. 51–52]

This is the first assertion in Hawthorne's writings that history is part of our lives. And though he soon began to depict the persistent past as a heavy burden rather than a contributor to human bliss, he retained his sense of its continuing presence in his writings through *The Marble Faun*.

The chair that stands in Grandfather's study came over to Massachusetts as the property of the Lady Arbella, at the original founding of the colony. Grandfather begins with her story and then follows the chair from one owner to the next through the history of Massachusetts to the Revolution. The children interrupt his narrative with questions and comments, and Grandfather shapes his narration in response to their expressed needs and interest. The frame, thus, enters into the history and becomes part of it. Fully detachable stories constitute less than half the bulk of *The Whole History*. Storytelling is seen as an interactive process between the teller and his audience, a process marked by mutual affection and respect as well as by a clear understanding of the appropriate behavior for teller and listener. It is a very comfortable and relaxed situation for Grandfather and the children, and one that idealizes the relationship between author and audience. Hawthorne too participates in this relationship, for he is present in the narrative, characterizing both Grandfather and the children and on occasion summarizing what Grandfather has said instead of giving his words. Hawthorne narrates *The Whole History* just as Grandfather tells the individual stories, and stands to the readers of the book in the same relationship that Grandfather stands to his auditors. The author is the beloved sage, that favorite Victorian persona.

In *The Whole History* we meet again historical figures whom Hawthorne had written about before—John Endicott, Ann Hutchinson, Roger Williams, Sir William Phips—and hear again some of the historical episodes that he has already recounted—the red cross, the Quaker persecution, the witchcraft delusion, Hutchinson's banishment, the humiliation of the royal governors, the taking of Louisberg. There is also much that is new—Lady Arbella, the Apostle Eliot, Mather and smallpox inoculation, the exile of the Acadians, the Boston massacre and many other pre-Revolutionary military skirmishes. The underlying movement in American history is like that in "Endicott and the Red Cross" and "The Legends of the Province-House." American history takes its meaning from the Revolution; earlier events are interpreted in the light of that great later one. Hawthorne is especially concerned to identify those early events that prefigure the Revolution, that contain its germ or somehow prophesy it. There is more than a trace in his method of an approach like that of the religious exegetes who saw the entire Old Testament as a foretelling of Revelation.

Each of Hawthorne's three little volumes corresponds to an era in Massachusetts history defined by a particular political relationship with England. *Grandfather's Chair* covers the Puritan era, when the people of Massachusetts governed themselves. *Famous Old People* takes up the era of the New Charter, when "Massachusetts ceased to be a republic, and was strictly a province of England" (p. 72). This era begins in 1692 with the governorship of Sir William Phips. Hawthorne makes no mention of the internal evolution (or decline) of Puritanism as expressed in its series of doctrinal modifications; he clearly implies that the nature of a society is determined by the nature of its political system and not by the content of its theological belief. Although some twentieth-century students of Puritan history see in Hawthorne a remarkable understanding of the psychological implications of Puritan doctrine, it seems evident that such understanding was a by-product of his own approach.[9] For him, espousal of any single doctrine was always connected with private error, with undisciplined imaginative excess, and all too often with public injustice.

In fact the theme of public injustice runs as a minor motif throughout the treatment of the Puritans in the first volume, *Grandfather's Chair*. The Puritans governed themselves, and

9. See in particular David Levin, "Shadows of Doubt: Specter Evidence in Hawthorne's 'Young Goodman Brown,'" *American Literature*, 34 (1962), 344–52; Michael J. Colacurcio, "Visible Sanctity" (cited in n. 5, above), and "Footsteps of Ann Hutchinson: The Context of *The Scarlet Letter*," *ELH*, 39 (1972), 459–94.

thus their political system was better than that under the New Charter. But their form of government was vastly inferior to the democracy established after the Revolution because it did not permit the free competition of ideas. Roger Williams, Grandfather explains, was banished because "the wise men of those days believed, that the country could not be safe, unless all the inhabitants thought and felt alike." To Laurence's query whether anybody still believes so, Grandfather answers that "possibly there are some who believe it . . . but they have not so much power to act upon their belief, as the magistrates and ministers had, in the days of Roger Williams. They had the power to deprive this good man of his home, and to send him out from the midst of them, in search of a new place of rest" (p. 26). If the Puritans' belief led to the banishment of a good man, something is wrong with the belief.

As a way of enlarging on this theme of Puritan totalitarian paranoia, Hawthorne greatly softens his handling of some of the heretics whom in earlier historical sketches he had treated more harshly. Ann Hutchinson, whom he had depicted from a strongly antifeminist perspective in the sketch of 1830 entitled "Mrs. Hutchinson," for example, now becomes the pathetic victim of Puritan antifeminism. "The Ministers did not think it safe and proper, that a woman should publicly instruct the people in religious doctrine." Passing over the content of her heresy as of no importance, Grandfather explains how a synod met and "declared that there were eighty-two erroneous opinions on religious subjects, diffused among the people, and that Mrs. Hutchinson's opinions were of the number." Pragmatic Charley draws the moral: "If they had eighty-two wrong opinions . . . I don't see how they could have any right ones." And little Alice, "who contrived to feel a human interest even in these discords of polemic divinity," makes the human response to Ann Hutchinson's punishment: "Dear Grandfather, did they drive the poor woman into the woods?" (pp. 27, 28).

The Quakers are no longer the fantasists they were in "The Gentle Boy." Only the Puritan imagination makes them seem so, for while "the rulers looked upon them as plotting the downfall of all government and religion," in truth they were "impelled by an earnest love for the souls of men, and a pure desire to make known what they considered a revelation from Heaven." Grandfather calls the Quaker persecution "one of the most mournful passages in the history of our forefathers" (pp. 40, 41), and as for the Salem witchcraft delusion, that was "the saddest and most humiliating passage in our history" (p. 79). Though much worse than the Quaker persecution, the Salem episode is of a kind with it; together they illustrate the ultimate result of Puritan narrowness. The uncorrected Puritan imagination led to periodic outbreaks of madness.

In his account of the Apostle Eliot, Grandfather uncovers other Puritan limitations. He contrasts Eliot's dealings with the Indians with that of the Puritans, to show the man of love versus the men of hate. And he contrasts the Puritans with the Indians, as narrow scholars with poets, when he pictures a young Indian boy reading Eliot's Bible to a group of ministers. The divines, he says, "had grown gray in study; their eyes were bleared with poring over print and manuscript, by the light of the midnight lamp. And yet, how much they left unlearned! . . . The Indian boy cast his eye over the mysterious page, and read it so skilfully, that it sounded like wild music. It seemed as if the forest leaves were singing in the ears of his auditors, and as if the roar of distant streams were poured through the young Indian's voice" (p. 46). The Puritans, then, have uncorrected and also unpoetic imaginations: a terrible combination. Theirs is a society of obsessed and fanatic people.

The source of the Puritan fault is their religious beliefs—not, of course, the specific content of that belief, but the exclusiveness of their faith. In other ways they are admirable people. They have the rugged strength to settle and endure in a wild land. The first story in *Grandfather's Chair* tells of Lady Arbella, the pale English flower who dies within a month of landing, lacking that essential strength. "Thinking mournfully of far-off England," she sits in Grandfather's chair and looks out at the settlers, building and sowing. She "feels that this new world is fit only for rough and hardy people. None should be here, but those who can struggle with wild beasts and wild men, and can toil in the heat or cold, and can keep their hearts firm against all difficulties and dangers." One like this is John Endicott, pressed into service again as the quintessential Puritan. "As bold and resolute as iron," he "had no time to look back regretfully to his native land. He felt himself fit for the new world, and for the work that he had to do, and set himself resolutely to accomplish it" (pp. 16, 17).

Epitome that he is, Endicott shows the connection between the strength to found a new country and the courage to resist encroachments on his rights. Grandfather tells the story of the red cross for much the same reason that Hawthorne told it in "Endicott and the Red Cross." Another Puritan virtue, not apparent until the epoch of the New Charter, is their simple, austere way of life. They were a hardheaded and realistic, but not a worldly, people. In the undemocratic situation of the second epoch of Massachusetts life, chronicled in *Famous Old People*, the new nation becomes oddly secular and decadent: "The iron race of Puritans . . . in the first Epoch of our History, have now given place to quite a different set of men. . . . Our old Chair, itself, loses the severe simplicity, which was in keeping with the habits of its earlier possessors, and is gilded and varnished, and gorgeously cushioned, so as to make it a fitting seat for vice-regal pomp" (p. 71).

The simplicity of the good old Puritan times was fast disappearing. This was partly owing to the increasing number and wealth of the inhabitants. . . . Another cause of a pompous and artificial mode of life, among those who could afford it, was, that the example was set by the royal governors. Under the old charter, the governors were the representatives of the people, and therefore their way of living had probably been marked by a popular simplicity. But now, as they represented the person of the king, they thought it necessary to preserve the dignity of their station, by the practice of high and gorgeous ceremonials. [P. 108]

On the credit side, this Epoch developed a spirit of enterprise and activity among the people and greatly broadened their intellectual and imaginative horizons. Inevitably, "in a third Epoch, we shall find in individuals, and the people at large, a combination of ideal principle and adventurous action" (p. 72). In the revolutionary era, the better aspects of the two preceding ages combine and find their apotheosis in George Washington: "As he sat there, with his hand resting on the hilt of his sheathed sword, which was placed between his knees, his whole aspect well befitted the chosen man on whom his country leaned for the defence of her dearest rights. America seemed safe, under his protection. His face was grander than any sculptor had ever wrought in marble; none could behold him without awe and reverence" (p. 186). After this great moment, toward which *The Whole History* has been directed, Hawthorne brings the work to a close with a humorous scene in which the chair speaks. He had never been in firmer control of matter and manner than in this series.

The *Biographical Stories for Children* is much inferior. Hawthorne attempts a variation on the same framing formula, but handles it much more mechanically. Again there is an audience of children and a parental narrator. Edward Temple, a young boy, has an eye disease that confines him to a darkened room. To divert him, his father tells stories about the childhood of famous people. A brother and an adoptive sister, as well as Mrs. Temple, join to form an audience. In contrast with *The Whole History*, which used the solid chair to stimulate associations, *Biographical Stories* puts all the burden on the inner eye of the imagination. That Edward's blindness forces him to see with his mind becomes a metaphor apparently intended to link the various stories. The first two stories, for example, about Benjamin West and Isaac Newton, pick up the motif of the inner vision; but the remaining four are heavily moralistic in the manner of Sunday school tracts and fail to cohere either with one another or with the frame.

Hawthorne's biography of Queen Christina is of some slight interest, in view of his later sympathy for unconventional heroines, because she is used as the occasion for a lecture on woman's place. All Christina's problems, the father explains, stem from her having been brought up as a man. "Gustavus should have remembered that Providence had created [her] to be a woman, and that it was not for him to make a man of her." In conclusion, he rhapsodizes: "Happy are the little girls of America, who are brought up quietly and tenderly, at the domestic hearth, and thus become gentle and delicate women! May none of them ever lose the loveliness of their sex, by receiving such an education" (p. 283). The children's mother immediately responds, that although "Christina was a sad specimen of womankind, indeed . . . it is very possible for a woman to have a strong mind, and to be fitted for the active business of life, without losing any of her natural delicacy. Perhaps, some time or other, Mr. Temple will tell you a story of such a woman" (pp. 283–84). Who might that woman have been? The intriguing question was never answered, because Hawthorne failed to produce a second volume in the series. He no longer worked in the Custom House, he was finished with his stint at Brook Farm, and as he prepared to marry Sophia Peabody he determined once again to try to make a living as a writer for adults. He wrote no more books for children until after his success with *The Scarlet Letter*. Then, under pressure to produce rapidly in order to cash in on his new fame, he carried out a long-held plan to retell some of the classical myths for modern children. During the years at the Old Manse and the Salem Custom

House, however, he did continue to produce an occasional juvenile piece, the most important of which is "The Snow-Image." Although he did not want his reputation to rest solely on his works for children, he was certainly pleased to have them known as his. Clearly he viewed his writing for children as part of his literary achievement.

Hawthorne's venture into "the world" had changed his life permanently. As he wrote to Evert Duyckinck on December 22, 1841, "during the last three or four years, the world has sucked me within its vortex, and I could not get back to my solitude again, even if I would."[10] After he and Sophia Peabody were married on July 9, 1842, they moved to the Old Manse in Concord, where they lived until October 1845, and here Hawthorne's life changed again. He had decided to try to support his household by writing for magazines; he had been unsuccessful in this attempt at Salem, but now he had some reputation and more literary contacts. He could count on publishing everything he wrote. But he discovered that the pay was so low (and so uncertain, since the magazines were financially straitened) that he had to write continuously. He had no time for fantasizing, for waiting until an idea ripened, for picking, choosing, and discarding.

This study has been following change and development in Hawthorne's writing from the outset of his career; the differences between the works composed at the Manse and Hawthorne's other writings are particularly striking and have been observed by several critics. Chiefly, critics point out that in the Manse period Hawthorne moved away from history and concentrated on contemporary material. But this view falsely implies a much greater proportion of historical writing in the earlier periods than Hawthorne actually produced, and it ignores his substantial attempt to relate to the world around

10. Quoted by John J. McDonald in " 'The Old Manse' and Its Mosses: The Inception and Development of *Mosses from an Old Manse*," *Texas Studies in Literature and Language*, 16 (1974), p. 80.

him in his sketches. According to another theory, the work of the Manse period is more artificial than earlier writings. This is certainly true in an important way, but again involves a certain distortion of the early work. "Rappaccini's Daughter," for example, is clearly more artificial than "Young Goodman Brown," but not more than "The Great Carbuncle" or "Dr. Heidegger's Experiment."

The work of the Manse period is fundamentally much more essayistic in tone than either Hawthorne's sketches or fictions dating from earlier years. The persona does not define himself as an imaginative or even a fanciful writer so much as a man of opinions, a critic, and commentator.[11] Imagination has not vanished in the works of this period, but has a function subordinate to the ideas that it illustrates and dramatizes. Fewer than one-third of the pieces Hawthorne wrote at the Manse are stories. One finds little development of individual character and almost no natural description. Perhaps the term "sketch" can be applied to the sort of work Hawthorne wrote at the Manse, but one has to distinguish it from the earlier kind of sketch. The sketches of the early Salem period were associative pieces grounded in observation. Only two Manse works fit this description—"Buds and Bird-Voices" and "The Old Apple-Dealer"—and these exhibit a different kind of speaker from the persona in *Twice-told Tales*.

The narrator in a typical Manse sketch is more worldly, self-assured, and ironic than Hawthorne's earlier speakers. He knows that he has a readership, and even seems to know who its members are. He tosses off topical allusions with a facility beyond the reach of Oberon or his successor in *Twice-told Tales*. He is a man of the world, an insider, an author who has arrived. He neither deprecates himself nor apologizes to his audience. He seems content with the reception he anticipates

11. McDonald, " 'The Old Manse' and Its Mosses," p. 79, contrasts the two personae as a "solitary wanderer" and a "critical observer."

and gives no impression of aspiring to more substantial literary accomplishment or a greater reputation. There is no sense of urgency, discomfort, or strain in the writing of this period. Quite possibly the absence of strain was actually the product of the speed with which Hawthorne was writing at this time. In earlier years he had worked at his own pace; now he was producing one or two sketches a month in order to pay his bills.[12] Perhaps beneath the self-assured mask Hawthorne suffered immense dissatisfaction with his still limited achievement and fame. Possibly he was simply trying out a new authorial stance to see how it worked: to assert himself as a successful man of letters might be to prevail as one.

Whatever the sources of the persona, the sketches do show Hawthorne's haste in the systematic repetition of their structure. Each piece develops from an initial contrivance, a clever device for presenting its idea. "Fire-Worship" is a defense of domesticity couched as an attack on the replacement of the hearth by the heating stove. "P.'s Correspondence" is literary criticism penned by a madman who thinks that all the living authors are dead and all the dead ones still living. "The Celestial Rail-road" comments on contemporary materialism by modernizing the narrative of The Pilgrim's Progress. "The New Adam and Eve" criticizes modern life by wiping out contemporary civilization and setting a newly created couple in the ruins. "A Book of Autographs" re-creates historical figures through an analysis of their penmanship. "Earth's Holocaust" talks ironically about reform by inventing a great bonfire in which all human errors are consumed. Only the source of error—the human heart—escapes the holocaust. In "The Procession of Life" we observe a series of parades of people linked by secret bonds such as illness, disappointment, alienation, and guilt. "A Select Party" gathers all the partici-

12. See John J. McDonald, "The Old Manse Period Canon," Nathaniel Hawthorne Journal, 1972, for a careful dating of the works Hawthorne wrote at the Manse.

pants in a person's fantasy life. "The Hall of Fantasy" assembles all those who have ever daydreamed. "The Intelligence Office" imagines a bureau where people go to express their hearts' deepest desires.

The success of these works depends on three elements: the wittiness of the fundamental image, the content of the idea being expressed through the image, and the linear structure of the sketch. Except for "The Celestial Rail-road," which has the advantage of Bunyan's plot, the sketches have no action. Each develops as an animated list, in which elements follow one another in no necessary or compelling order, and no tension accumulates or dissipates. The controlling images in the sketches vary in their wit and aptness, but even the best of them is essentially a gimmick and therefore cannot be the vehicle of a deep reflection. Given the way in which he wrote these pieces, and the places in which they were published (chiefly the *Democratic Review*), Hawthorne could not possibly have meant them to be profound statements. They are, rather, statements that seem proper to a successful man of letters, as conventional in their way as the moralizing of the *Twice-told Tales* had been. It is unfortunate that the discursive quality of these works has led critics repeatedly to use them as evidence of Hawthorne's deepest thoughts on the issues discussed in them.

Hawthorne clearly expects his audience to consist of literate Bostonians and New Yorkers attached to the Democratic Party. Since he had made his reputation among New Englanders and was now writing for the *Democratic Review* (a partisan New York journal), his expectations seem to be realistic. His comments on the issues of the day steer a course between New York pragmatism and Boston idealism. He is a critic of society from a transcendental viewpoint ("The New Adam and Eve") and a critic of transcendentalism from a socially pragmatic viewpoint ("Earth's Holocaust"). He thinks America a progressive nation and finds progress a generally good thing; but he doubts that true progress is a quick or easy matter. He deplores those who spend their lives in idle fantasies detached from reality. He deplores even more those whose lives are entirely materialistic, who never know the elevating influence of an ideal. He agrees that reformers are foolish, but ranks them among the noblest of human beings. Thus, on the two social issues to which he addresses himself—reform and materialism—he takes a negotiator's attitude. There is good on both sides. If excess is avoided, men of goodwill can see validity in the opposing position. But we should not imagine Hawthorne to be motivated in these writings by altruism. The broader his own views, and the more diplomatically expressed, the broader the readership he can attract.

Within this context of literary Realpolitik, Hawthorne's approach to the domain of imagination is as equivocal as ever. It is possible to abstract a series of statements asserting the primacy of imaginative experience over material actuality. The passengers on the celestial railroad are wrong when they take the material goods of Vanity Fair for realities. "The Procession of Life" asserts that people are connected through like feelings and thoughts, not similar social rank or material possessions. In "The Intelligence Office" we are told that the aggregation of human wishes "is probably truer, as a representation of the human heart, than is the living drama of action, as it evolves around us."[13] The Hall of Fantasy, in the sketch of that title, "is likely to endure longer than the most substantial structures that ever cumbered the earth. . . . It may be said, in truth, that there is but half a life—the meaner and earthlier half—for those who never find their way into the hall" (pp. 173, 179). Of another castle in the air Hawthorne writes, in "A Select Party," that "the dominions

13. *Mosses from an Old Manse*, p. 333. Subsequent references to stories from this volume given parenthetically in text.

which the spirit conquers for itself among unrealities, become a thousand times more real than the earth whereon [people] stamp their feet, saying 'This is solid and substantial!—this may be called a fact!' " (p. 58).

But even as he says these things, Hawthorne cautions his readers to make only occasional visits to the Hall of Fantasy or to their castles in the air. Even though reality may lie in the depths of the heart or on the heights of ideal wishes, the appropriate atmosphere for human life is the busy world of surfaces. Or so it appears. But we should not try to force Hawthorne's writings from this period into a meaningful statement about the relationship between imagination and life. Here as in his social commentary he is mediating between opposed positions with an eye to attracting the largest audience.

"Buds and Bird-Voices" lacks the formulaic structure of the other Manse sketches and its movement seems more associative. In this work Hawthorne draws from journal entries on the arrival of spring to produce a seasonal essay in the transcendental mode. He uses natural facts as signs of spiritual facts: "Summer works in the present, and thinks not of the future; Autumn is a rich conservative; Winter has utterly lost its faith, and clings tremulously to the remembrance of what has been; but Spring, with its outgushing life, is the true type of the Movement!" (p. 158). Allegorist that Hawthorne is, this maiden attempt at transcendental symbolizing has a certain stiffness, and the kinds of observation that he makes, as well as the uses to which he puts them, reflect a less hopeful sensibility than the transcendentalists': "Persons who can only be graceful and ornamental—who can give the world nothing but flowers—should die young, and never been seen with gray hair and wrinkles. . . . Human flower shrubs, if they will grow old on earth, should, beside their lovely blossoms, bear some kind of fruit that will satisfy earthly appetites" (pp. 151–52). Much as he tries to conjure the appropriate spirit, he continues to see autumn and winter behind the spring:

One of the first things that strike the attention, when the white sheet of winter is withdrawn, is the neglect and disarray that lay hidden beneath it. . . . How invariably, throughout all the forms of life, do we find these intermingled memorials of death! . . . Why may we not be permitted to live and enjoy, as if this were the first life, and our own the primal enjoyment, instead of treading always on these dry bones and mouldering relics, from the aged accumulation of which springs all that now appears so young and new? Sweet must have been the springtime of Eden, when no earlier year had strewn its decay upon the virgin turf, and no former experience had ripened into summer, and faded into autumn, in the hearts of the inhabitants! That was a world worth living in!   [Pp. 152–53]

Faintly, the concerns of *The House of the Seven Gables* and *The Blithedale Romance* are foreshadowed; unlike most of the work of the Manse period, "Buds and Bird-Voices" anticipates Hawthorne's later works, both in its illumination of the surface with symbolic meanings and in its theme of the oppressive persistence of the past.

In "The Old Apple-Dealer" Hawthorne writes an essay about the difficulty of bringing to life a colorless character. His subject, who sells apples in the railroad station, lacks a character because he lacks inner life. Lacking imagination, he has aged without responding to experience and thus essentially has had no experience; there is nothing in the surface he presents that an author can use as an index of the person. This sketch has both psychological and literary implications, for it locates both the human essence and the author's subject in the inner life. The empty shell that is the old apple dealer looks ahead to Hawthorne's depiction of the old men of the Salem Custom House.

"The Christmas Banquet," a generic mixture of sketch and fiction, makes the same point: to lack inner life is to lack life altogether. Hawthorne imagines an annual Christmas banquet to which each year are invited the most wretched people who can be found. Only one man, Gervayse Hastings (who has no connection with the Gervayse Hastings of "Lady Eleanore's Mantle"), returns year after year. He must be the most miserable man on earth, and yet he has money, fame, power, talent, family, and friends. The mystery is resolved when Hastings confesses that he is utterly without inner life; experience has failed to touch him, and therefore it is as though nothing had ever happened to him. Life, then, is the same as inner response. In a way, "The Old Apple-Dealer" and "The Christmas Banquet" are iterating Hawthorne's predictable theme of the precedence of the imaginative life over outer experience. But Hawthorne's intention—to define the quality of life by the richness of the imaginative response to it—is rather different from the intention in those earlier fictions that expose the dangers of the uncorrected imagination. Evidently, he was beginning to absorb some transcendental ideas into his thematic scheme.

The expository persona that Hawthorne developed in these sketches is an unlikely fabulator; story, when he utilizes it, serves to illustrate or enliven his discursive point. Putting aside two children's pieces—"A Good Man's Miracle," about the founding of Sunday schools, and "Little Daffydowndilly," a parable about a little boy who tries to avoid work but finds it everywhere and learns at last that life is synonymous with labor—we find only six fictions written in the Manse period. These are "The Antique Ring," "Egotism; or, the Bosom Serpent," "The Birth-mark," "Rappaccini's Daughter," "The Artist of the Beautiful," and "Drowne's Wooden Image." It is difficult to find consistency of matter or manner in the group. But except for "The Antique Ring," which is a gothic fiction set in a satiric frame, these stories are among the most interesting and puzzling in Hawthorne's canon. All of them are characterized by an intervening, prosy narrator; but this narrator's commentary is often inadequate to and sometimes even incompatible with the narrative and symbolic content of the fiction. It seems most unlikely that Hawthorne was experimenting with the device of an obtuse narrator, for such a procedure would implicitly undermine the position of the speaker in the Manse sketches; nevertheless, the persona of the Manse does become obtuse when he is pressed into service as a narrator of fiction. The material escapes his attempts to control it.

In at least one case Hawthorne appears to recognize this fact, for he presents the story as though not the persona, but another author, were the creator. "Rappaccini's Daughter" begins with an introduction in which the persona takes the role of the translator and critic of the fiction composed by the French writer M. de l'Aubépine (French for Hawthorne). This author, he says, "must necessarily find himself without an audience" because "if not too refined, he is at all events too remote, too shadowy and unsubstantial in his modes of development, to suit the taste of the [multitude], and yet too popular to satisfy the spiritual or metaphysical requisitions of the [transcendentalists]" (p. 91). But despite his failure in popularity, M. de l'Aubépine "is voluminous; he continues to write and publish with as much praiseworthy and indefatigable prolixity, as if his efforts were crowned with the brilliant success that so justly attends those of Eugene Sue" (p. 92). A list of more than fourteen of his books is cited, including a three-volume "Le Voyage Céleste à Chemin de Fer" and a five-volume "L'Artiste du Beau, ou le Papillon Mécanique."

How is one to take this facetious introduction? Obviously, its ironies refer to certain objective truths, touching on Hawthorne's dissatisfaction with the meagerness of both his audience and his output. But at the same time the analysis is just the sort of well-meaning but imperceptive commentary that a critic like Oliver Wendell Holmes or James Russell Lowell might impose on a romantic or visionary author. The split between Hawthorne the Manse persona and Aubépine the writer of fiction exposes the shortcomings of both, and makes especially clear the underlying discomfort that Hawthorne experienced with his Manse voice because of its inhospitality to fiction.

Aubépine, however, is not a perfect narrator for "Rappaccini's Daughter," for this is one of the richest stories in the canon, at once a visionary tale and a commentary on the visionary imagination, calling for a narrator firmly based in the camps of both the real and the ideal. The story may even be too rich, in the sense that it is susceptible of a number of partial explanations but seems to evade any single wholly satisfactory reading. It offers itself as an allegory of faith, an allegory of science, and an allegory of sex all at once. At first it proceeds along the familiar Hawthorne track. Young Giovanni is another obsessed protagonist who brings harm to himself and others by persisting in his delusion, which is that the beautiful Beatrice has been made poisonous, like a deadly plant, by her father's experiments and that she is poisoning him. This delusion is the product, we are made to think, of Giovanni's basically cynical and shallow mind. But at a certain point it becomes absolutely clear that Giovanni is not deluded; Beatrice really is poisonous. Still, the narrator continues to scold Giovanni, and the design of the plot exposes him as terribly in error, for his attempt to cure Beatrice has the effect of killing her.

This plot becomes less puzzling if the story is read as an allegory of faith. The question is not Giovanni's delusion but his belief. Had he believed in Beatrice, she would not have been poisonous. The statement that Hawthorne is making about faith is not merely that one must persist without evidence. It is far more extreme—one must persist in belief *despite* evidence. If this is one meaning of "Rappaccini's Daughter," then it is antithetical to the familiar Hawthorne story of visionary delusion, for it urges Giovanni to reject the corrective influence of his senses and hold instead to his intuitions. Although it is not likely that Hawthorne intended this story to refer to any particular doctrinal question, given his lack of interest in theological niceties, "Rappaccini's Daughter" is a story with which Christian critics have felt especially comfortable, because the kind of idealism it endorses is certainly compatible with orthodox belief.

If "Rappaccini's Daughter" makes an uncharacteristic defense of the visionary imagination, it appears to do so at the expense of science, the alternative world view. Rappaccini, Baglioni, and Giovanni are all nineteenth-century scientists of a sort, their approach to life determined by their premise that sensory evidence is real. But as a criticism of science the story comes full circle, for these scientists are not men of reason but visionary fanatics after all.[14] They are criticized not for their rationality but for their delusion that they are rational. They believe that they have detached their minds from their emotions, while all the time it is their emotions that determine their behavior: Giovanni is governed by his lust, Baglioni by his rivalry with Rappaccini, and Rappaccini by his wish to put his daughter beyond the reach of ordinary human experience.

The story is also an allegory of sex, and because writing about sex is so rare in Hawthorne's time this may be its most interesting aspect to a modern reader. It is evident in many ways that Beatrice's poison is her sexuality, particularly in the image of the deadly erotic flower with which she is identified. Her attraction for Giovanni is largely sexual, and he fears that attraction because it suggests that Beatrice has power over him. Thus, "poison" may be seen as a symbol for the power of sex. The interpretative dilemma is whether this sex is real and good or horrible but (fortunately) delusory. When Hawthorne writes that "all this ugly mystery was but an earthly illusion, and . . . whatever mist of evil might seem to have

14. M. D. Uroff has pointed out this lack of scientific objectivity in "The Doctors in 'Rappaccini's Daughter,'" *Nineteenth-Century Fiction*, 27 (1972), 61–70.

gathered over her, the real Beatrice was a heavenly angel" (p. 122), does he mean that in essence Beatrice was free of the "ugly mystery" of sex; or that properly seen, sex is not an ugly mystery? The question is not resolved, and rightly not, because Giovanni is a type of the sexually confused Victorian male, struggling between his wish to accept sex as a beneficent part of life and his strong conviction that it is unnatural and evil.

Given these multiple meanings, one must conclude that no persona Hawthorne had yet developed in his career was adequate to tell the tale. It would have been better presented unmediated by a narrative voice, like the earliest stories. In fact, however, it is heavy with authorial interpolation. One might suspect also that the short form was becoming a confinement, for although one may celebrate the richness and complexity of "Rappaccini's Daughter," one may also feel that its method represents a kind of shorthand notation for what by rights could have been a much longer, and correspondingly richer (even though perhaps less suggestive), work. There is a better fit in "Egotism; or, the Bosom Serpent" and "The Birth-mark" between teller and tale, largely because these are simpler fictions. They are both pure, undigressive stories about the obsessional imagination and lend themselves to unitary interpretations. "Egotism," which substitutes for a specific *idée fixe* the conventional notion of a serpent in the breast, is clearly an allegory, paradigmatic of all Hawthorne's other stories of estranged protagonists. In "Egotism," as in most of the stories of this type, the cure for the hero's disease rests in a loving woman who connects—or can connect, if he accepts her—the lonely male with the social order and gives him a chance to develop his own capacities for altruism and love. The figure of the woman is highly idealized.

In "The Birth-mark" Hawthorne examines more specifically than he had done before the sexual problems that underlie the protagonist's social alienation, as well as the sexual reasons for his inability to take the help offered by the woman. Critics have found adumbrations of the motif of rejection of the female in such stories as "Roger Malvin's Burial," "Young Goodman Brown," and "The Minister's Black Veil,"[15] but this is the first instance in which Hawthorne identifies the male obsession overtly with a revulsion against women and specifically with a revulsion against her physical nature. "Rappaccini's Daughter" was written almost two years after "The Birth-mark"; its treatment of the sexual theme is more ambiguous because the earlier story states simply that sex is good and that Aylmer's revulsion is perverse. His idealism is nothing more than a rationalized distaste for sexuality.

Another woman-hater is Owen Warland, the protagonist in "The Artist of the Beautiful." In this story the narrator and the narrative flatly contradict each other, demonstrating again the inadequacy of the Manse voice for fiction. When the narrator brings the tale to a close with the assurance that "when the artist rose high enough to achieve the Beautiful, the symbol by which he made it perceptible to mortal senses became of little value in his eyes, while his spirit possessed itself in the enjoyment of the Reality" (p. 475), he claims a dignity for Owen Warland that the story will not support. The conflict here is directly related to Hawthorne's own literary dilemma, for if Owen's audience is faulted for its indifference to his art, so is he faulted for devoting himself to the realization of ideas that have so little connection to the life around him.

Indeed, in scene after scene Hawthorne shows that Warland's impulse to attain the beautiful springs not from a desire to enrich life but from the need to escape it. To Danforth's strength, to Hovenden's acuity, even to Annie's warmth, he responds with fear. The ideal that takes shape is a mechanical miniature, exquisite to be sure, but lifeless and depthless: a fragile, cold bauble. In a literal sense, the miniature that he

15. Especially, of course, Frederick C. Crews in *The Sins of the Fathers* (New York: Oxford University Press, 1965).

produces represents the belittling of imagination. The heart of this story lies neither in the pathetic situation of the unappreciated artist nor in his ultimate triumphant indifference to reputation. At the core of "The Artist of the Beautiful" is Hawthorne's recognition of how inadequate a figure Owen is for the vocation he has chosen, how timid and shrunken his conception of art. The narrative belies the narrator's claim for Owen's artistic stature and calls for another kind of artistry than his.

"Drowne's Wooden Image," the story Hawthorne wrote immediately before "The Artist of the Beautiful," proposes passion as the source of a truly great art. More than any other work of the Manse period, this story looks ahead to the long romances. Comfortably situated in a port town as a carver of ship's figureheads, Drowne is a mechanic and businessman rather than an artist. He turns out crude but serviceable figureheads in a prompt and efficient manner. He aspires to no artistic heights and has no conception of his medium—wood—as other than material. Is he lacking that sense of nonmaterial essence, that devotion to the exquisite, exemplified in Owen Warland? Perhaps, but Drowne's lack of spirituality is not his shortcoming as an artist; what he needs is a powerful emotion. When he falls in love with the beautiful woman he has been asked to represent in a figurehead, his art is transformed. Wood becomes an expressive form, fluid to his emotions as it never was to his tools. The completed figure is almost frighteningly real, exhibiting a skill far beyond Drowne's ordinary capabilities. Beauty combines with force, idea with material, purpose with craft. Such art needs no justification, is beyond apologies and manifestos. Such art convinces by its very existence; it does not so much please as conquer its audience.

Nothing before in Hawthorne's work resembles this concept of art and the artist. It shares little with the sensitive gentleman of *Twice-told Tales* or the cosmopolitan man of letters writing from the Old Manse. A romantic conception, it differs from Fanshawe's style of painful aloofness and Oberon's defiant *Stürm und Drang*. It requires an exertion and dedication beyond anything that has been demanded of Hawthorne's author figures; it taxes the whole range of the artist's emotions and experience and channels his whole existence into the creation of his work. The artist lives at the intersection of his imaginative life and his work; no other considerations matter.

This is the idea against which Hawthorne is measuring Owen Warland; and in comparison to this idea he would also have to judge his own work thin and superficial. One can only speculate about the cumulative dissatisfactions that generated this sudden expression of romantic feeling. It seems a reaction to long years of working within an idea of authorship that failed to satisfy him. Hawthorne had curtailed his powers in order to please an imagined audience, and an audience had materialized; but the exchange was uneven. He had given up more than he had received. "Drowne's Wooden Image" points the way to a vision of art as a fully serious, absorbing enterprise, and to the artist as an independent person responsible only to his art and to himself. Of course, Drowne receives far greater recognition for this self-reflexive work than for all the obedient productions of his studio. This was to be precisely Hawthorne's experience in *The Scarlet Letter*. Unique among Hawthorne's writings at this time, "Drowne's Wooden Image" is not a proclamation or a declaration of independence, but it is an augur of the future.

Mosses from an Old Manse, published in two volumes in 1846, contains twenty-two works, not much more than half the total in *Twice-told Tales*. From his writings at the Manse Hawthorne omitted only "Little Daffydowndilly," "A Good Man's Miracle," "The Antique Ring," and "A Book of Autographs." Among earlier works he chose "Roger Malvin's Burial," from *Provincial Tales*, "Young Goodman Brown" from *The Story Teller*, and "Mrs. Bullfrog" and "Monsieur du Miroir" from the *Twice-told Tales* period. These pieces increase the range of work in *Mosses*, bringing in historical, gothic, and comic elements. They strengthen the imaginative side of the collection while diluting the dominance of the Manse persona, who has much less presence in the collection than one might have anticipated. The arrangement of work in both volumes follows the rhetorical scheme of associative clusters varied by contrast, with intent to create the greatest possible impression of variety in the material. Hawthorne revised some of his most topically allusive pieces by cutting out several specific references to his contemporaries, and excised some sectarian commentary from "Monsieur du Miroir." Such references might suit the ephemeral nature of magazine publication, but seemed inappropriate to a volume designed for permanence.

Nothing Hawthorne did in designing the shape of *Mosses from an Old Manse* was more important, however, than his writing of a long essay to introduce and unify the collection. First mention of this essay occurs in a letter of April 7, 1845, when he and his publisher began to discuss plans for the collection. He wrote that he had in mind an essay to serve as "a sort of framework . . . for the series of stories already published, and to make the scene an idealization of our old parsonage, and of the river close at hand, with glimmerings of my actual life—yet so transmogrified that the reader should not know what was reality and what fancy."[16] This framework—technically not a frame, since it was only to introduce but not conclude the work—would unify the separate pieces by connecting them to the life Hawthorne had lived at the Old Manse. The stories and sketches would then be interpreted as the product of a single mind interacting with its surroundings. In a sense, this framing intention returns to the scheme of *The Story Teller*, although in a much simplified way; it

16. Quoted in McDonald, " 'The Old Manse' and Its Mosses," p. 87.

also includes an autobiographical element that is quite new for Hawthorne, who always before concealed himself behind his various personae.

Perhaps because the conception of this sketch was inherently retrospective, Hawthorne found that he could not actually write it at the Manse. He began it in May 1845, but did not finish it until April 1846, several months after he had left the Manse. As he wrote, "Nothing that I tried to write would flow out of my pen, till a very little while ago—when forth came this sketch of its own accord, and much unlike what I had purposed."[17] "The Old Manse" is clearly unlike what Hawthorne originally intended, because it shows not how the work in *Mosses* reflects Hawthorne's life at the Manse, but just the opposite: how it fails to do so. In a way not at all schematic, Hawthorne identifies three aspects of his experience at the Manse. The Manse itself, the old house where he and his family lived, represents social institutions and (through the people who lived there before the Hawthornes) the human past. His transcendental friends represent a breathtaking freedom of speculation and stand for the brave mind contemplating the promise of the future. Finally, the natural beauty of Concord with its river, orchards, and even Hawthorne's vegetable garden reminds one of the ongoing and yet timeless rhythms of the natural world that sustain human beings and their social organizations. In a scene that twines all these together Hawthorne describes a river trip with Ellery Channing, who was to Hawthorne the most representative transcendentalist:

The winding course of the stream continually shut out the scene behind us, and revealed as calm and lovely a one before. We glided from depth to depth, and breathed new seclusion at every turn. . . . Amid sunshine and shadow, rustling leaves, and sighing waters, up-gushed our talk, like the babble of a fountain. . . . The chief profit of those wild days, to him and me, lay . . . in

17. Quoted by J. Donald Crowley in the "Historical Commentary" to the *Mosses*, p. 519.

the freedom which we thereby won from all custom and conventionalism, and fettering influences of man on man. . . . And yet how sweet—as we floated homeward adown the golden river, at sunset—how sweet it was to return within the system of human society, not as a dungeon and a chain, but as to a stately edifice, when we could go forth at will into statelier simplicity! [Pp. 23–25]

Looking out from such experience at his work, Hawthorne judges it severely. "These fitful sketches, with so little of external life about them, yet claiming no profundity of purpose,—so reserved, even while they sometimes seem so frank,—often but half in earnest, and never, even when most so, expressing satisfactorily the thought which they profess to image—such trifles, I truly feel, afford no solid basis for a literary reputation" (p. 34).[18] As he compared the life he had led with the work he had produced he saw an enormous disparity. Even the account of the Old Manse itself as he pens it strikes him as superficial. "How narrow—how shallow and scanty too—is the stream of thought that has been flowing from my pen, compared with the broad tide of dim emotions, ideas, and associations, which swell around me from that portion of my existence!" (p. 32).

Of course, Hawthorne had been deprecating himself as far back as The Story Teller. But the tone of the criticism in "The Old Manse" is entirely different from the humble and self-effacing note of the earlier strategy, which operated to

18. These words may seem like a literary pose; but Hawthorne wrote to Evert Duyckinck in much the same way a few months before composing "The Old Manse": "As the first essays and tentatives of a young author, they would be well enough—but it seems to me absurd to look upon them as conveying any claims to a settled reputation. I thank God, I have grace enough to be utterly dissatisfied with them, considered as the productions of a literary life. . . . I am ashamed—and there's an end" (quoted by Crowley in the "Historical Commentary" to the Centenary Mosses, p. 517).

ingratiate the author with his audience. Part of Hawthorne's earlier claim to attention was that he asked so little of his readers. Now it is precisely on the score of their littleness that Hawthorne excoriates his own productions. There is nothing humble about the criticism Hawthorne makes of his own work, because his censure implicitly makes the highest demands on the literary artifact. Behind Hawthorne's earlier self-criticism lay the assumption that not only his own work but the whole profession of literature was perhaps an idle or worthless enterprise. Now, however, he sharply distinguishes his own work from another kind of literature—literature that he might have written, that he ought to have written, that he greatly fears he is incapable of writing. "The Old Manse" itself is a first attempt at this other kind of writing, with its much more personal voice and its infinitely richer texture than the work from the Manse period.

Retrospectively idyllic as life at the Manse may have been, and secure as Hawthorne might have felt in a moderate literary reputation, the fact is that his magazine work did not pay and that, even if he had wished to take the plunge into a long work, the necessity to turn out short works for monthly pay checks made it impossible for him to do so. Finally, he could no longer afford to live at the Manse. In October 1845 he took his family to his mother's house in Salem, where he waited for a government position. In April 1846 he was appointed surveyor in the Salem Custom House, and he worked there until his dismissal in June 1849, after his party had been defeated in the elections. During these years in Salem he wrote very little—only four pieces besides "The Old Manse," including "The Snow-Image," "Main-street," "The Great Stone Face," and "Ethan Brand." Two of these works, "The Snow-Image" and "The Great Stone Face," have child protagonists and may have been intended as stories for children, although they were eventually published in adult magazines. "Main-street" was written for the *Aesthetic Papers*, compiled by his sister-in-law Elizabeth Peabody (the same collection in which Thoreau's "Civil Disobedience" appeared). "Ethan Brand" is a puzzle: Hawthorne is known to have completed it in December 1848, but some scholars have supposed it to be exactly what the subtitle proclaims it to be, "A Fragment from an Abortive Romance," and therefore dating from an earlier time.

Hawthorne said toward the end of "The Old Manse" that *Mosses from an Old Manse* would be "the last collection of this nature, which it is my purpose ever to put forth. Unless I could do better, I have done enough in this kind" (p. 34). His limited output may represent the implementation of this resolve; perhaps he was simply demoralized by the tedious work routine of the Custom House and lacked the motive to write. In any event, the long phase of his career in which he had confined himself entirely to short works was coming to an end, some twenty years after the failure of *Fanshawe*. After these few pieces composed in the Custom House period, Hawthorne wrote only one more independent short fiction, "Feathertop."

Its plot developed from a journal entry of 1838, "Ethan Brand" is more appropriate to that date than for ten years later. Brand is another protagonist victimized by his own uncorrected imagination as it relentlessly drives him into a self-enclosed universe. Continual assaults on his fantasy enrage him and lead him to increasingly extreme affirmations of his own delusion. Horrified at every hint that he has wasted his life in pursuit of a false idea, he moves at last to the final, unanswerable attempt to validate the meaning he has imposed on his life: he kills himself. This gesture gives his life the meaning he wants it to have while forever putting him beyond the reach of a regulating reality. Of course, the real world, completely untouched by his madness, wakes up the next morning and goes about its business unperturbed.

Interpretations of this story that concentrate on the theological implications of Brand's delusion (the Unpardonable Sin) miss Hawthorne's emphasis. For his purposes, one delusion is as good as another; they all illustrate the same point. In many ways, "Ethan Brand" is not as good as other variants of this motif, and in the context of Hawthorne's changing views about imagination it is something of an anachronism in 1848. Perhaps he actually did write it at an earlier date and put it aside because he found it too stiff and schematic in its presentation. But if so, we do not know why he revived it.

If "Ethan Brand" is a throwback in its identification of the imagination with solipsism and insanity, so is "The Snow-Image" a reprise in its equation of imagination with the insubstantial and perishable. Like "The Artist of the Beautiful," the story presents a conflict between imagination and common sense; it also shows imaginative creation to be evanescent and fragile. In contrast to "The Artist of the Beautiful," the story lacks a corrective irony and therefore suggests no other type of imagination than that which it depicts in the activities of the children as they create their snow maiden. Its weakness is not so much the identification of imagination with the mental operations of children (approvingly supervised by their mother) as its portrayal of the mother and children in sentimental, stereotypical terms. Within their cozy domestic world, these pure and tender beings bring their wonderful snow companion to life. No sympathy is expressed for the bumbling though well-meaning father of the family, who mistakes the imaginative creation for a real being and brings her into the house to be warmed before the fire. He is only to be laughed at for his obtuseness and blamed for destroying the fragile artifact. But this same obtuseness enables him to go out daily into the rough world and earn the means on which the protected domestic world depends for the very insularity that develops its imaginative capacities. Beneath its delicately articulated surface, then, "The Snow-Image" is a crudely and carelessly conceived work.

So, too, in a different way is "The Great Stone Face," although this story strives to imbue the idea of imagination with more power and virtue. Ernest's natural, artless life conforms with the natural forces that have carved the great stone face, while all the false candidates have shaped their lives for social ends, wealth, fame, power. Even the poet, closer than any worldly man to fulfilling the requirements of the Face, has passed too much time among what he calls "realities." Evidently, the least brush with reality forever destroys the purity the face demands. Thus, though couched in moral and ethical rather than aesthetic terms, "The Great Stone Face" takes the same fastidious attitude toward actuality that underlies "The Snow-Image." The world is a dirty place, it says. Imagination should keep itself pure and have nothing to do with actuality. In these two stories Hawthorne, who in the irony of "The Artist of the Beautiful," in the image of the passionate artist in "Drowne's Wooden Image," and in the intense directness of "The Old Manse," was moving toward a profound connection between actuality and imagination, swings almost violently backward.

"Main-street" is, after "The Old Manse," much the most interesting of Hawthorne's writings from the Custom House. This is a history of Salem presented as a series of tableaux by an itinerant showman, framed by interchanges between the showman and members of his audience. The historical representation recapitulates much that we have seen before in Hawthorne's historical writings, but brings in fascinating new material as well. The frame takes up some new aesthetic considerations. The exchanges between the irritated showman and his dissatisfied audience appear at first to oppose the man of imagination to the commonsense literal mind once again. But, in fact, the showman's audience is not unliterary; it has aesthetic expectations that the showman is not satisfying. Apparently the audience wants realism. The showman admits that his effects might be more forcefully managed, but insists that the sort of verisimilitude requested is altogether detrimental to his purposes, which involve the imaginative stimulation of his audience. This is a sign that Hawthorne recognizes an emerging audience trained up in the aesthetic of the novel rather than that of the romance.

Along with much familiar historical narrative, Hawthorne offers a strikingly different historical organization in "Mainstreet." Salem history divides into two stages, and each stage falls again into two segments. First comes pre-European civilization and the settlement; then come two successive stages of Puritan community. A view of pre-European America is unprecedented in Hawthorne's works, and it is of great interest in terms of his later treatment of women—especially the conflict of Hester with the Puritan oligarchy—that he describes pre-European America as a matriarchy. The Puritans, when they come, impose a staunchly patriarchal attitude, hostile to nature, on a landscape that for untold centuries has harmoniously integrated man and nature under the rule of a woman:

You perceive, at a glance, that this is the ancient and primitive wood,—the ever-youthful and venerably old,—verdant with new twigs, yet hoary, as it were, with the snowfall of innumerable years, that have accumulated upon its intermingled branches. The white man's axe has never smitten a single tree; his footstep has never crumbled a single one of the withered leaves. . . . What footsteps can have worn this half-seen path? . . . We discern an Indian woman,—a majestic and queenly woman, or else her spectral image does not represent her truly,—for this is the great Squaw Sachem, whose rule, with that of her sons, extends from Mystic to Agawam.[19]

After the rule of the Queen comes a brief Edenic time of individual pioneering settlement, wherein each family is a separate unit, a world to itself. Personal freedom and human

19. *The Snow-Image*, pp. 50–51. Subsequent references given parenthetically in text.

relation combine in a natural world free from social institution. In the second phase of history, the Puritan community establishes itself and destroys both the matriarchy and the life of the yeoman family. The earliest Puritans have the virtues and defects that Hawthorne always discovered in them. "Stern, severe, intolerant" as ever, they nevertheless act in the "zeal of a recovered faith" that "burns like a lamp within their hearts." For the second and third generation, whose religion is "inherited from the example and precept of other human beings," it is impossible "to grow up, in heaven's freedom, beneath the discipline which [the first generation's] gloomy energy of character had established." Consequently, "the sons and grandchildren of the first settlers were a race of lower and narrower souls than their progenitors" (pp. 58, 67–68). To the influence of these children and grandchildren Hawthorne attributes much of the worst in American life and character even in the nineteenth century.

The distinction between a felt and an inherited religion is new to Hawthorne and clearly an outgrowth of his exposure to the transcendentalists, for such a distinction lay at the very heart of Emerson's teachings. Still, and characteristically, the content of the religious belief is of no interest to Hawthorne; the issue is whether the belief is felt, so that its rituals are expressive, or is externally imposed and therefore repressive. Repressed themselves, the later Puritans have only the bad qualities of their ancestors. Taken together, the four phases of Salem history comprise a complete political and psychological mythology. The pre-European phase is childhood, ruled over by the mother; the Edenic pioneering period represents youth, independent, enterprising, and individualistic; the first Puritan generation is maturity; and subsequent generations symbolize decay. Both Puritan phases are patriarchal and institutional. At this point in the showman's disquisition, his machinery breaks down, forcing him to end his presentation. But the historical cycle has already been completed, and the minor mishap simply facilitates the ending of the sketch. What would Hawthorne have said about his own time? Would it have appeared a further decline or a new beginning? All four of his major romances focus on this question, particularly *The House of the Seven Gables* and *The Blithedale Romance*. In "Main-street" Hawthorne is approaching his major phase.

⊰ 4 ⊱

The Major Phase I
1850

Hawthorne took his post at the Salem Custom House under the impression that the position had been removed from the patronage rolls and that it would be his regardless of the results of future elections. When, after the Democratic defeat in 1848, the local Whigs determined to turn him out, they raised questions about his administrative competence as a means of justifying their action and removed him from the post. Hawthorne detested his work in the Custom House, but it was a living. To lose it—especially in a publicly humiliating way—was a traumatic experience. As long as the Whigs remained in office he could not expect another political appointment; he had no profession but writing, and writing had failed to support him at the Manse. In the period immediately following his dismissal the Hawthorne family lived on such household money as Sophia Hawthorne had saved, on the sale of her hand-decorated lampshades and hand screens, and on the contributions of friends. Hawthorne was poor, out of work, unfairly disgraced—and his terrible crisis was exacerbated yet further by the death of his mother (to whom he was deeply tied despite the emotional reserve that characterized their relationship) on July 31, 1849. *The Scarlet Letter* was written in a mood of grief and anger and seems to have had a therapeutic effect on him. "He writes immensely," Sophia re-

123

ported in a letter to her mother. "I am almost frightened about it. But he is well now and looks very shining."[1]

Before he finished *The Scarlet Letter*, he set it aside to compose "The Custom-House," so that in effect the two were written concurrently.[2] He designed "The Custom-House" for many purposes: to balance the mood and tone of *The Scarlet Letter*, which, he feared, was monotonous in its single effect; to increase the length of the volume in which *The Scarlet Letter* would be published; to take revenge on the politicians who had caused his removal from the Custom House. But above all he wrote it as a commentary on, and a frame for, *The Scarlet Letter*. The essay tells the story of how Hawthorne came to write *The Scarlet Letter* and in so doing tells us a good deal about how to read it. If "The Custom-House" makes an introduction to *The Scarlet Letter*, so does *The Scarlet Letter* provide the conclusion for "The Custom-House."

In *The Scarlet Letter* Hawthorne defined the focus of all four of his completed long romances: the conflict between passionate, self-assertive, and self-expressive inner drives and the repressing counterforces that exist in society and are also internalized within the self. In this romance he also formulated some of the recurrent elements in his continuing exploration of this theme. In Hester he developed the first of a group of female representatives of the human creative and passionate forces, while in Dimmesdale he created the first of several guilt-prone males, torn between rebellious and conforming impulses. These two characters operate in *The Scarlet Letter*

1. Stewart, *Nathaniel Hawthorne*, pp. 91, 93–94; see also Hubert H. Hoeltje, "The Writing of *The Scarlet Letter*," *New England Quarterly*, 27 (1954), 326–46.

2. William Charvat, in his introduction to the Centenary *Scarlet Letter*, shows that "The Custom-House" was completed by January 15, 1850, on which date three chapters of *The Scarlet Letter* remained to be written (p. xxii).

in a historical setting, which was not repeated in any of Hawthorne's later romances, but the historical setting is shaped according to thematic preoccupations that do recur. Nominally Puritan, the society in *The Scarlet Letter* in fact symbolizes one side of the conflict.

None of his many treatments of the Puritans depicted them in their own terms—that is, as a group bound together by a covenant among themselves and with God, to establish "a due form of government both civil and ecclesiastical," in accordance with "a special overruling providence." (The words are John Winthrop's, from "A Model of Christian Charity.") The historical first generation of Puritans made constant reference out from their every act to the divine purpose for which they acted and the greater will they were bound to serve. Hawthorne, however, always treated the Puritans within an entirely secular framework. His early works constantly balance their punitive intolerance against their strong sense of their own rights and their hardy endurance. "Main-street" manifested, for the first time, a discrimination between them and their descendants on the grounds of their pure religious faith, but his treatment did not operate *within* that faith. The formulation in *The Scarlet Letter* is different from both of these, but retains the same secularity.

In *The Scarlet Letter*, unlike Hawthorne's stories about Ann Hutchinson, the Quakers, Roger Williams, or the Salem witches, the Puritans are not punishing a heresy but an act that in its essence does not appear to quarrel with Puritan doctrine. What Hester and Dimmesdale have done is not a crime against belief but against the law. Many critics have maintained that, since the act violates one of the Ten Commandments, it is necessarily seen by Hawthorne as a crime against Divine Law. But in *The Scarlet Letter* he considers the act entirely as a social crime. Precisely because he does not take up the issue of whether the law broken is a divine law, the issues center on the relations of Hester and Dimmesdale to their community and to themselves as they accept or deny the judgment of the community on them. They differ from one another, not as beings more or less religious, more or less "saved," but as beings differently bound to the community and differently affected by it.

Such a thematic situation is created in *The Scarlet Letter* by the virtual absence of God from the text, and in this respect the romance is a very poor representation of the Puritan mental life as the Puritan himself would have experienced it. Divinity in this romance is a remote, vague, ceremonially invoked concept that functions chiefly to sanction and support the secular power of the Puritan rulers. And—another difference from Hawthorne's earlier formulation of Puritan psychology—these rulers are not transfigured by the zeal of a recovered faith burning like a lamp in their hearts. Remove the sense of communal purpose and service in behest of God, and a self-satisfied secular autocracy remains; this is what we find in *The Scarlet Letter*. The Puritans of this community are sagacious, practical, realistic; they are lovers of form and display; they even tend toward luxury—consider Hester's many opportunities for fancy embroidery, and the elegance of Governor Bellingham's residence.

The ruling group is composed of old males, aptly epitomized in the Governor, "a gentleman advanced in years, and with a hard experience written in his wrinkles. He was not ill fitted to be the head and representative of a community, which owed its origin and progress, and its present state of development, not to the impulses of youth, but to the stern and tempered energies of manhood, and the sombre sagacity of age; accomplishing so much, precisely because it imagined and hoped so little."[3] This patriarchy surrounds itself with displays of power, and when Hawthorne writes that this was "a

3. *The Scarlet Letter*, p. 64. Subsequent references to the Centenary *Scarlet Letter* and "The Custom-House" are given parenthetically in text.

period when the forms of authority were felt to possess the
sacredness of divine institutions" (p. 64), he makes the point,
crucial for his story, that the Puritans venerate authority, not
because it is an instrument in God's service, but because they
believe secular authority itself to be divine.

What Hawthorne says of this group at the beginning of the
romance he repeats at the end. In the final scene we see them
as men of "long-tried integrity," of "solid wisdom and sad-
colored experience," with "endowments of that grave and
weighty order, which gives the idea of permanence, and
comes under the general definition of respectability" (p. 238).
The portrait is by no means wholly unfavorable (although
respectable or authoritarian types will become increasingly
unattractive in the subsequent romances) because Hawthorne
feels, as he felt in *Grandfather's Chair*, that men of this type
were required to establish a new nation: "They had fortitude
and self-reliance, and, in time of difficulty or peril, stood up
for the welfare of the state like a line of cliffs against a tem-
pestuous tide" (p. 238). But such men are totally unfit to
"meddle with a question of human guilt, passion, and anguish"
(p. 65)—to meddle, that is, with the private, inner, imaginative life of the person. They are purely formal, purely public
men; the society they devise accordingly recognizes no private
life, and it is against this obtuseness that Hester and Dimmesdale must try to understand their own behavior and feelings.

A community that embodies the qualities of aging public
males must necessarily repress those of the young and female.
Dimmesdale is a brilliant young minister who, in order to
maintain himself as a favorite among the oligarchs, has repressed himself—made himself prematurely old by resolutely
clinging to childhood. He "trode in the shadowy by-paths,
and thus kept himself simple and childlike; coming forth,
when occasion was, with a freshness, and fragrance, and dewy
purity of thought, which, as many people said, affected them

like the speech of an angel" (p. 66). In this dewy innocent we
recognize faint traces of Hawthorne's earlier men of fancy,
and like them Dimmesdale does not so much want power as
approval. He is a dependent personality. But he is still a young
man, and to forgo the engagement with life characteristic of
youth he must continually hold himself back. His "sin" is an
impulsive relaxation of self-restraint and a consequent assertion
of his youthful energies against the restrictions established by
the elders. He does a passionate, thoughtless, willful thing.
Precipitated out of his protected security as much by fear as
by guilt, he must now confront the conflicts of adulthood. It
is not only that he has been initiated into sex; it is less the
sexual than the mental and emotional that interests Hawthorne, the inner rather than the outer aspects of the experience. Dimmesdale must now recognize and deal with previously hidden, subversive, and disobedient parts of himself.

Hester begins from no such position of security as Dimmesdale, and her relative lack of protection is at once a disadvan-
tage and a blessing. He is the darling insider while she is in
many ways an outsider even before her deed exposes her to
public disgrace. She has been sent to Massachusetts by her
husband, there to await his arrival; her own will is not implicated in her residence in the community. She thus has
nothing like Dimmesdale's tie to the group at the outset. If, as
the unfolding of the romance demonstrates, she is a far more
independent character than Dimmesdale, her independence
may be partly the effect of her relative unimportance in and
to society and her consequent paradoxical freedom within it.
To judge by the development of a certain feminist ideology in
Hester's thinking over the years, it would seem that Hawthorne intended to represent a basic difference in the status of
men and women within a patriarchal structure. Since women
are of less account than men—are not fully members of the
society—they are coerced physically rather than psychologi-

cally. Forced to wear a symbol of shame in public, Hester is left alone behind that symbol to develop as she will.

The story of *The Scarlet Letter* evolves from the sin of omission that has occurred before the narrative begins to a much more important sin of commission that takes place in the same place seven years later. The original sexual encounter between Hester and Dimmesdale was an act neither of deliberate moral disobedience nor of conscious social rebellion. The characters had forgotten society and were thinking only of themselves. But seven years later when they meet again, they deliberately reject the judgment society has passed upon them. "What we did had a consecration of its own," Hester says, and "what hast thou to do with all these iron men, and their opinions?" (pp. 195, 197) Deciding to leave the community, they in effect deny its right to punish them. Hester is mainly responsible for this decision; seven years of solitude have made of her a rebel and a radical. The consequent catastrophe originates with Dimmesdale, whose fragile personality cannot sustain the posture of defiance once Hester's support has been removed and he is back in the community. He reverts—rather quickly—to the view that society has the right to judge and therefore that its judgment is right. His dying speech does not convince Hester. "Is not this better," he demands, "than what we dreamed of in the forest?" "I know not! I know not!" she replies (p. 254). She undertakes alone the journey they had planned together and secures the fruit of her sin from the consequences of a Puritan judgment. Then, surprisingly, she returns.

But by returning, even though she takes up the scarlet letter and wears it until her death, she does not acknowledge her guilt. Rather, she admits that the shape of her life has been determined by the interaction between that letter, the social definition of her identity, and her private attempt to withstand that definition. Her life is neither the letter nor her resistance—neither the inner nor the outer—but the totality. But by again wearing the letter after her return—a gesture nobody would have required of her after so many years—and thus bringing the community to accept that letter on her terms rather than its own, Hester has in fact brought about a modest social change. Society expands to accept her with the letter—the private life carves out a small place for itself in the community's awareness. This is a small, but real, triumph for the heroine.

Hester and Dimmesdale work through their seven-year purgatory accompanied by alter egos, partly supernatural and parasitic beings related in several symbolic ways to their hosts: for Hester, Pearl; for Dimmesdale, Chillingworth. These subsidiary figures embody the sin that has been committed as it is felt and understood by each of the two actors; they are figures of the imagination made real. Since Hester and Dimmesdale imagine their act quite differently, the deed assumes a radically different shape in each one's inner life. Hester perceives her "sin" in the shape of the beautiful child, wild, unmanageable, and unpredictable, who has been created from it; Dimmesdale sees his in the form of the vengeful and embittered husband who has been offended by it.

Splintered off from the characters with whom they are associated, Pearl and Chillingworth indicate disharmony and disunity within Hester's and Dimmesdale's emotional lives, a direct result of the conflict between their sense of themselves and their awareness of how the community perceives them. Each character is alienated from a different part of his nature; crudely, Hester is tormented by her passions and Dimmesdale by his conscience. At the end of the romance the two shattered personalities become whole again and the symbolic characters disappear. Dimmesdale dies and so does Chillingworth; Hester, free at last from social stigma, becomes a whole person and so does Pearl.

For the seven solitary years that she remains in the community, Hester tries to come to terms with its judgment. She actually wants to accept that judgment, for, if she can, she will see purpose and meaning in her suffering. But her attempts cannot shake her deepest conviction that she has not sinned—that is, that the social judgment is not a divine judgment: "Man had marked this woman's sin by a scarlet letter, which had such potent and disastrous efficacy that no human sympathy could reach her, save it were sinful like herself. God, as a direct consequence of the sin which man thus punished, had given her a lovely child, whose place was on that same dishonored bosom, to connect her parent for ever with the race and descent of mortals, and to be finally a blessed soul in heaven!" (p. 89).

As an embodiment of Hester's sin, Pearl is a kind of variant of the scarlet letter. Hester perceives her as such, and dresses her to bring out the identity, "arraying her in a crimson velvet tunic, of a peculiar cut, abundantly embroidered with fantasies and flourishes of gold thread. . . . It was a remarkable attribute of this garb, and indeed, of the child's whole appearance, that it irresistibly and inevitably reminded the beholder of the token which Hester Prynne was doomed to wear upon her bosom. It was the scarlet letter in another form; the scarlet letter endowed with life!" (p. 102). In dressing Pearl to look like the letter, Hester appears to be trying to accept the Puritan idea that Pearl is a creature of guilt. But her behavior is subversive and cunning, for she has already transformed the letter into a work of art with her gorgeous embroidery, and it is to this transfigured symbol that she matches Pearl.

Hester's art—and that she is an artist, Hawthorne leaves no doubt—though ornamental in form, must not be confused with the delicate prettiness of Owen Warland's butterfly or the cold fragility of the snow-image. Her art is not pretty but splendid, and not cold but fiercely passionate, for it stems directly from the passionate self that engendered Pearl and is now denied all other expression: "She had in her nature a rich, voluptuous, Oriental characteristic,—a taste for the gorgeously beautiful, which, save in the exquisite productions of her needle, found nothing else, in all the possibilities of her life, to exercise itself upon" (p. 83). Now this expressive activity, which is fundamentally nonsocial, must be realized in shapes that are perceived and classified and judged by society. Hester's activity is permissible when it is employed in giving "majesty to the forms in which a new government manifested itself to the people," that is, by creating "deep ruffs, painfully wrought bands, and gorgeously embroidered gloves" (p. 82). With these items her gift is brought into the service of authority. But when Hester employs this same activity on her own letter, it is quite another matter. By making the letter beautiful, Hester is denying its literal meaning and thereby subverting the intention of the magistrates who condemn her to wear it. Moreover, by applying this art to her own letter, she puts her gift to work in the service of her private thoughts and feelings rather than in support of public rituals. The Puritan women understand at once what she has done: "She hath good skill at her needle, that's certain . . . but did ever a woman, before this brazen hussy, contrive such a way of showing it! Why, gossips, what is it but to laugh in the faces of our godly magistrates, and make a pride out of what they, worthy gentlemen, meant for a punishment?" (p. 54). Fortunately for Hester—fortunately for the artist—the magistrates lack this ironic perception. They are not imaginative men, and if this failing has led them to deny expression to the imagination, it also prevents them from recognizing it when it manifests itself in subtle or indirect forms.

But in a society that does not recognize and provide forms for imaginative expression, the artist of the private must always make her statement covertly by distorting the available public forms of expression. The executed product therefore involves a compromise, sometimes a very radical one, between the conception and its final shape. In the interplay between

Pearl and the letter, Hawthorne and Hester both wrestle with the problem of bringing together the artist's "idea," which is nonsocial and even nonverbal, and the eventual product. At the most basic level the writer must use language, a social construct, for his expression. Thereby his product becomes social even if his idea is not. Pearl, the antisocial creature, must be transformed into the letter *A*. Ultimately, artistic conceptions that are expressive but perhaps not meaningful in a declarative sense must acquire meanings through the form in which they are expressed, meanings that may be irrelevant to and even at odds with the conception. The undecorated scarlet letter would certainly be a form false to Hester's conception of what she has done. Her recourse is to play with that form in order to loosen it, expand it, undercut it, and thereby make it capable of a sort of many-layered communication. Her artist's activity is directly contrasted to the operation of the Puritan mind, forever anxiously codifying the phenomena of its world into the rigid system of its alphabet.

If Pearl is Hester's imagination of her sin, she also symbolizes the sinful part of Hester's self—the wild, amoral, creative core. Hester is at odds with this part of herself (though she probably would not be if society had not judged as it did) and, until she comes to some sort of resolution, is a divided personality. Truly to assent to her punishment, Hester must come to judge her own nature, or that part of it, as society has judged it. She does try to feel guilty, and hopes that by behaving like a guilty person she will eventually create a sense of guilt within her. She tries to restrain and discipline the child according to society's judgments, but her passionate nature—pushed by ostracism into defiance—continues to assert itself. Pearl expresses all the resentment, pride, anger, and blasphemy that Hester feels but may not voice, and perhaps does not even admit to feeling. One recalls the famous catechism scene where Pearl, to Hester's mortification, proclaims that "she had not been made at all, but had been plucked by her mother off the bush of wild roses, that grew by the prison-door" (p. 112). Pearl repudiates all patriarchs: God, the magistrates, her actual father. Boldly, the child aligns her mother with the persecuted and martyred, for the rosebush is said to have sprung from the footsteps of "sainted" Ann Hutchinson (p. 48).[4] Pearl locates herself within a world inhabited entirely by women, figuring her birth as an event that occurred without men. She confirms the conflict in Hester's case as one between a woman and a patriarchal social structure.

Hester's ultimately unshakable belief in the goodness of this wild and nonsocial core of her being, frightening though it may sometimes be, saves her from taking the readily available and far less imaginative route of witchcraft. This path, which leads straight from the governor's door in the person of his sister, Mistress Hibbens, is in fact a legitimate Puritan social institution. The witches are rebels, but their rebellion arises from accepting the Puritan world view and defining themselves as evil. Yes, they say, we are indeed terribly wicked creatures, and we rejoice in our badness. Because they view themselves as society views them, the witches indirectly validate the social structure. Hester's defiance is another thing entirely.

Alone, her emotions repressed, she does her needlework and thinks. She "assumed a freedom of speculation . . . which our forefathers, had they known of it, would have held to be a deadlier crime than that stigmatized by the scarlet letter" (p. 164). Had she spoken her thoughts, she probably would "have suffered death from the stern tribunals of the period, for attempting to undermine the foundations of the Puritan

4. On the basis of Hawthorne's treatment of Ann Hutchinson in the early biographical sketch, some critics have read this passage as ironical. But there is no rhetorical reason for irony in the passage in *The Scarlet Letter;* and, as we have seen, Hawthorne greatly modified his harsh depiction in later accounts of Ann Hutchinson.

establishment" (p. 165). Naturally, her mind dwells much on her condition as a woman, especially because caring for a girl-child forces her to see her situation in more general terms: "Was existence worth accepting, even to the happiest among [women]?" Pursuing her thought, she is overwhelmed by the magnitude of the changes that must occur before woman's lot becomes generally tolerable. There is certainly no individual solution; there is only individual escape into happy love.[5] But love for Hester is the instrument of misery rather than an escape into bliss, for it is love that keeps her in Boston close to Dimmesdale all those long, sad years. And when she proposes to leave, it is not for herself but for him that she is concerned. The limitation imposed by love on freedom is an aspect of woman's (as distinct from the general human) condition, and this is partly why Hester, returned to Boston, hopes for the revelation of a new truth that will "establish the whole relation between man and woman on a surer ground of mutual happiness" (p. 263).

Hester, labeled guilty by society, gradually rejects the meaning of that label although she cannot reject the label itself. Dimmesdale, thought to be innocent, eventually displays himself in public as a guilty man. His character contrasts completely with Hester's, except in one crucial respect: both of them must ultimately, at whatever cost, be true to the imperatives of their own natures. No matter how she tries to assent to it, Hester cannot help but reject the judgment of the letter. Dimmesdale must finally stigmatize himself no matter how

5. Some critics have taken Hawthorne's comment that these speculations vanish in a woman's mind "if her heart chance to come uppermost" as a patronizing antifeminist comment which undercuts the validity of Hester's thinking. But such an interpretation is too simple, for it is precisely Hawthorne's point that the existing system very rarely allows the heart to come uppermost. The fact that one woman in a thousand (let us say) is happy and therefore not a radical says nothing to the urgency of the need of the other nine hundred and ninety-nine.

much a part of him longs to concur in the idea of his innocence. As I have already briefly observed, Hester is naturally independent and romantic, Dimmesdale dependent and conservative, and these tendencies are reinforced by their different places in the social structure.

"Mr. Dimmesdale," Hawthorne writes, "was a true priest, a true religionist, with the reverential sentiment largely developed, and an order of mind that impelled itself powerfully along the track of a creed, and wore its passage continually deeper with the lapse of time. In no state of society would he have been what is called a man of liberal views; it would always be essential to his peace to feel the pressure of a faith about him, supporting, while it confined him within its iron framework" (p. 123). Observe how, characteristically for Hawthorne, the particular content of a creed is seen as irrelevant to its essential purpose of satisfying the psychological needs of a certain kind of personality. In any society, Dimmesdale would have been a "religionist" because he is a reverent person—that is, he requires authority over him. Although he happens to be a Puritan, Dimmesdale's type is not confined to the Puritan community or bounded by the specific nature of Puritan doctrines. This is a psychological, and not an ethical or philosophical, portrait.

Because of his dependent nature, Dimmesdale is profoundly sincere in his wish to conform. He has apparently remained ignorant of his own passions until his encounter with Hester reveals them. But the passion has been there all the time. Hester must not be misread, as D. H. Lawrence so egregiously misread her, as a dark lady with an appetite for corrupting pure men. She occasions Dimmesdale's passion but does not create it. There are physical signs of struggle in Dimmesdale— his perpetual paleness, the tremor of his mouth denoting both "nervous sensibility and a vast power of self-restraint" (p. 66). In fact, Hawthorne shows what the minister can never accept: the true source of his power over the people is not the spirituality to which he sincerely attributes his success but his denied and despised passionate nature.

Dimmesdale reaches his audience not by argument but by emotion. His instrument is the music of his voice: "This vocal organ was in itself a rich endowment; insomuch that a listener, comprehending nothing of the language in which the preacher spoke, might still have been swayed to and fro by the mere tone and cadence. Like all other music, it breathed passion and pathos, and emotions high or tender, in a tongue native to the human heart, wherever educated." It ranges from a "low undertone, as of the wind sinking down to repose itself," through "progressive gradations of sweetness and power" to a climax of "awe and solemn grandeur. And yet, majestic as the voice sometimes became, there was for ever in it an essential character of plaintiveness" (p. 243). The voice bypasses language to become a direct expression of unmediated feeling.

After his encounter with Hester, Dimmesdale becomes a much more effective preacher, because his feelings have surfaced and cannot entirely be suppressed thereafter. Dimmesdale's congregation is no more aware than he of the source of his power: "They deemed the young clergymen a miracle of holiness. . . . The virgins of his church grew pale around him, victims of a passion so imbued with religious sentiment that they imagined it to be all religion, and brought it openly, in their white bosoms, as their most acceptable sacrifice before the altar" (p. 142). The passionate man arouses passion in others. In spite of himself, Dimmesdale has become an artist. But an artist is not what he intended to be. He is bewildered and horrified by his success. A man like this, deeply committed to the furthering of the social aims of permanence and respectability, who yet finds himself possessed of this subversive power, is necessarily a psychologically ravaged human being. Before he knew Hester, his profession had provided him with a refuge. Afterward, the refuge becomes his prison.

Unable to identify his "self" with the passionate core he regards as sinful, he is even less able to admit that this sinful core can produce great sermons. He is obsessed with a feeling of falseness. His act with Hester almost immediately becomes loathsome to him. The part of him that is Puritan magistrate, and which he thinks of as his "self," condemns the sinful "other."

The guiltiness of his act, as it appears to him, is well expressed in the hideous figure of Chillingworth, who materializes out of thin air and, after establishing a superficial connection with Hester, moves on to his true mission of persecuting Dimmesdale. This monster becomes his constant companion and oppressor. If Pearl, to borrow a Freudian metaphor, may be seen as representing Hester's "id," so Chillingworth can be interpreted as Dimmesdale's "superego." That he is intended as a part of Dimmesdale's personality is made clear not only by the magical ways in which he appears on the scene and disappears from it, and his unrealistic fixation (for a cuckolded husband) on the guilty *man*, but also by the spatial disposition of the two together in a single dwelling, just as Hester and Pearl are housed together. Chillingworth is the watchful eye of the personality, linked with both intellect and conscience.

Fearing the punishment of society, and yet afraid of going unpunished, Dimmesdale has substituted an internal for a social punishment. The replacement of his kindly, benevolent mentor Reverend Wilson by this malevolent inner demon symbolizes the self-imposed punishment. Chillingworth's cruelty represents Hawthorne's idea that the internal judge, freed (exactly as Pearl at the other end of the spectrum is freed) from "reference and adaptation to the world into which it was born" (p. 91), is unmitigatedly merciless: "All that guilty sorrow, hidden from the world, whose great heart would have pitied and forgiven, to be revealed to him, the Pitiless, to him, the Unforgiving!" (p. 139).

By virtue of his age and relation to Hester, Chillingworth invites a classical Freudian explanation for Dimmesdale's feelings of guilt. In a larger, more mythic framework, to characterize Chillingworth as a sort of father is to establish his connection to the patriarchal structure of the Puritan society. Dimmesdale feels guilty because he has offended the "fathers," the male gods of his universe. But he did not offend them by stealing one of their women, for they are all men without women and do not appear to covet Hester for themselves. His offense is to have repudiated their rule by acknowledging her dominion. In the forest she is, like the great Squaw Sachem in "Main-street," an alternative to the patriarchy: "O Hester, thou art my better angel! I seem to have flung myself—sick, sin-stained, and sorrow-blackened—down upon these forest-leaves, and to have risen up all made anew, and with new powers to glorify Him that hath been merciful! This is already the better life! Why did we not find it sooner?" (pp. 201–2). Here Hester fulfills the image of "Divine Maternity" that she suggested at the scaffold (p. 56). Here is the pre-civilized nature goddess opposing western civilization, the impulsive heart defying the repressive letter of the law. Here, in brief, is a profoundly romantic mythology.

The protracted relationship with Chillingworth during the seven-year span of the romance represents Dimmesdale's strategy to keep from confessing. Nothing frightens him more than the idea of public exposure. He pacifies his inner thirst for punishment by self-castigation. Of course, he fails to confess partly because he cannot bear the thought of social ostracism. For a being who defines himself largely by the image he sees reflected back from the watching eyes around him, loss of social place implies loss of identity. It would be far more difficult for him than for Hester to survive a public disgrace. But confession would mean more than this. It would be a final capitulation to his sense of guilt. No matter how he persecutes himself, no matter what masochistic free rein he allows his overbearing conscience, he does not fully assent to his guilt until he admits it openly, because open admission has irreversible consequences.

Observe that public confession has in fact never been demanded of Hester. She has never had to say "I am guilty," because, for the Puritans, to have done the deed and to be guilty are synonymous, and Hester has obviously done the deed. Dimmesdale has no such escape. If he confesses, he must confess his guilt. Chillingworth as a substitute for social judgment actually forestalls that judgment and protects Dimmesdale from an ultimate condemnation. Once he confesses, he has no psychological alternative but to die. Quite literally, Chillingworth the physician has kept him alive all these years, even if only to torment him.

Dimmesdale's resistance is roundabout and neurotic, but it keeps him functioning and is appropriate to his deep internal divisions. The aftermath of the forest scene breaks his will to resist, convincing him that he is as evil as he had feared. Leaving the forest, Dimmesdale is possessed by a flood of impulses, which, although amusingly puerile to the reader, are horrifying to him. He wants to teach obscene words to a group of little boys, blaspheme before a devout old woman, and solicit the sexual favors of a maiden in his congregation. At long last freeing his passionate self, he finds freedom expressed in a series of silly, wicked wishes. Lacking Hester's long evolution of thought and independence, the "free" Dimmesdale is no more than a naughty boy. In his own eyes he is a monster. He ceases, therefore, to resist social judgment. He turns his new burst of life into the writing of his greatest sermon, still not recognizing the source of his power, still bewildered that "Heaven should see fit to transmit the grand and solemn music of its oracles through so foul an organ-pipe as he" (p. 225). He delivers the sermon to great approbation and, at the height of his triumph, confesses. By that confession, he executes himself.

The final scene on the scaffold seems to suggest that the public institutions of society and the private needs of the personality are irreconcilable. Dimmesdale, revealing his inner nature, has died. Hester, in order to express herself at last and to permit Pearl to develop freely, must leave the community. But her return to Boston and the consequent loosening of the community to accommodate her lighten the gloomy conclusion. A painfully slow process of social relaxation may, perhaps, be hoped for. The human heart may not need to be an outcast forever.

The Puritan community in *The Scarlet Letter* is a symbol of society in general. It is portrayed as a set of institutions unresponsive to personal needs and deliberately repressive of the private experience. Puritan institutions define the human being as all surface, all public. So far as the inner life is made public, it must be submitted to social definitions. Social institutions, however, may not be defined in the language of individual needs. The Puritan magistrates are not hypocrites. For them, the business of establishing and perpetuating a society demands the full energies of all the members of the community; there is no time for the indulgence of a private dimension of the personality. Self-expression is therefore a threat to the community.

Since the magistrates believe that self-expression is a threat, they make it a crime. Thereby, of course, they make it a threat as well. *The Scarlet Letter* asks whether this state of opposition between passion and authority is necessary; it expresses the hope that a society allowing greater individual expression might evolve, but it does not commit itself to a certain conclusion. It makes clear, however, that in a society such as the romance describes, the relationship of the artist who speaks for passion to the social institutions that suppress it can only be one of estrangement, duplicity, or subversion.

Dimmesdale's voice and Hester's letter enunciate and undermine the social creed. Disguised as a social document, the work of art secretly expresses the cry of the heart. Doing this, it covertly defies society in response to hidden but universal needs.

Two questions arise: what relation does the situation depicted in *The Scarlet Letter* bear to Hawthorne's idea of his own contemporary society? And what relation does the thematic design of the romance bear to his own function as an artist? /Clearly, *The Scarlet Letter* is quite different from all of Hawthorne's earlier work, which had argued that the individual finds rich fulfillment when integrated into society, that society expresses the personality. Now although Hawthorne does not suggest in *The Scarlet Letter* that there is any joy in isolation, he does show that the individual pays a very high price to be a member of the group. The earlier fictions and sketches exhibited the imagination at work in the service of society; *The Scarlet Letter* makes it clear that imagination serves the self. The earlier works tended to define serving the self as obsession, egotism, or eccentricity; *The Scarlet Letter* asserts that the self has needs and claims that must be satisfied. The earlier works restricted the exercise of imagination to the surface of events, while *The Scarlet Letter* ties imagination to the life beneath appearances. Evidently, Hawthorne jettisoned the whole load of commonsense assumptions about imagination and art and replaced them with a romantic vision.

If the vision of *The Scarlet Letter* is romantic, then Hawthorne must be presenting his own role and function in an entirely new way. One wonders whether Hawthorne actually underwent some sort of conversion or simply adopted another in a long series of authorial stances designed to find favor with an audience. Clearly, a romantic view was more up-to-date than the late eighteenth-century ideology his works had been expressing. And Hawthorne was too great a realist ever to publish a work that he thought might actually harm his reputation. One might conclude that in *The Scarlet Letter* he was accommodating himself to the taste of the times. The conception of art, imagination, and the artist implicit in this romantic formulation is nevertheless intellectually and aesthetically far richer and more vigorous than the formulation he had abandoned; consequently, it might have given him the support and justification for his professional commitment that he had not found before. Since it propelled him into the most productive decade of his career and thrust him immediately into the forefront of living American authors, this romantic vision certainly was usable.

"The Custom-House" invites us to view it as a deeply held belief as well. The essay tells the story of a conversion to the idea of literature as self-expression, in defiance of external and introjected social demands. It suggests that the psychological survival of the "I" depended upon that conversion. A product, Hawthorne says, of the same "autobiographical impulse" that motivated "The Old Manse," "The Custom-House" takes up his story where the earlier essay left it. Ignoring what we know to have been the economic imperatives that took him back to Salem, Hawthorne projects a psychological story in the conventions of romance. Appropriately, then, we may label "The Custom-House" an autobiographical romance.

Hawthorne interprets his return to Salem and his employment at the Custom House as the answer to psychological longings that his life at the Manse failed to satisfy and in part created. After three years of living in a transcendental cloudland, it was time to return to solid earth. He needed to participate in the ongoing work of the world, to prove himself a contributing member of society. He had to confront what might be called the persisting influence of Salem on his artistic life. By "Salem" is meant the combined environmental and personal pressures that made him think writing an idle and sinful craft.

Hawthorne personifies Salem in his Puritan ancestry, whose

imagined judgment on him as a writer survives all his attempts to overcome it: "What is he? . . . A writer of story-books! What kind of a business in life,—what mode of glorifying God, or being serviceable to mankind in his day and generation,—may that be? Why, the degenerate fellow might as well have been a fiddler!" (p. 10). Hawthorne's attempts to resist these imagined strictures by castigating his ancestors in turn for their bitter persecuting spirit and hard severity (p. 9) have no effect, because these Puritan ancestors, of course, represent a part of Hawthorne himself. "And yet, let them scorn me as they will, strong traits of their nature have intertwined themselves with mine" (p. 10). There is nothing to do but accede to the pressures they exert and return to Salem.

So far as these ancestors (or that part of Hawthorne they represent) are concerned, the sojourn in the Custom House has a twofold benefit. To work there is to satisfy their demand that he be serviceable. And the Custom House may provide Hawthorne with materials for a literature to mediate between the requirement of service and his self's need for imaginative expression. It is implicit in Hawthorne's treatment of life at the Custom House that a successful literature would likely be realistic, with imagination subordinated to external reality and dedicated to the service of the other. At the outset of "The Custom-House" Hawthorne leaves open the question of retiring from the surveyorship eventually to translate his experiences into literature or remaining in the position permanently. Ultimately, the decision is never made because he is dismissed from office.

Hawthorne makes no attempt to hide the fact that he did not choose to leave his position, but we are never meant to think that he enjoyed it. We know from the biographies that he stayed because he could not afford to go; in "The Custom-House," however, Hawthorne presents himself as remaining because he sincerely wants to do what the ancestors expect of him. Like Dimmesdale, he is trying to be socially acceptable.

But he is increasingly miserable, and the dismissal, he says, is fortunate. Far from plunging him into the midst of social life, the Custom House thoroughly isolates him. Everybody there appears to exist in a state of suspended animation. All are old men, of torpid imaginations and emotionally atrophied. The work itself is trivial, monotonous, and dispiriting.

The Custom House building, Uncle Sam's institution, quickly becomes a metaphorical prison. Working for society instead of himself, the Custom House officer loses his manhood:

> While he leans on the mighty arm of the Republic, his own proper strength departs from him. He loses, in an extent proportioned to the weakness or force of his original nature, the capability of self-support. . . . Uncle Sam's gold—meaning no disrespect to the worthy old gentleman—has, in this respect, a quality of enchantment like that of the Devil's wages. Whoever touches it should look well to himself, or he may find the bargain go hard against him, involving, if not his soul, yet many of its better attributes; its sturdy force, its courage and constancy, its truth, its self-reliance, and all that gives the emphasis to manly character.
>
> [Pp. 38–39]

The ejected officer, left "to totter along the difficult footpath of life as best he may," is one who "forever afterwards looks wistfully about him in quest of support external to himself" (p. 39), and sounds a good deal like Arthur Dimmesdale. The iron framework of the Puritan oligarchy has been replaced by a more benevolent but ultimately equally debilitating kind of paternalism.

Hawthorne represents his romance, *The Scarlet Letter*, as originating in the attempts of his imagination to make itself felt and keep itself alive in the deadly atmosphere of the Custom House. His withdrawal from the tedium of the first-floor routine into the cluttered chambers of the upper story signifies Hawthorne's withdrawal into his own mind, his escape into fantasy. But in these circumstances, fantasy is an escape to freedom rather than a retreat from life. It is an affirmative rather than a denying gesture. In one of his flights of fancy, Hawthorne comes upon a roll of parchment enclosed within "a certain affair of fine red cloth" wrought "with wonderful skill of needlework" and "intended, there could be no doubt, as an ornamental article of dress" (p. 31). Examination proves it to be a fabric representation of the letter *A*.

"My eyes fastened themselves upon the old scarlet letter, and would not be turned aside. Certainly, there was some deep meaning in it, most worthy of interpretation, and which, as it were, streamed forth from the mystic symbol, subtly communicating itself to my sensibilities, but evading the analysis of my mind" (p. 31). Impulsively, Hawthorne puts the letter to his breast and experiences "a sensation not altogether physical, yet almost so, as of burning heat; and as if the letter were not of red cloth, but red-hot iron" (p. 32). In this electric moment, which many critics have recognized as central to both "The Custom-House" and *The Scarlet Letter*, Hawthorne senses with a mixture of fear and excitement that he has found his subject. The letter—a verbal sign, a symbol, and the channel of inspiration—becomes the type of Art.

Because in *The Scarlet Letter* the *A* signifies a social crime, Hawthorne suggests that the writing of his romance is in some sense an analogously guilty act. My analysis of *The Scarlet Letter*, stressing the self-expressive and passionate nature of Hester's and Dimmesdale's act, indicates why there is an analogy. For Hawthorne, the romance originated as expression of his own feelings of social defiance and discontent, as a reaction to the stifling position of surveyor in the Custom House at Salem. The decision to write the romance, or to try to write it, involves a transference of Hawthorne's allegiance from his Puritan conscience to his imagination, personified in "The Custom-House" by Surveyor Pue. Adopting this figure as his "official ancestor," Hawthorne accepts the former surveyor's charge that he publicize Hester's story.

Now Hawthorne discovers that to generate a fantasy is not the same thing as to give it body. As he attempts in his free hours to compose his tale, he becomes aware in a frighteningly new way of the terrible effect the Custom House is having on his imaginative faculties. And he realizes how profoundly he values these faculties. "My imagination was a tarnished mirror. . . . The characters of the narrative would not be warmed and rendered malleable, by any heat that I could kindle at my intellectual forge. . . . 'What have you to do with us?' [they] seemed to say. 'The little power you might once have possessed over the tribe of unrealities is gone! You have bartered it for a pittance of the public gold. Go, then, and earn your wages!' " (pp. 34–35).

I had ceased to be a writer of tolerably poor tales and essays, and had become a tolerably good Surveyor of the Customs. That was all. But, nevertheless, it is any thing but agreeable to be haunted by a suspicion that one's intellect is dwindling away; or exhaling, without your consciousness, like ether out of a phial. . . . I began to grow melancholy and restless; continually prying into my mind, to discover which of its poor properties were gone, and what degree of detriment had already accrued to the remainder. I endeavoured to calculate how much longer I could stay in the Custom-House, and yet go forth a man. [Pp. 38–40]

Clearly, then, it is impossible for Hawthorne to continue to be a writer of romances while placating the inner Puritan. The unexpected fruits of the Custom House interlude are the authentication of just those theories he laid aside when he left Concord for Salem and the validation of a definition of happiness as living throughout the whole range of one's faculties and sensibilities (p. 40)—in brief, living the fullest inner life.

Yet Hawthorne, in accepting Hester as his subject, does not return to the transcendentalists so much as go beyond them. She represents everything the transcendentalists believe and more besides, for in her Emerson's "Spirit" is transformed into

Eros and thus allied to sex, passion, eroticism, flesh, and the earth. The Puritans seek to repress Spirit not only because of their dedication to permanence and form, but also because as shrewd men of hard experience they are aware of its sexual sources. Thus, the sin in *The Scarlet Letter* is sexual, and a sexual sin can symbolize Hawthorne's writing of romances. This is why Hawthorne epitomizes Puritan severity in a depiction of their persecution of women. In women they see the occasion of a dangerous passion. Their opposition to sex is not prudish but pragmatic. As he goes beyond transcendentalism in his rejection of the concept of an unearthly spiritualism, Hawthorne goes beyond most of his earlier work, but echoes some of the themes expressed in "The Birth-mark," "Drowne's Wooden Image," and, ironically, "The Artist of the Beautiful." In *The Scarlet Letter* he also presents an advocate of unearthly spiritualism, Dimmesdale.

Hawthorne's servitude in the Custom House generated, as a reactive defense, the fantasy of the scarlet letter; his dismissal led to its creation. In both idea and execution, the romance is related to maladjustment between Hawthorne and his society. Miserable as Hawthorne had been in the Custom House, to be forced out of it represented an evident failure: "The moment when a man's head drops off is seldom or never, I am inclined to think, precisely the most agreeable of his life. . . . In view of my previous weariness of office, and vague thoughts of resignation, my fortune somewhat resembled that of a person who should entertain an idea of committing suicide, and, altogether beyond his hopes, meet with the good hap to be murdered" (pp. 41–42). Observe the ambivalence of the images. Hawthorne's thoughts of resigning from the Custom House are like thoughts of suicide. Why should this be, if the Custom House is so unpleasant? Obviously Hawthorne is torn.

Like Hester, he becomes a rebel because he is thrown out

of society, by society: "Meanwhile, the press had taken up my affair, and kept me, for a week or two, careering through the public prints, in my decapitated state. . . . So much for my figurative self. The real human being, all this time, with his head safely on his shoulders, had brought himself to the comfortable conclusion, that everything was for the best; and, making an investment in ink, paper, and steel-pens, had opened his long-disused writing-desk, and was again a literary man" (pp. 42–43). Anxious for so long to "be of some importance in [my good townspeople's] eyes, and to win myself a pleasant memory in this abode and burial-place of so many of my forefathers" (p. 44), Hawthorne has finally accepted his destiny. The Custom House self, the man of affairs and the world, the public servant, becomes a figurative self, and Hawthorne accepts the conjunction of the real being with the literary man. The autobiographical episode has a happy ending, for in composing *The Scarlet Letter* he found himself "happier, while straying through the gloom of these sunless fantasies, than at any time since he had quitted the Old Manse" (p. 43). The direct attack of "The Custom-House" on some of the citizens of Salem adds a fillip of personal revenge to the theoretical rebellion that it dramatizes.

In the current state of biographical knowledge we cannot be sure to what degree the symbolic representation in "The Custom-House" corresponds to the facts. We do not know, for example, whether the germ of *The Scarlet Letter* actually occurred to Hawthorne in the Custom House or was conceived entirely in the months after his dismissal. Many readers have noted the foreshadowing appearance of a beautiful young woman with an embroidered *A* on her bosom in "Endicott and the Red Cross"; it is at least possible that the story had, in some form, been in his mind for years. We also do not know if Hawthorne really tried to write *The Scarlet Letter* before he was dismissed from the Custom House and, failing, actually became distracted and gloomy over the loss of his powers. But if, in fact, the story is not a symbolic representation of the truth, then it is all the more striking that Hawthorne should wish to represent *The Scarlet Letter* as a gesture of insubordination.

Even at his most defiant, Hawthorne could not entirely avoid the tone of self-deprecation. But in "The Custom-House" he almost appears to satirize his own formerly characteristic apologetic mode. "It was a folly," he writes, "with the materiality of this daily life pressing so intrusively upon me, to attempt to fling myself back into another age; or to insist on creating the semblance of a world out of airy matter, when, at every moment, the impalpable beauty of my soap-bubble was broken by the rude contact of some actual circumstance" (p. 37). These are metaphors apt for Owen Warland's butterfly, but not for *The Scarlet Letter*. And he goes on to theorize that it would have been "wiser . . . to diffuse thought and imagination through the opaque substance of to-day, and thus to make it a bright transparency." But "The Custom-House" has shown that it was not folly, but absolute necessity, to turn into his own mind for sustenance. And his humorous portraits of the inhabitants of the Custom House have done the job of diffusing thought and imagination through them. Despite the apparent humility of his conclusion to this paragraph—"A better book than I shall ever write was there"—Hawthorne was never less humble.

This lack of humility is clearly evident in his preface to the second edition of *The Scarlet Letter*, dated March 30, 1850, some two weeks after his romance had been published. The book had already sold well enough to assure Hawthorne that he had, at last, a solid success. He acknowledges the furor caused by "The Custom-House" with evident delight. He has learned the interesting lesson that to create a scandal is not necessarily to hurt sales. For years he had dependently courted public approbation; now he has been rewarded for independence:

> As the public disapprobation would weigh very heavily on him, were he conscious of deserving it, the author begs leave to say, that he has carefully read over the introductory pages, with a purpose to alter or expunge whatever might be found amiss, and to make the best reparation in his power for the atrocities of which he has been adjudged guilty. But it appears to him, that the only remarkable features of the sketch are its frank and genuine good-humor, and the general accuracy with which he has conveyed his sincere impressions of the characters therein described. . . . [The sketch] could not have been done in a better or more kindlier spirit, nor, so far as his abilities availed, with a livelier effect of truth. [Pp. 1–2]

And then, with relish, he pens his final sentence: "The author is constrained, therefore, to republish his introductory sketch without the change of a word."

❦ 5 ❧

The Major Phase II
1851

Hawthorne's new romanticism did not diminish his sensitivity to his readers' responses or give rise to the expectation that he had a right to success, whether or not he pleased his audience. He was concerned that *The Scarlet Letter* was too gloomy, and too single in effect, to suit most readers. He thought it should probably be published in the company of other works, so that, as in his earlier volumes, balance and variety might be attained. He wrote to James T. Fields, his publisher:

If the book is made up entirely of "The Scarlet Letter," it will be too sombre. I found it impossible to relieve the shadows of the story with so much light as I would gladly have thrown in. Keeping so close to its point as the tale does, and diversified no otherwise than by turning different sides of the same dark idea to the reader's eye, it will weary very many people and disgust some. Is it safe, then, to stake the fate of the book entirely on this one chance? . . . However, I am willing to leave these considerations to your judgment, and should not be sorry to have you decide for the separate publication.[1]

Fields did opt for separate publication, and we can thank him that the effect of *The Scarlet Letter* was not dissipated

1. Quoted in Stewart, *Nathaniel Hawthorne*, pp. 94–95, and partly in Charvat's introduction to the Centenary *Scarlet Letter*, p. xxi. The letter, dated January 20, 1850, exists only in transcript.

by balancing it against "The Snow-Image" and "Little Daffy-downdilly." Even after accepting his publisher's decision, Hawthorne remained anxious, writing to Bridge on February 4, 1850, for example: "Judging from its effect on [Sophia] and the publisher, I may calculate on what bowlers call a ten-strike. Yet I do not make any such calculation. . . . [It] lacks sunshine, etc. To tell you the truth . . . it is positively a hell-fired story, into which I found it almost impossible to throw any cheering light."[2] Even the success of *The Scarlet Letter* did not entirely put his mind at rest, for he subsequently determined to produce a more variegated and cheerful work in his next romance.

Ostensibly, Hawthorne's concern was wholly for his audience; but a letter of July 22, 1851, to Bridge suggests something different: "I think it a work more characteristic of my mind," he says of *The House of the Seven Gables*, "and more proper and natural for me to write, than 'The Scarlet Letter'; but for that very reason, less likely to interest the public."[3] Here Hawthorne is apparently less concerned with the audience than with fidelity to his own temperament. Yet in November 1850, while at work on *The House of the Seven Gables*, he had written to Fields: "It darkens damnably towards the close, but I shall try hard to pour some setting sunshine over it."[4] Here Hawthorne is guided not by what is natural to him, but by what he wishes were natural to him. A conflict emerges thus between the writer Hawthorne wants to be and the writer he has discovered himself to be.

Attempting in *The House of the Seven Gables* to blend the different types of writing he had set side by side in previous volumes, Hawthorne interspersed with the gothic mode of the

2. Bridge, *Personal Recollections of Nathaniel Hawthorne*, pp. 111–12.

3. Bridge, p. 126.

4. Quoted by Charvat in the introduction to *The House of the Seven Gables*, Centenary Edition, Vol. II (1965), p. xxii.

romance sketchlike and moralistic interludes and comic and sentimental touches. After he had done so he had second thoughts that anticipate what many modern readers feel about the book: "I should not wonder . . . if the romance of the book should be found somewhat at odds with the humble and familiar scenery in which I invest it."[5] The difficulty today seems to be more than a clash of effects. The comic surface appears untrue to the gloomy import of the romance, and looks like Hawthorne's effort to conceal his own meaning.

Yet in some ways the disjunction corresponds to the meaning. For the romance assumes that behind or beneath the actual world is an unseen world of motive and meaning, which actually controls the shape of the visible. When one limits oneself entirely to observation of the actual world, it appears comic, pathetic, charming, or sentimental, and the invisible world makes itself known only by an aura of the uncanny. But this same actual world breaks down into a series of discrete items, because it lacks the coherence of a meaningful action. The unseen world manifests itself in action, which erupts into the actual world like a gothic plot. In *The House of the Seven Gables* the visible world exists in the romance's present time and is controlled by the invisible world which is the past. As it becomes increasingly clear that the seen present is controlled by the unseen past, the mood of the book darkens. The sense of the present changes; its lack of freedom becomes clear. The feeling of confinement, exemplified in the imprisoning power of the house itself, eclipses the series of pleasantries that comprises the novelistic surface of *The House of the Seven Gables*.

The action of this romance pursues the theme Hawthorne had enunciated in *The Scarlet Letter*—that of the romantic conflict, at once social and private, between forces of passion, spontaneity, and creativity and counterforces of regulation

5. Bridge, p. 125.

and control. In *The House of the Seven Gables* these forces are embodied respectively in Maule and Pyncheon and are represented emblematically in Maule's fountain and Pyncheon's house. The fundamental action of the novel revolves around a struggle for possession of land first occupied by Maule and then appropriated by Pyncheon, and possession in various senses is the book's major metaphor. The antagonism between Pyncheon and Maule implies many social and ideological struggles—aristocrat versus democrat, conservative versus radical, institutionalist versus transcendentalist, for example—and these have been duly noted by critics. These readings all depend, however, upon the romance's psychological core, where the struggle occurs within the single self, with authority trying to suppress passion and passion to depose authority. The apparent stability of the situation as it exists in the novel's present time is clearly unhealthy, for Maule's fountain has turned brackish and Pyncheon's house become a prison, a dead shell expressing no one's nature and deforming the lives trapped within it.

Moreover, the stability is illusory. The Maules still retain and exercise strange forms of control over the Pyncheons, who, "haughtily as they bore themselves in the noonday streets of their native town, were no better than bond-servants to these plebeian Maules, on entering the topsyturvy commonwealth of sleep."[6] Though they may be repressed and distorted, the energies represented by Maule cannot die until the self dies, for they are original energies. Observe Hawthorne's myth of the beginnings of the conflict between Maule and Pyncheon. Maule was the first and the only rightful owner of the land at issue in their dispute. He brought it from a state of nature into the Edenic garden state with the labor of his own hands. Both settler and cultivator, he made the land express

6. *The House of the Seven Gables*, p. 26. Subsequent references given parenthetically in text.

his being, and entered into a useful relationship with it.[7] His symbol, appropriately, is the pure fountain, emblem of the sources and energies of life. In contrast, Pyncheon is a formalist, a man of writs, deeds, and documents, having no true relationship with the land he desires to own. He arrives on the scene after Maule, with the expansion of the village boundaries, and he claims the land not from nature but from the legislature. In every crisis, Pyncheon resorts to the law, which supports his claims.

Thus, Pyncheon represents the advent of civilization, and civilization replaces a creative and expressive relation to nature with one wholly materialistic. Land is now desired as a material possession rather than an expressive medium. Apparently, the whole apparatus of law exists to further and protect the aims of materialistic greed; it is created by men like Pyncheon and serves their interests. Pyncheon's criminal acquisition of Maule's land, by having him dispossessed and executed as a witch, is legal. Jaffrey Pyncheon has Clifford legally imprisoned for a term of years and, when it appears that Clifford will not reveal the location of the deed to the Maine lands, threatens to commit him legally to a mental asylum.

In brief, Hawthorne's myth of the origins of civilization founds it on a crime. The fact and nature of that crime irrevocably determine the character of the civilization. Maule and the qualities he represents are officially driven out of civilization and seem to disappear. The remaining civilized beings are oppressed, distorted, and incomplete. Moreover, the structure itself begins immediately to decay, because, by refusing to permit the open existence of energy and creativity, the civilization cuts its own lifelines. Because societies are composed of people and not things, the Pyncheon civilization,

7. One senses here the influence of Thoreau, whom Hawthorne had known well in Concord. Behind that is the influence of Locke.

based on a hard materialism and formalism that are destructive to people, must eventually destroy itself. As *The House of the Seven Gables* opens, that destruction is at hand.

The social and psychological strands of the romance are closely entwined, so that any event may be referred either to the individual psyche or to the structure of the civilization. And the story is different for those imprisoned within the structure—the house, commissioned by Pyncheon but built naturally enough by Maule since all creative and constructive powers belong to him—and those who are dispossessed outside it. Psychologically speaking, Maule has lost his identity and is in some existential sense outside himself, forced to hover on the periphery of his own personality—ghostlike, sinister, misunderstood: an underground man. The Pyncheons, on the other hand, are locked into rigid identities with no opportunity for innovation, spontaneity, or refreshment. Hepzibah, who occupies so much of the foreground of the romance, is the embodiment of social forms that have lost their capacity for change or growth. Change and growth are not possible without Maule; but for Maule nothing is possible unless he can take a rightful place above ground.

The story, then, poses two interrelated questions: can Maule make a place for himself in the social structure without destroying it? Alternatively, can he join society without destroying himself? Ultimately, this romance asks the same question that *The Scarlet Letter* asks: is civilization necessarily the tombstone of the spirit? These are transcendental queries, but *The House of the Seven Gables* does not offer transcendental answers. The foreground of the romance concerns itself with the victims within the social structure; this focus is designed to create reader approval of Maule, or Holgrave, who, in the present time of the narrative, has returned to claim what is rightfully his. His spectatorship, which Phoebe (and many critics, following her lead) mistakes for intellectual coldness, is in fact his pose. The returned exile waits for the right moment to make himself known. The right moment occurs after Pyncheon's death, and not only as a matter of strategy: Holgrave cannot really resume his identity as Maule until the obstacle to his selfhood has been removed.

It is a commonplace of interpretation that Hawthorne disapproves of radical reformers, and for this reason Holgrave's is generally read as a critical portrait. But in reading it thus, the critics must ignore Hawthorne's unambiguous praise for his young protagonist and the implicit approval of his radical ideas. Holgrave's radicalism is defined as a sense of human possibility, "which a young man had better never been born, than not to have, and a mature man had better die at once, than utterly to relinquish" (p. 179). Perhaps he is naive, but his errors are noble. To Hawthorne's generally weak male protagonists Holgrave is an exception, in his courage, high principles, ideals, kindheartedness, self-reliance, and sensitivity. He has "never violated the inmost man," has "carried his conscience along with him," combines inward strength with enthusiasm and warmth. He conveys a total "appearance of admirable powers" (pp. 177, 180, 181).

At his entrance into the novel he is made to contrast with Hepzibah, who, as I have said, is the symbol of Pyncheon strength become withered and impotent: "Coming freshly, as he did, out of the morning light, he appeared to have brought some of its cheery influences into the shop along with him" (p. 43). He continues throughout the romance to diffuse vigor and joy into the pervasive atmosphere of gloom and fatigue. Tending and planting the Pyncheon garden, he recalls the original Maule, and he is associated with metaphors of fertility and sexuality, especially in the remarkable image of the bean poles vivid with scarlet blossoms and attracting to them multitudes of vibrating hummingbirds (p. 148). In other, less sensuously charged scenes he diverts and enspirits the melancholy inhabitants of the house; on occasion he is so stimulating that even Clifford's somnolent soul awakens and gives off winged thoughts (p. 157).

Holgrave does lack one quality that many critics, applying to *The House of the Seven Gables* an inappropriate scheme derived from Hawthorne's earlier fictions, have identified as his ruling characteristic: intellectuality. True, "he considered himself a thinker, and was certainly of a thoughtful turn," but he "had perhaps hardly yet reached the point where an educated man begins to think" (p. 180). The narrator does not consider this a serious shortcoming, in view of Holgrave's youth, but he does have one doubt about this otherwise admirable character. He wonders whether Holgrave will fulfill his promise or, "like certain chintzes, calicoes, and ginghams," will "assume a very sober aspect after washing-day" (p. 181). It is possible that his powers will not survive their first serious testing.

Because Holgrave represents creative energy he is also a type of the artist. Through him Hawthorne returns to some of the questions suggested in *The Scarlet Letter* and "The Custom-House" about the nature of art and the problems of the artist in a repressive society. Holgrave is a kind of archetypal artist, for he has mastered a variety of media and is unattached to his productions. Hawthorne often refers to him as "the artist." He is presented as a contrast, in his artistry, to previous Maules, in whom artistic energies were perverted; he is also contrasted with Clifford, who appears to be an artist (and unfortunately is too often taken for one in the criticism on this romance) but is in reality a travesty of one, a castrated artist such as society will allow to exist.

Hawthorne illustrates Holgrave's superiority to earlier Maules—and incidentally explains a good deal about the equation between art and wizardry (the black art)—in the scene where Holgrave reads his narrative about Alice Pyncheon to Phoebe. As he reads, the present-day characters assume the identities of those in the fiction. Holgrave becomes the wizard

Maule, and Phoebe becomes Alice. Phoebe shows the same susceptibility to Holgrave that Alice felt for Maule and gives Holgrave the opportunity to repeat Maule's abuse of them. In Holgrave's narrative, Alice Pyncheon feels and unconsciously manifests a physical attraction to Maule, which he inflames into a violent physical passion. Alice, as in all cases of demonic possession, is in fact controlled by internal, invisible forces—invisible because denied. She refuses to recognize her sexual nature, and Maule takes advantage of that refusal. "This fair girl deemed herself conscious of a power—combined of beauty, high, unsullied purity, and the preservative force of woman-hood—that could make her sphere impenetrable, unless be-trayed by treachery within" (p. 203). Her inability to con-ceive of internal treachery delivers her to Maule.

Like all Pyncheons, she rejects, suppresses, or denies the passions that underlie human nature, with sex primary among them. Her later torments, too, result from the continued frustration of this inadmissible and yet obvious passion, for "so lost from self-control, she would have deemed it sin to marry" (p. 209); and she is killed, aptly enough, by the irrevocable loss of her passion's object when Maule marries, and by Maule's astounding sadism in forcing her to attend the bride on his wedding night.

Alice is partly victimized by her self and partly by her father. His greed for possessions (like all the Pyncheons after the first, he is forever trying to find the lost deed to the Maine lands) and the Pyncheon habit of regarding people as things have induced him to permit Maule to use Alice in an experi-ment that promises knowledge of the deed's whereabouts. The Maule guilt in her degradation is nevertheless obvious and terrible. His behavior is of the meanest, at once arousing and denying Alice. This nastiness figures his own degradation into a destructive Eros, which expresses itself in malicious acts, subversive thrusts that produce no release. Denied free and open expression, the fountain becomes a source of self-pollution.

Holgrave's reading re-creates Alice's erotic response in Phoebe; so Hawthorne demonstrates the sexual power of art and its near relation to witchcraft. Art and sex are both expressions of the creative energy which, ideally, they should celebrate. The common origin of art and sex in the Eros of the personality makes possible a kind of interchange of artistic and sexual metaphors, as we have already seen in *The Scarlet Letter* and "The Custom-House." Great works of art in Hawthorne's fictions are often unabashedly sensuous representations of beautiful women—one can think back to the figurehead in "Drowne's Wooden Image" and ahead to the Cleopatra of *The Marble Faun*. And as Hawthorne preaches so he practices—witness Hester, Zenobia, and Miriam.

But in a repressive society, art and sex are both inhibited and go underground. Denied legitimate expression, they erupt not only in actions that are deemed criminal by the society, but in acts that are deliberately perverse. In *The Scarlet Letter* the governor's mansion itself is the abode of Mistress Hibbens; witchcraft is a debased, perverse creativity, and it is debased because—as we recall from Hester's dialogue with Mistress Hibbens—the witch and wizard have accepted the idea that they are evil. Wizardry destroys rather than creates, controls rather than liberates, degrades instead of celebrating the life force. The self-mocking and yet deadly serious wizard, seeking to "possess" through misuse of the powers of art, is a parodist of the tyrant. He betrays his own nature by aping repressive forms. He destroys art by using it to oppress. And ultimately he reinforces the social power he defies because he offers only another version of it.

The optimist Holgrave, while recognizing that he operates in a repressive society, refuses to twist his art. He believes that the world is striding toward a Utopia where Eros will be free to express itself. He imagines art in the interim to have a certain liberating and constructive effect through its power to expose the truth. His daguerreotypes, taken with the help of the sunlight that is his friend and ally, show Pyncheon's true nature, illuminating his villainy and identifying him with his persecuting ancestor. His tale of Alice Pyncheon, developed with the help of the moonlight, which for Hawthorne always accompanies romance, exposes the depravity of the Maules and shows Holgrave's awareness of his own situation. His refusal to take advantage of the opportunity given him by Phoebe's response demonstrates his moral worth. He withstands temptation, and not only Phoebe but art as well is saved by his forbearance. "Let us, therefore—whatever his defects of nature and education, and in spite of his scorn for creeds and institutions—concede to the Daguerreotypist the rare and high quality of reverence for another's individuality. Let us allow him integrity, also, forever after to be confided in; since he forbade himself to twine that one link more, which might have rendered his spell over Phoebe indissoluble" (p. 212).

The cleansed vitality that Holgrave brings to the old conflict seems attributable to his mobility. He has severed ties with the house, abandoned the place, and refused to commit himself to any fixed form of life. He has made the particularly American response to the past—left it behind, even to the extent of creating a new identity by taking on a new name. He has escaped history by avoiding the forms through which it is preserved and transmitted. Distance has given him objectivity toward his origins. But can he maintain this vitality and objectivity if he comes back? He must now discover if freedom is possible on any terms other than perpetual rootlessness and flight. He hopes to reattach himself to his sources without forfeiting any of his spiritual independence and flexibility, to be, like the fountain, at once fixed and fluid.

Therefore he must return to Salem and confront the figure who has forced the Maules into their long exile. He is serene at the prospect of his ordeal, because he trusts himself. He does not doubt that he will triumph in this confrontation; he has no inkling of internal weakness, of "treachery within." Establishing himself in an attic gable, tending the garden—taking possession, so to speak, of the house's peripheries—he calmly bides his time, waiting, we must assume, for Maule's curse to claim its last victim. Pyncheon is naturally unaware of the other's presence and has no sense of impending doom. His attention is focused on the returned Clifford, and the possibility of wresting from him, at last, the secret of the deed to the Maine lands.

For his more practical-minded readers, Hawthorne supplies (as is customary in a gothic plot) a natural explanation for Pyncheon's death: a hereditary disposition to apoplexy. But the truth of the matter in the invisible world is that the Pyncheons are killed by Maule's curse. Through the curse, the power of the suppressed Eros is communicated to the oppressor. In any of three readings of the story—that every generation of Pyncheons and Maules repeats the story; that there is really only one Pyncheon and one Maule; or that both Pyncheon and Maule are parts of a single personality—Holgrave, as Maule, must assume some responsibility for Jaffrey Pyncheon's death. Holgrave's serenity implies that he is prepared to face that death and accept that responsibility.

Holgrave is especially interested in Clifford, in whom Hawthorne depicts the alternative—for an artistic personality—to exile. Many critics have understood Clifford as one of Hawthorne's most complete, and critical, analyses of the artist. But such an approach misses Hawthorne's point, which is that Clifford is not an artist because he has not been permitted to become one.[8] In Clifford he shows the degradation of the

8. There are many specialized studies of Hawthorne's artist figures, and one book-length treatment of the subject: Millicent Bell, *Hawthorne's View of the Artist* (Albany: State University of New York, 1962). Although one finds many interesting observations in this ma-

artistic impulse when it is not permitted creative expression but is forced into a lifelong attitude of passive receptivity. Although physically and chronologically an old man, Clifford has the psyche of an infant. His cousin's tyranny has kept him passive, dependent, absorbed in immediate sensual (but non-sexual) gratifications, uncontrollably moody, permanently impotent, a mental somnambulist. Exile has enabled the Maules to attain some sort of warped manhood, but Clifford has been kept a child. Not allowed to grow, he atrophies.

From Clifford's first appearance we see that he has no inner resources and, apparently, no expressive needs. He achieves satisfaction through a sort of absorption of the world into himself, for which eating is the best metaphor: Hawthorne dwells much on his voracious and indelicate appetite. Such appetites imply an incompleteness which is precisely the opposite of the artist's creative urge to overflow. Clifford loves beauty, but in the manner of Owen Warland he fears energy. He approaches beauty as a materialist, wishing to possess and seeing no further than the surface. The spiritual beauty of his sister goes unseen by him, because she is outwardly an ugly, aging woman. Here, much more clearly than in "The Artist of the Beautiful," and in contradistinction to the theme of "The Snow-Image," Hawthorne rejects the equation of artistry with childishness. There is no art until childhood has been left behind.

At some point in its development, the child moves from a fascination with and dependence on forms to the desire to create them; after this, forms become dependent on him. If this point is not reached, the artist remains unborn. Art is thus associated with the adult personality, as a progressive force

---

terial, as a whole it is distorted by its emphasis on Hawthorne's Christian presuppositions—an emphasis with which the present study obviously takes issue—and even more by its inclusion among artists many characters who are not artists but merely resemble artists in one or another aspect of their personalities.

that confronts reality rather than a regressive activity that tries to evade it. The child, as Clifford demonstrates, presents no threat to the social structure; he is easily pacified, diverted, and controlled. The artist, on the other hand, driven from within, cannot be easily placated. He threatens the stability and permanence of institutions by his continual indifference to them in the creation of his own forms. Even if he were not a deliberate rebel, the artist would quickly become one inadvertently—witness Hester.

Though he lacks the force to make art, and is terrified of raw energy, Clifford is also greatly attracted to it. Perhaps this attraction is the seed from which artistry normally matures. As soon as he escapes from the house of the seven gables Clifford runs to the railroad that has always frightened him, recognizing on this occasion, as he does sporadically, that his salvation can come only by embracing what he fears. His sympathy with the force behind the form led him, in the past, to the secret hiding place of the deed to the Maine lands (hidden by Maule when he built the house for Colonel Pyncheon). Of course, he has also forgotten his knowledge, for his insights are weak and intermittent—it is not for *him* to tumble Colonel Pyncheon's portrait from the wall. But sign of such sympathy is the signal for Jaffrey Pyncheon's oppression. Jaffrey's death means Clifford's liberation, and his essentially lightweight nature, relieved of the pressures that have constricted it for so long, achieves some fraction of the pleasing development originally possible to it. But his crushed soul can never expand into true art.

In theory the death of Jaffrey Pyncheon should liberate all the characters in the romance from their long oppression. And so it does, except in one case. For Holgrave that death is the beginning of oppression. Between the evening that he enters the parlor, prepared to face the judge, and the morning of Phoebe's return, Holgrave changes strikingly. His social radicalism disappears; he is ready to give up art and adopt the life of a country landowner. Instead of finding himself in the dark parlor, he loses himself, reclaiming the name of Maule but taking on the form of Pyncheon. We see this change at once in his new behavior toward Phoebe.

The love that he declares for her is a barely disguised plea for solace and protection: "Could you but know, Phoebe, how it was with me, the hour before you came! A dark, cold, miserable hour. . . . I never hoped to feel young again! . . . But, Phoebe, you crossed the threshold; and hope, warmth, and joy, came in with you! The black moment became at once a blissful one. It must not pass without the spoken word. I love you!" (p. 306). His betrothal to Phoebe, entered into in such a frame of mind, is the appropriate means by which he becomes the owner of the Pyncheon estate, for it expresses a wish to be limited by, and supported within, social responsibilities.

Phoebe, with all her appealing freshness and softness, is a law-abiding and limit-loving Pyncheon. She is a great comfort to Hepzibah and Clifford, but in the manner of one making prison life more tolerable rather than as an agent of release. Indeed, confined to the house, she too has been fading and drooping. At the same time she feels, like Clifford, attracted to what she fears. She loves Holgrave. Even as she tells him she is afraid to marry him, she shrinks toward him, asking him without words to help her move beyond her own limits (p. 306). But Holgrave is no longer a liberator. This relationship does not signal the beginning of a new era between men and women; the two exchange their vows in the presence of a corpse. They drive off later to Pyncheon's country estate loaded with goods and dependents. Clifford, Hepzibah, Uncle Venner, and all the neighbors rejoice, but Holgrave has become a brooding, melancholy man. Would it have been a better symbol of his victory if he had built his own house or, remaining in the house of the seven gables, had made it truly his own? He abandons, however, the precious ground for which he has struggled—the ground of his own self—and goes to live in the Judge's country mansion, astonishing everyone by his lament that the wooden structure is not built of more durable material. Moving into this house, Holgrave identifies himself with all those parts of the personality he had previously been trying to overcome.

Many critics argue that Holgrave's conversion from radical to conservative opinions has been effected by love. His relationship with Phoebe ties him for the first time to the human world and gives him a new appreciation of how much is worth preserving. But behind this argument is a critical conviction that Holgrave's conversion is a good thing, and this conviction can be maintained only by ignoring the character of Pyncheon as Hawthorne created it. Moreover, the plot shows Holgrave's love as subsequent to, and indeed caused by, his change to conservatism. Love is not the agent, but the expression, of a change. The critical argument also assumes that Holgrave finds a new happiness in his love and his set of complex, stable relations to the social order; Holgrave himself appears to concur when he says that he will no longer be radical because "the world owes all its onward impulse to men ill at ease. The happy man inevitably confines himself within ancient limits" (pp. 306–7). But Holgrave's words are belied by the facts. He was happy before the Judge's death; he is not happy afterward. In the opening sequence of the romance he brought the sunlight indoors with him; now he has been permanently darkened by the shadows of the house. He turns to Phoebe for comfort, as we have seen. Later, with a "half-melancholy laugh," he will pass judgment on himself for this conversion, which he calls "especially unpardonable in this dwelling of so much hereditary misfortune, and under the eye of yonder portrait of a model-conservative, who, in that very character, rendered himself so long the Evil Destiny of his race" (p. 315). The point could not be more clearly stated. But the dynamics of Holgrave's conversion remain mysterious. Instead of following Holgrave's mental processes during the night he spends with the corpse, Hawthorne writes one of his nightmare-procession sequences, having troops of phantoms pass by the dead man in his chair. Are these fantasies meant to be those of the distraught Holgrave, in the manner of "The Haunted Mind"? One is left to guess at the connection between these images and the state of mind of the protagonist. Readers thinking ahead to the preoccupations of *The Blithedale Romance* and *The Marble Faun* might explain Holgrave's change as the result of guilt feelings incurred by the Judge's death. The first Maule, who antedated society, was the only Maule who did not have to commit a crime in order to gain his own independence. All subsequent Maules have found an authority figure blocking the path to selfhood. If, in even the slightest degree, they accept the validity of that figure, they must necessarily feel guilt for the act that deposes it. Feeling guilty, they lose the sense of their own rightness; implicated in the guilt-ridden structures of society, they acquiesce in them. Feelings of guilt are assuaged by accepting the values of the system one has overthrown; energies that were to have been expended in self-expression are diverted to atonement. The system survives the overthrow of any particular person who symbolizes authority within it; the revolutionary becomes an oppressor in his turn.

As Holgrave attempts to reattach himself to the past, he finds that he can do so only by accepting the past's whole burden. Having committed the fatal deed, he cannot return to his earlier free state. His new vision sees the whole world under the shadow of the guilt he feels: "The presence of yonder dead man threw a great black shadow over everything; he made the universe, so far as my perception could reach, a scene of guilt, and of retribution more dreadful than the guilt" (p. 306). Is it not death itself that has changed Holgrave? Knowing the present only, and impelled by transcendental idealism, Holgrave imagined himself to exist through an infinity of present moments. In effect, he thought himself immortal. In his impassioned speeches he used death as a trope, as though he did not feel its reality: "The case is just as if a young giant were compelled to waste all his strength in carrying about the corpse of the old giant, his grandfather, who died a long while ago, and only needs to be decently buried. Just think, a moment; and it will startle you to see what slaves we are to by-gone times—to Death, if we give the matter the right word!" (pp. 182–83). But of course we are slaves to death; only the very young could be startled by that perception.

Implicit in Holgrave's language is the certainty that once we remember the past is dead, we will throw off our bondage to it with an incredulous laugh at our own stupidity. But precisely because the past has given the present its shape, it continues to exist; just as death, by giving life its shape, is in this sense also a part of life. The real existence of death parallels the real existence of the past. Dying, Judge Pyncheon becomes Death itself, the ultimate, unconquerable, tyrannizing force.

But if Pyncheon is ineluctable, he is no less hateful. Holgrave can hardly be said to embrace his destiny; he accepts it with weary melancholy. At the end of the romance he is a sad man. In him Hawthorne depicts the life of the individual as a journey away from the illusion of freedom. As the self awakens to its personal history, it becomes implicated in that history. Still, if the story is sad from the private point of view, it is perhaps less so for society. Though Maule has turned conservative, he will not be an evil tyrant like Jaffrey Pyncheon. Certainly Hepzibah, Clifford, and Phoebe are all better off living in his house than in Judge Pyncheon's. Perhaps we see here a qualified meliorism like that represented in the conclu-

sion to *The Scarlet Letter*, the hope not of a sudden overthrow
of powerful repressive institutions, but of their gradual relaxation—a relaxation evidently brought about by much human
suffering and sacrifice.

The plot of *The House of the Seven Gables*, opposing
passion to authority, is certainly meant to embody a universal
drama in particular terms; yet since it is set in the American
present and linked to the American past, some social commentary must be intended as well. Jaffrey Pyncheon is a
modern representative of the Puritan character, which is now
simplified—in comparison to Hawthorne's earlier treatments
of the Puritans—into a dominant materialism. This type is
centered on ownership, on things, and does not believe in the
existence of Spirit. This is the type that naturally builds for
permanence and that, if it does not create new forms, makes
sure that the old ones last. By definition, this is the type that
builds a civilization, and thus the American nation has been
built not by lovers of freedom but by lovers of form. Hawthorne's own criticism of this materialism receives strong expression in the preface (whose import is generally ignored by
his critics, *because* it is so radical), where he says that "he
would feel it a singular gratification, if this Romance might
effectually convince mankind (or indeed, any one man) of
the folly of tumbling down an avalanche of ill-gotten gold, or
real estate, on the heads of an unfortunate posterity, thereby
to maim and crush them, until the accumulated mass shall be
scattered abroad in its original atoms" (p. 2). If this is the
author's view, then he cannot but see the story of his hero as a
defeat.

Of course, Hawthorne is much too skeptical to imagine that
reading *The House of the Seven Gables* will reform anybody,
but he does make his reformist sympathies clear. But, oddly
enough—and to the surely inadvertent end of generating dozens of critical articles about his intentions—he is at pains in the

conclusion to present that story, by means of its floridly happy ending, as a triumph. As I have suggested, there is no way to interpret the conclusion as triumphant within the logic of the story. Holgrave did not get what he wanted, and what he got was much inferior to what he desired. Why, then, does Hawthorne manipulate the rhetoric of the last chapter to give the impression of a happy ending? One's first thought might be that he intended to conceal his radicalism. But, then, the preface would not have expressed his radicalism so strongly. And too, his radical hopes are so confined by his sense of the unlikeliness of their being realized that they hardly require concealment.

In all probability the explanation for the strategy of the finale involves a kind of concealment different from the hiding of radical political views. Political and social radicalism was probably more acceptable in the 1840s and 1850s than at any other time in American history, before and after. It was not his radical opinions that he wished to hide, but his apparent temperamental pessimism. It is one thing to see society as full of evils, but quite another to see absolutely no hope of their ever being corrected. Those who were conservative and those who were radical in these decades publicly shared the one quality of optimism. Hawthorne did not like his inability to participate in the hopeful temperament. He wanted to be a writer of happy books. He had struggled, unsuccessfully, to lighten the gloom of The Scarlet Letter. He felt sure that his readers would not like so dark a tale. When they liked it, he persisted in his discomfort, asserting that so unrelieved a dark story was not healthy or natural. As The House of the Seven Gables began to darken toward the close, he became uneasy. Writing closer to himself as he now was doing, he was uncomfortable with the sort of writer he was finding himself to be. But why? More than reader response was involved, evidently, since The Scarlet Letter had succeeded. Apparently, some inner censor, rather than a wish to please his audience, directed him to be a writer of happy stories, and judged him lacking when he failed to do so.

Not succeeding in the intention to make *The House of the Seven Gables* a pleasant and variegated book—at least, not as fully as he had hoped—he next undertook a project in which success along these lines would be virtually certain: a collection of stories for children. While Hawthorne was writing *The House of the Seven Gables*, his publishers (Ticknor, Reed, and Fields) were busy consolidating and expanding the reputation he had achieved with *The Scarlet Letter*. Late in 1850 they reissued all four of his children's books in a volume called *True Stories from History and Biography*. Early in 1851 they reissued *Twice-told Tales* with a new preface wherein the established author bid an amused farewell to one of his earlier personae. Fields now suggested to Hawthorne that another, new collection of short works be published, and that he write another book for children. Thus, three facets of Hawthorne's ability would be brought before the public simultaneously: the romancer, the writer of tales and sketches, and the children's author. Hawthorne responded on April 7, 1851, that he had thought of both things himself.[9]

He began work on the children's book in June 1851, barely two months after *The House of the Seven Gables* was published. He finished it within six weeks. He used an idea that had long been with him, which had developed from an aborted plan of 1838 to collaborate with Longfellow on a book of fairy tales for children. In 1843 he wrote to Sophia that he hoped to write "one or two mythological story books" to be published by John L. O'Sullivan, editor of the *Democratic Review*, and in 1846 he proposed such a project in more detail to Evert Duyckinck, whose firm was publishing *Mosses from an Old Manse*.[10] Since it had been in his mind for so

9. Centenary, VI, p. 303.
10. Centenary, VI, pp. 297–304, passim.

long, realization came easily, but as he outlined his project to
Fields on May 23, 1851, he had complicated his 1846 scheme
by including the tales in the framework of "a young college-
student telling these stories to his cousins and brothers and
sisters, during his vacations, sometimes at the fireside, sometimes in the woods and dells."[11] Out of the past, the structure
of *The Story Teller* combined with that of *The Whole History* to enable Hawthorne to write *A Wonder Book for Girls
and Boys*, his most complex and successful framed narrative.

The scene opens in autumn at Tanglewood Manor, in the
Berkshires (Hawthorne had been living at Lenox, in the
Berkshires, since leaving Salem in May 1850), where "not less
than nine or ten . . . nor more than a dozen" children "of all
sorts, sizes, and ages . . . brothers, sisters, and cousins, and a
few of their young acquaintances" are going on a nutting
party.[12] Their chaperon and leader is Eustace Bright, eighteen
years old and a student at nearby Williams College. During a
break in the expedition he amuses the children by fashioning
an extemporaneous version of one of the Greek myths with
which, presumably, his college education is making him familiar. (In reality, Hawthorne used Anthon's *Classical Dictionary* as his sole source.)[13] Each of the six myths narrated
involves a similar interchange between Eustace and his audience, and each is connected with a season and an occasion of
frolic at Tanglewood. A full year elapses during the course of
the work, and Hawthorne sets scenes inside and outdoors, on
the hillside, in the playroom, and by the fireside.

Besides connecting the myths one to another, this frame

11. Centenary, VI, p. 304.
12. *A Wonder Book for Girls and Boys*, Centenary Edition, Vol.
VII (1972), p. 6. Subsequent references given parenthetically in text.
13. See Calvin Earl Schorer, "The Juvenile Literature of Nathaniel
Hawthorne" (Diss., University of Chicago, 1948), and Hugo Mc-
Pherson, *Hawthorne as Myth-Maker* (Toronto: University of Toronto
Press, 1969).

involves a good deal of landscape description, for which Hawthorne drew from his notebooks, thereby realizing one unfulfilled intention of *The Story Teller*. The frame also captures the comfortable and leisurely ways of a pleasant affluent style of life. The myths, indeed, derive their value precisely from what they can contribute to this way of life, and thus are truly functions of the occasions that call forth their narration. They are clearly a product, too, of the youthful, energetic optimism of Eustace, and Hawthorne writes in a style that suggests spoken discourse. Lastly, the myths are directed toward the group of children, who, though they do not interject questions and commentary as do those in *The Whole History*, make their presence very much felt. They are depicted as lively, joyous, and playful beings, with names like Blue Eye, Primrose, Sweet Fern, Dandelion, Clover, and Squash-Blossom to stress the innocent, blossomy qualities of childhood.

It had been Hawthorne's intention as far back as 1846 to present the myths in a gothic manner, and this plan is reiterated in the letter of May 23, 1851, to Fields, in which he speaks of "substituting a tone in some degree Gothic or romantic . . . instead of the classic coldness which is as repellent as the touch of marble."[14] He carries out this intention in *A Wonder Book*. Within the context of quotidian leisure, sentimentalized childhood frolic, and extensive word paintings of the Berkshires, the myths add a note of the supernatural and fantastic, imparting a slight shiver, a hint of moonlight, a touch of magic to the sunny round of homely pleasures. All this is achieved without a trace of the macabre and terrifying, which are hallmarks of the true gothic. Indeed, the myths are gothicized but also tamed. Divested of their emotional ferocity and their archaic moral and religious significances and refer-

14. Centenary, VI, p. 304.

ences, they are refashioned into products to while away the leisure hours of advantaged children.

Homeric Greeks would have been astonished at the virtues these tales are made to demonstrate. Three of them—the stories of Hercules, Bellerophon, and Perseus—become simple adventure stories. Their heroes display appropriate manly virtues, courage, modesty, ambition, and a gentlemanly competitive spirit. The other three tales—of Pandora, King Midas, and Baucis and Philemon—are developed as domestic stories centering on simplified family relationships: the childish squabblings of Pandora and Epimetheus (both children in Hawthorne's version, whose troubles begin when they cannot play together nicely), the love between King Midas and his little daughter Marygold (Hawthorne's invention), and the sedate, grandparently, mutual devotion of Baucis and Philemon. It is not difficult to see that the adventure stories are directed toward boys, the domestic stories toward girls, and that in both types Hawthorne is inculcating appropriate feminine and masculine virtues for the places assigned to the sexes in society.

However, one should not overstress the didacticism of Hawthorne's intention, for in general the children are not distinguished by sex but grouped together as possessors of a certain kind of imaginative sensibility. Appealing to this imagination, Hawthorne's chief strategy is to embroider the myths with masses of fanciful, piquant, concrete visual detail. Eustace mainly describes. He describes Mercury's staff, Perseus's shield, Pandora's box, Midas's golden roses, until *A Wonder Book* becomes, as its title promises, a treasury of marvelous objects. In a sense Hawthorne does not so much narrate as decorate these stories. The gothic is modulating into something resembling the works of the pre-Raphaelites (although Hawthorne probably did not yet know them).[15]

15. It is possible that he was reading some Ruskin at this time, but he certainly did not know any pre-Raphaelite painting.

In addition to the audience, the narrator, the tales, and the setting, *A Wonder Book* contains another element that had appeared in *The Story Teller*—a mild version (as Eustace is a mild version of Oberon) of Parson Thumpcushion. Mr. Pringle, the master of Tanglewood Estate, adheres to Enlightenment values and disapproves of Eustace's versions of the myths. But the conflict between Parson Thumpcushion and his ward was moral, while Eustace and his host clash entirely on aesthetic grounds. The artist has a place in this comfortable, satisfied, tolerant, commonsense world of the American gentry that he did not have in the sterner New England of some twenty years earlier. Half patronized and half patron, he is a member of the family. He can talk back to authority.

After listening to Eustace tell the story of the three golden apples, Mr. Pringle advises the youth "never more to meddle with a classical myth. Your imagination is altogether Gothic, and will inevitably gothicize everything that you touch. The effect is like bedaubing a marble statue with paint. This giant [Atlas], now! How can you have ventured to thrust his huge, disproportioned mass among the seemly outlines of Grecian fable, the tendency of which is to reduce even the extravagant within limits, by its pervading elegance?" (p. 112). These are traditional Enlightenment ideas about the virtue of such qualities as balance, order, harmony, abstraction, and rationality; and here is the Enlightenment conviction that the Greeks possessed such qualities. Eustace distorts their classicism, creating a different effect by concentrating on details at the expense of proportion. He picks his details for picturesque and striking qualities rather than for intellectual or moral seemliness or for their ability to harmonize with each other.

Curiously, Eustace does not deny the correctness of Mr. Pringle's analysis of the Greek mind, though as one who has worked with the original texts he might have been expected to. He does not appear to know, any more than does Mr. Pringle, that the Greeks did indeed bedaub their statues with paint. And he acquiesces in Mr. Pringle's characterization of his own imagination. Eustace defends himself by maintaining that the fables "are the common property of the world, and of all time," and that he is not bound to reproduce them in the terms of another age. He argues that "the Greeks, by taking possession of these legends . . . and putting them into shapes of indestructible beauty, indeed, but cold and heartless, have done all subsequent ages an incalculable injury" (pp. 112–13). The older man argues for fidelity to the original not because he is a scholar but because he prefers those values he thinks of as classical. Eustace, asserting his right to handle the myths as he chooses, is making a transcendental statement about the separability of the idea from the historical forms in which it manifests itself, and is characterizing the dominance of the classical mode as a sort of aesthetic tyranny. Here, on an aesthetic field, the young radical encounters the old conservative and defends youth against age, expression against restraint, emotion against reason, the present against the past.

Defending the gothic, Eustace appears to be defending the taste of the age. But Hawthorne is somewhat devious here, for in 1851 gothicism was hardly the aesthetic of the moment. There is, in fact, a curious disparity between Eustace's theory and his practice. For he claims to be attempting to reimbue the myths, through a gothic presentation, with their original warmth of heart, passions, and affections. But his kind of gothicizing achieves none of these effects. Where human emotions are involved these myths are intentionally superficial. Eustace's imagination expends itself in wonders, and the liveliness in the stories is the product of ingenuity. His imagination is cunning and fertile but lacks depth, distinguishing itself by cleverness rather than insight. The gothic imagination, as Eustace embodies it, is a cold faculty. The disjunction between a theory of gothic warmth and a practice of gothic coldness is to be explained largely—although not entirely—by the controlling stereotype of the child's imagination.

The child's imagination is more impressionable, intuitive, perceptive, and "poetic" than the adult imagination, which has become deadened by experience and routine. We have seen such a conception of childish fancy in Hawthorne's writings as far back as "Little Annie's Ramble," and even there it does not represent an original idea. The child as visionary is a significant cultural concept, bridging the gap between romantic and Victorian sensibilities and between elite and popular literature. In the story of Bellerophon Hawthorne has a fascinating example of a childish visionary in the little boy who waits by the well with the hero—a silent, lonely, intense person, who alone among all the people has seen Pegasus, and whose faith sustains the more skeptical Bellerophon. The little boy symbolizes Bellerophon's imagination. The inexperienced child has no reason to doubt the existence of winged horses; the adult who knows better may still value that receptive naiveté.

Still, the childish imagination operates and must operate in an experiential void. This void is precisely what facilitates its ready belief and constitutes its moral innocence; therefore it must not be disturbed. Literature for the child, in this view, must not bring the child any unwelcome experience. It must be purely imaginative in that it presents a better world than the human one, and is therefore directed away from reality rather than toward it. To preserve innocence literature must be escapist, but without those qualities of fear and horror that the literature of a gothic writer like Poe depends upon for effect. As Hawthorne suggests in the story of Pandora, suffering is not inherent in the child's life; knowledge of suffering, or the experience of it, signals adulthood.

The view of children's literature here differs from that implicit in *The Whole History*, where Grandfather thought somberly of his responsibility in conveying so much knowledge of suffering and error to his auditors. Eustace Bright is quite a different narrator from Grandfather, and his character suits his idea of literature as protection rather than revelation. An inexperienced lad barely out of childhood himself, Eustace is distinguished from his young auditors only in a slight degree; his tales emanate from the same sort of imagination as that for which they are designed. From this point of view Eustace, though a limited and perhaps partly satiric character, is a technical triumph, for he tells the story in a way that Hawthorne most certainly could not. In creating a narrator like Eustace, Hawthorne was able to transcend his own temperamental affinity for the dark side of experience and enter into the simple and sunny world view he desired to represent.

I have suggested that it was Hawthorne's earnest wish after *The Scarlet Letter* to write a cheerful book, and in *A Wonder Book for Girls and Boys* he certainly succeeded. One of its reviewers commented that "the spirit of the book is so essentially sunny and happy, that it creates a jubilee in the brain as we read."[16] Unfortunately, when he attempted to replicate his achievement eighteen months later in *Tanglewood Tales*, he lost his magic touch; the second book of children's myths is a much more grim affair.

A Wonder Book, dated 1852, actually appeared late in 1851, as did *The Snow-Image and Other Twice-told Tales*, the third and final gathering of short works. Thus, within one year several old works were reissued (*Twice-told Tales* and the children's histories), a major romance completed and published, a new children's book written, and a volume of previously uncollected stories compiled. This was the busiest year of Hawthorne's literary life, and he was preparing now for a long and busy career as a major author. He had written on July 22, 1851, to Bridge: "As long as people will buy, I shall keep at work, and I find that my facility for labor increases

16. From *Graham's Monthly Magazine*, quoted in Centenary, VI, p. 306.

with the demand for it."[17] The election of Franklin Pierce to the presidency and his subsequent offer of a diplomatic post to Hawthorne changed these plans.

In the preface to *The Snow-Image* (prefaces had now become a regular feature in his work), Hawthorne speaks to his friend Horatio Bridge and expresses his conviction that all his earlier writings worth preserving had now been collected. His assertion that "these are the last" was not quite true, as it turned out, though no doubt he meant it as firmly as he had meant it when he said in "The Old Manse" that he would do no more of that kind of work. He wrote just one more short piece, "Feathertop," late in 1851. This he added to the 1854 reissue of *Mosses from an Old Manse*, along with two descriptive segments of *The Story Teller*, which were given the titles "Sketches from Memory" and "Passages from a Relinquished Work." But he did compose virtually no more short fiction, and the best of it had been republished in his collections. Little of the uncollected work has aroused critical interest. "Fragments from the Journal of a Solitary Man" has been studied by those trying to reconstruct *The Story Teller* as well as by those who consider Oberon a purely autobiographical statement. "Mrs. Hutchinson" has been used by a few critics to draw conclusions about Hester; several scholars have been interested in the ideas about history and fiction in "Alice Doane's Appeal." The other uncollected works have been ignored.

The Snow-Image itself is unlike the two earlier collections because it contains work from the whole sweep of Hawthorne's career without emphasizing a single period. He used nothing from his earliest project, *Seven Tales of My Native Land,* but took two stories from *Provincial Tales:* "The Wives of the Dead" and "My Kinsman, Major Molineux," dating around 1830. There is work from *The Story Teller* ("The

17. Bridge, p. 127.

Canterbury Pilgrims," "The Devil in Manuscript," "Old News," "Old Ticonderoga"), the *Twice-told Tales* years ("A Bell's Biography," "The Man of Adamant," "Sylph Etherege," "John Inglefield's Thanksgiving"), the Manse period ("Little Daffydowndilly"), and the Custom House period ("Main-street," "The Snow-Image," "Ethan Brand," "The Great Stone Face"). The four most recent pieces appear at the beginning of the collection, and in general Hawthorne appears to have arranged the stories on a principle of reverse chronology, so that the earliest are read last.

He may have done so to support his prefatory statement that the early pieces "come so nearly up to the standard of the best that [he] can achieve now," to show how much of a piece his writing was. There is also a predictable pattern of contrast and variety in the arrangement. Since *The Snow-Image* does not represent the output of one specific phase of Hawthorne's career, the collection does not have so strongly marked a character as either *Twice-told Tales* or *Mosses from an Old Manse*. Almost all the sketches and moralized fictions were published in *Twice-told Tales*, and almost everything written at the Manse went into *Mosses*; Hawthorne had little left to collect except early fiction that he had passed over before and the four pieces he wrote at the Custom House. Of the early pieces collected in *The Snow-Image*, only "My Kinsman, Major Molineux" has attained a strong critical reputation, and that reputation is a creation of Freudian criticism after 1950. Besides this story, the most interesting item in *The Snow-Image* is its preface, which tackles directly in its statement and indirectly in its form (it is a dedicatory letter to Horatio Bridge, Hawthorne's closest friend) the problem of how personal a writer may or must be in his work.

From the beginning of his career Hawthorne had conceptualized the literary profession as a meeting of author and audience, where the burden was largely on the author to make himself understood and to make himself pleasing and acceptable. In such an endeavor there are two limits: at one extreme, the writer must not put forward material of so private a nature, or so privately articulated, that it is offensive or incomprehensible to others. At the other extreme, he must not elect a rhetoric, or a form, so conventional that there is nothing whatsoever of himself in what he does. The reason for this limit is not a belief in the ideal of sincerity—or at least it was not at the outset of Hawthorne's career—but a practical awareness that if an author has nothing of his own to offer he can make no claim on an audience's attention. In defining the boundaries precisely and in succeeding within them, the writer has nothing to guide him but his own literary tact and his sensitivity to audience response.

Writing in a vacuum for so many years in Salem, his works published anonymously and almost never receiving any notice, Hawthorne could not depend on audience reaction to locate himself. His imagination had to do the whole job. During these years he hid, so to speak, behind several different masks that had some pertinence to his own situation but did not purport to represent him in his own person. In the Old Manse period he began to make direct autobiographical statements. He wanted to assume his own identity and felt he had established an audience that would be glad to have him do so. But he was careful to insist that he was not violating any fundamental principles of decorum; his statements were always tasteful and did not impinge on his own fundamental privacy or the reader's. He repeated this insistence in "The Custom-House," and restated it again in the preface to *The Snow-Image*; but in the latter his statement is ironic and played off against a different definition of his work:

And, as for egotism, a person, who has been burrowing, to his utmost ability, into the depths of our common nature, for the purposes of psychological romance,—and who pursues his researches in that dusky region, as he needs must, as well by the tact of sympathy as by the light of observation,—will smile at incurring such an imputation in virtue of a little preliminary talk about his external habits, his abode, his casual associates, and other matters entirely upon the surface. These things hide the man, instead of displaying him. You must make quite another kind of inquest, and look through the whole range of his fictitious characters, good and evil, in order to detect any of his essential traits.[18]

Before *The Scarlet Letter* Hawthorne would not have characterized his work as psychological romance, and such early work as fits the definition does so because "in youth, men are apt to write more wisely than they really know or feel" (p. 6). From the vantage point of psychological fiction, the prefatory notation of a few autobiographical details is a superficial activity; but the works themselves are put forward as intensely private documents. Indeed, Hawthorne implicitly invites the reader to approach his work as private revelation. Still, he has not abandoned his idea of a meeting of reader and author, for there is a public intention behind such private revelation; it is the unveiling of the depths of our common nature. In Hawthorne's major period, reader and author are imagined to meet not on the common ground of conventional rhetoric or socially sanctioned morality, but on the ground of their deepest shared secrets. Hawthorne has gone very far from his starting point, but he remains a distinctly unmodern author because he does not attempt to enter the great domain of the unshared secret, that which is private and unique to each person. He reveals nothing that is merely his own.

18. *The Snow-Image*, p. 4.

⊷ 6 ⊶

The Major Phase III
1852–1853

The unrelieved gloom of *The Scarlet Letter* troubled Hawthorne; he was uneasy at the idea of a reputation identified
with a single mode of writing, associated with catering to
morbid or melancholy tastes. But his attempts to correct the
situation ran up against the bias of his own temperament. *The
House of the Seven Gables* swerved aside from his intentions.
Having then achieved a thoroughly jubilant work in *A Wonder Book*, Hawthorne gave up the battle gracefully. "I don't
know what I shall write next," he observed to Bridge in the
letter of July 22, 1851. "Should it be a romance, I mean to
put an extra touch of the devil into it, for I doubt whether
the public will stand two quiet books in succession without
my losing ground."[1]

Hawthorne did no work for several months, because he
was leaving the Berkshires and looking about for a permanent
residence. Late in November 1851, however, he began working on the new romance which he completed some five months
later (five months seems to have been his normal time to write
a long work).[2] *The Blithedale Romance* is, notwithstanding
its title, a very gloomy book indeed. But aside from its tone,

1. Bridge, *Personal Recollections of Nathaniel Hawthorne*, p. 127.
2. According to Pearce in the introduction to Vol. III, Centenary
Edition, p. xviii, he began work in November 1851; Stewart says he
completed it on April 30, 1852 (*Nathaniel Hawthorne*, p. 122).

which relates it to *The Scarlet Letter*, it is much more closely tied to *The House of the Seven Gables*. Like *The House of the Seven Gables*, it is set in the present and involves a group of people whose activities place them somewhat apart from "the highway of ordinary travel" and who therefore must not be exposed to "too close a comparison with the actual events of real lives."[3] The action in both romances proceeds from a hidden, gothic plot. This plot takes its meaning from the social and psychological oppositions of freedom and structure, passion and oppression, shared by all the major romances, but it attacks quite directly some of the questions raised by the ending of *The House of the Seven Gables*.

The House of the Seven Gables concluded with the overthrow of a tyrant that turned out to be a Pyrrhic victory; the act of overthrow encumbered the free imagination with guilt, and the radical who entered the house left it a conservative. If such an event is inevitable, it was nevertheless managed in the romance so rapidly and with such ambivalence that the reader who feels uncertain about Hawthorne's intentions at the conclusion is quite justified. In *The Blithedale Romance* Hawthorne returns to a point before that of the ending of *The House of the Seven Gables* and repeats the event. Giving the other side every benefit of the doubt, Hawthorne imagines a group of people who assert that they are not slaves to an oppressive personal history but are oppressed entirely by social institutions, which can be discarded at will because they have no organic relation to the self. These people leave society, as Holgrave left the house of the seven gables, but without his debilitating sense of complicity in the evils that inform the structures they are abandoning. They withdraw to construct their own expressive forms, free in theory of bias or entanglement. Like Holgrave, they move away from the city into the

3. *The Blithedale Romance*, Centenary Edition, Vol. III (1965), p. 1. Subsequent references given parenthetically in text.

country, but they are more evidently attempting to reproduce the situation of the original Maule, by finding some plot of ground still in a natural state and working it into organic representations of their own ideals.

With this opportunity to live in freedom, what happens to these people? The answer is, of course, that they re-create the oppression they left behind, because they are not free. Hawthorne devotes the whole of *The Blithedale Romance*, then, to making the point reserved for the last two chapters of *The House of the Seven Gables*. People are civilized, which means that they bring with them, because they have within them, attitudes that they thought were purely external. If repression and oppression are not original nature, they have become, in a long course of socialized life, second nature.

Because in *The Blithedale Romance* a Utopian ideal falls victim to human weakness and depravity, the work is read over and over again—with virtual critical unanimity until fairly recently—as Hawthorne's text on original sin. For this reason it cannot be too much emphasized that the "sin" is not one of disobedience, but of tyrannizing and repressing. The snake in this Eden, as well as its greatest sinner, is Hollingsworth, the authoritarian fatherly figure who stands against everything the Blithedale people believe in. The sin is the father's against the children, and not the children's against the father. Hollingsworth literally subverts the Blithedale enterprise, joining the community merely in order to gain access to its property and approach Zenobia for financial gain. His motives may seem exalted, but his relation to the property and the people who live on it is no less materialistic or ruthless than Pyncheon's.

As in *The House of the Seven Gables*, there is a basic territorial symbolism, in which a plot of land is identified with the self's body, and the self's potential is represented in the relation between the human being and land. As Hollingsworth takes over the role of Pyncheon, so the Maule-figure in *The*

Blithedale Romance is Coverdale, its narrator. An artist, like Holgrave, Coverdale differs from his predecessor because he is not socially alienated and he has not preserved a radical self free from institutional influence. But he retains enough spark to wish to achieve freedom; *The Blithedale Romance* is the story of his quest and his failure. The world of Blithedale is the realization of his story, and all the events and characters take their fundamental meanings from their pertinence to his goal. Since it is Coverdale's story that we are following, the innumerable critical analyses of his character as detached voyeur are very much beside the point; but Coverdale's passivity is much to the point. Not only is Coverdale represented in the romance to some extent as the dreaming mind passively observing the images of its own creating (as in "The Haunted Mind"); his passivity indicates his oppression and inhibition.

He is the product of a middle-class cosmopolitan way of life that sees no goals beyond comfort and pleasure and has confused the necessary material means of human existence with its ends. He thinks that by leaving behind his bachelor apartment, his sherry, and his urban entertainments, he will become a strong free man. But of course he is wrong. The characters and their interrelations tell the story of his error. The gradual drift from harmonious relations toward polarization and eventual violent antagonism represents the fragmentation of a personality. Imagery of masks and veils, much noted in the criticism, contributes to the dreamlike atmosphere of uncertain identities and reminds one of the indirect, misleading, and elusive ways in which truth is both asserted and disguised in fantasy. The carnival, or pageant, during which Zenobia is repudiated by Hollingsworth is not play-acting at all, but the moment of revelation when the characters cease to pose as people and appear in their symbolic meanings for Coverdale. Zenobia is the repudiated queen of the soul, Hollingsworth its wrathful judge. Recalling the mythology of "Main-street," we might see in Zenobia the great Squaw Sachem dispossessed and obliterated from memory by the Puritan patriarchy that Hollingsworth, cast as a Puritan judge, suddenly comes to represent. The event echoes Pyncheon's strategy of labeling his opponent a wizard; and when we remember the Salem persecutions we find a role for Priscilla in this transaction as well, as Zenobia's accuser. The catastrophic conclusion leaves Coverdale a permanently passive character. The spark that drove him to Blithedale has been altogether extinguished. He withdraws his allegiance from Zenobia and bestows it on Priscilla.

In the opening chapters Coverdale takes the familiar literary journey of the self into its own depths, hoping to make contact with the sources of energy and life within and to return to the surface a new man. In Boston he has enjoyed the "sweet, bewitching, enervating indolence" (p. 19) of a genteel bachelorhood, parceling out his social days: "My pleasant bachelor-parlor, sunny and shadowy . . . [with] centre-table, strewn with books and periodicals . . . writing-desk, with a half-finished poem in a stanza of my own contrivance; my morning lounge at the reading-room or picture gallery; my noontide walk along the cheery pavement, with the suggestive succession of human faces, and the brisk throb of human life, in which I shared; my dinner at the Albion . . . my evening at the billiard-club, the concert, the theatre, or at somebody's party, if I pleased" (p. 40). This life is pleasant indeed, but effete; in its tepidly hedonistic atmosphere, art is but another languid pastime. Coverdale leaves it behind to liberate and test his talent. He wants to become a true poet, "to produce something that shall really deserve to be called poetry—true, strong, natural, and sweet" (p. 14). Presiding over the decadent life of the city is a mysterious idol, the Veiled Lady, who represents a decadent exploitation of spirituality; at the farm, Zenobia is the goddess in residence.

The movement from Boston to Blithedale represents a personal liberation, Coverdale's turning within himself, his abandonment of artificial forms in search of natural expression. As in the other romances of Hawthorne's major period, there is behind this personal story the question of the possibility of reconstructing society on larger and more generous principles than a narrow and repressive materialism. Boston is an institutional prison. Leaving the city with others about to join the community, Coverdale notes: "The buildings, on either side, seemed to press too closely upon us, insomuch that our mighty hearts found barely enough room to throb between them. The snow-fall, too, looked inexpressibly dreary, (I had almost called it dingy,) coming down through an atmosphere of city-smoke, and alighting on the sidewalk only to be moulded into the impress of somebody's patched boot or overshoe." And he draws a transcendental moral: "Thus, the track of an old conventionalism was visible on what was freshest from the sky" (p. 11).

In contrast, Blithedale aims to establish forms of labor and love that will permit the expression of the human spirit instead of inhibiting and distorting it. In an atmosphere of informality and innovation, it hopes to restructure human relations on the principle of "familiar love" and to "lessen the laboring man's great burthen of toil." Life will be "governed by other than the false and cruel principles on which human society has all along been based" (p. 19). But the community's economic aims have no deep interest for Coverdale, and the romance does not pursue the socialist dimension of the experiment, restricting itself to the drama of the inner life.

The springtime in which Coverdale leaves for Blithedale symbolizes (as has often been noted in the criticism) the rejuvenating purposes of his social withdrawal as well as his initial optimism. The severe snow that he encounters represents the necessary death of the social self prior to spiritual rebirth. Coverdale attributes the severity of his illness directly to the "hot-house warmth of a town-residence and the luxurious life" in which he indulged (p. 40). Recovered, he joins the community officially on May Day, confident that he is a new man and that his trials are all behind him:

> My fit of illness had been an avenue between two existences; the low-arched and darksome doorway, through which I crept out of a life of old conventionalisms, on my hands and knees, as it were, and gained admittance into the freer region that lay beyond. In this respect, it was like death. And, as with death, too, it was good to have gone through it. No otherwise could I have rid myself of a thousand follies, fripperies, prejudices, habits, and other such worldly dust as inevitably settles upon the crowd along the broad highway, giving them all one sordid aspect, before noontime, however freshly they may have begun their pilgrimage, in the dewy morning. The very substance upon my bones had not been fit to live with, in any better, truer, or more energetic mode than that to which I was accustomed. So it was taken off me and flung aside, like any other worn out or unseasonable garment; and, after shivering a little while in my skeleton, I began to be clothed anew, and much more satisfactorily than in my previous suit. In literal and physical truth, I was quite another man. [P. 61]

In fact, Coverdale's serious struggle is about to begin. He has replaced the flesh upon his bones, to be sure, but the attitudes that are wrought in the bone have yet to reveal themselves. The outer man has been renewed, but the inner man persists the same.

Coverdale's intention of tapping the soul's reservoir of energy, of contacting its passionate, creative, active principle, requires a representation in the romance of that underlying principle. Zenobia, who unites sex, art, and nature in one image, is that symbol. As the true aim of Coverdale's quest, she is waiting to greet him at Blithedale; and again Hawthorne creates the illusion, soon to be dispelled, that Coverdale's aims are easily and quickly realized. More than the community, Zenobia is the reality Coverdale seeks, and that is why in comparison with her the rest of the enterprise pales and looks unreal, becomes "a masquerade, a pastoral, a counterfeit Arcadia" (p. 21). The opposition between her and the rest of the community recalls the contrast, in "The Custom-House," between the transcendentalists, who represent an unerotic cloudland idealism, and Hester, who combines imagination and Eros in one figure. Sexual and poetic energy are varying forms of the same drive. In her symbolic function Zenobia stands for the creative energy of both nature and the self, equivalent in this romance to the fountain in *The House of the Seven Gables*.

In using a woman for this symbolism, Hawthorne returns to an important concept in *The Scarlet Letter* that he had put aside in *The House of the Seven Gables:* the idea that a man's liberation and fulfillment require his accepting a more fully sexual image of woman than the culture allows. The woman's sexuality (she is a secondary being in a patriarchal system) is suppressed in society as a means of inhibiting the male; both sexes suffer. Zenobia is described in unambiguously admiring physical images of softness, radiance, warmth, and health. She has a "fine, frank, mellow" voice, a "very soft and warm hand," and her smile "beamed warmth upon us all." Her laugh is "mellow, almost broad," her modes of expression "free, careless, generous" (pp. 14–16). Observing her, Coverdale thinks: "We seldom meet with women, now-a-days, and in this country, who impress us as being women at all; their sex fades away and goes for nothing, in ordinary intercourse. Not so with Zenobia" (p. 17). Later he rhapsodizes over "the native glow of coloring in her cheeks . . . the flesh-warmth over her round arms, and what was visible of her full bust" (p. 44). One astute critic of *The Blithedale Romance* has observed that Zenobia is linked to Phoebe through frequent sun images,[4] and the point is certainly valid; but Phoebe's is a

4. Rudolph Von Abele, *The Death of the Artist* (The Hague: Martinus Nijhoff, 1957), p. 78.

capacity for decorating the surface, while Zenobia can radiate from within.

Coverdale understands much better than many modern readers of the romance that his morbid and oversensitive shrinking from the force and energy of Zenobia's personality indicates his own "illness and exhaustion" and not a flaw in Zenobia (p. 44). Many critics interpret the hothouse flower that she always wears as Hawthorne's sign of her sensual evil. But when one reads that the flower was "so fit, indeed, that Nature had evidently created this floral gem, in a happy exuberance, for the one purpose of worthily adorning Zenobia's head" (p. 45), one must abandon the idea that the bloom is either unnatural or evil, although it is certainly sexual. To impose the idea of evil on sexuality is in fact to fall into the cultural trap that Coverdale hopes to escape. He will be recovered, he realizes, when Zenobia no longer embarrasses him. His energies are blocked because he cannot accept the passionate foundation of the human character and the inextricable union of art and Eros. Zenobia should be his poetic inspiration and subject. Until she becomes so, Coverdale will remain a childish man and (to borrow Whitman's term) a mere "poetling."

The relationship between Zenobia and Coverdale begins auspiciously as the two sit comfortably together before the blazing kitchen fire. But the fire is only brush; it will not endure, nor will Coverdale's easy frame of mind. Their companionable solitude is broken by the knock on the door that announces the arrival of Hollingsworth and Priscilla, whose destruction of Zenobia will put out the fires of Blithedale permanently for Coverdale. Zenobia soon laughingly forecasts her own death and even the manner of her dying when she calls Hollingsworth the "sable knight" and Priscilla the "shadowy snow maiden who . . . shall melt away at my feet, in a pool of ice-cold water and give me my death with a pair of wet slippers" (p. 33).

From the beginning, Hollingsworth is imaged in terms of fire, ice, animals, and iron. In his great snow-covered coat he looks like a polar bear. The imagery of cold is clear enough, and the experienced reader of Hawthorne will know by the iron metaphors that another Puritan has entered the scene. To Priscilla, the docile maiden, he displays a face that "looked really beautiful with its expression of thoughtful benevolence" (p. 30), but to the unconventional Zenobia his aspect is "stern and reproachful"; so he enters at once into the business of judging and reproving. "It was with that inauspicious meaning in his glance," Coverdale remarks, "that Hollingsworth first met Zenobia's eyes, and began his influence upon her life" (pp. 28–29). The outcome of the story is implicit in this first meeting, but Coverdale is long reluctant to believe what he has seen because he wants to believe that Hollingsworth is a benign and loving person.

And why does this matter to him? Because Hollingsworth is a figure of authority, and Coverdale wants to believe in the goodness of authority. This is the other side of his weakness: he denies passion, he respects authority. Thus, he wants authority to give its blessing to his Blithedale venture, and until it does he hesitates to commit himself. It is completely unrealistic of him to imagine that authority might countenance his radical aims, of course, and he finds this out. He understands at last that Hollingsworth desires nothing from individuals but their submission, that his high morality conceals and serves his wish to dominate others. The apex of Coverdale's development occurs when he refuses to join Hollingsworth in the scheme to betray the Blithedale community and thereby loses the friendship that is so valuable to him.

From the first he has known that Hollingsworth's heart "was never really interested in our socialist scheme, but was forever busy with his . . . plan" (p. 36). Coverdale thinks that Hollingsworth has joined the community because as an outcast he feels more at home with other outcasts (p. 55).

But this is a sentimental view. Hollingsworth has come, as one critic puts it, to "bore from within."[5] He is the counter-revolution. His purpose is to acquire the Blithedale property for himself, as the site of his reform school. This school could not be in greater contrast to the Blithedale community and appropriately requires dispossessing the Blithedalers as a first step. Far from envisioning a free relation between man and nature, Hollingsworth would shut people away from nature in an institution, a building, which conforms not to the spirit of the individuals within it but to *his* spirit.

Forever busy planning his structure to the last detail, Hollingsworth allows absolutely no freedom to those whom he proposes to reform. His solid material edifice negates the organic ideal of the Blithedale group, who wish institutions to take shape from inner motives and to remain sensitive to inner flux. Once again Maule is to be supplanted by Pyncheon. While the Blithedalers are programmatic nonconformists, Hollingsworth's plan imposes sameness on all. People may not grow their ways, but must grow his way. Starting with the premise that men are criminals, Hollingsworth denies the basic transcendental belief in the inherent divinity of the human being; setting himself apart from his criminals, he rejects human brotherhood. Perhaps most important, in accepting the social judgments that define some as criminals and others not, Hollingsworth's scheme rests on the social and institutional perceptions of human nature that the romantic soul rejects. In sum, Hollingsworth is not a romantic extremist but a representative of the authoritarian principle. To confuse his kind of reform with the goals of Blithedale is to miss the entire point of *The Blithedale Romance*.

His attachment to Zenobia, based wholly on his interest in her money, reveals his materialistic approach to human beings more clearly than anything else. When the fortune shifts from

5. Irving Howe, *Politics and the Novel* (New York: Horizon Press, 1957), p. 167.

Zenobia's to Priscilla's possession, so does Hollingsworth's allegiance, and he rescues Priscilla from the clutches of the villain only a few days after he had agreed that she might be delivered to him. Despite his rhetoric, Hollingsworth is a man of things, power, money, and material. The disparity between his self-righteous dismissal of Zenobia and the nature of his own motives shows his sanctimonious morality to be sheer, if unconscious, hypocrisy.

The rerouting of the fortune is more than a device to expose Hollingsworth's depravity and disloyalty. Although throughout most of the romance Zenobia is wealthy, she operates in a frame independent of money. Her wealth is in the abundance of her natural gifts. Priscilla, on the other hand, is very much a creature of money or the absence of it. Whether one thinks of her as a seamstress or as the Veiled Lady, one finds her characterization intimately bound up with economic questions, for she serves an environment that demands artifice and exploits its suppliers. As seamstress, she makes one highly specialized luxury item—a finely wrought silk purse. This object, whether interpreted sartorially or sexually, appeals to a jaded taste. As the Veiled Lady, Priscilla herself is an artificial construct appealing to sated appetites.

The contrast between the one sister's naturalness and the other's artificiality is brought out ironically in the Boston interlude of the romance (chapters 17–20). Zenobia, beautiful as ever, seems curiously artificial and dead despite the astonishing luxury of her costume, indeed because of it. The hothouse flower has been replaced by a jewel. The metamorphosis signifies that her attractions appear unnatural in an urban setting. Coverdale, while talking to her, feels that she is playing a part (p. 165).

But Priscilla comes to life. The city is her element. Although Coverdale opines that her beauty is of the delicate sort that would be falsified by the art of dress, he declares almost in the same breath that her perfection in the city is due to consummate art: "I wondered what Zenobia meant by evolving so much loveliness out of this poor girl." Art or artifice has turned Priscilla into a symbol of purity and innocence, but this meaning is inseparable from her situation in the city. "Ever since she came among us, I have been dimly sensible of just this charm which you have brought out. But it was never absolutely visible till now." And then Coverdale expresses one of the romance's bitter insights: "She is as lovely," he rhapsodizes, "as a flower" (p. 169). In other words, Priscilla is the story's true artificial flower, the bloom that seems natural in the city domain of repression and unnatural pleasure. In the distorting glass of civilization Zenobia's flower looks fake. She does not belong here. It is right that the fortune be taken from her and given to Priscilla.

As Zenobia is the natural or precivilized woman, or the future possibility of woman, Priscilla is the woman in history, distorted by her social role and misrepresented by the ideals derived from her. She is considered an inferior being and is subjugated and exploited; at the same time she is idealized. The ideal is obviously pernicious because it derives from woman's subject status and ultimately ennobles an enslaved condition. As a seamstress Priscilla represents the whole range of exploited female roles in society, and particularly the fact of female labor in an age that pretended women were too feeble to work. She may or may not have been a prostitute, but the possibility is forcefully suggested.[6]

Her economic servitude is recapitulated on a psychosexual level in the murky symbol of the Veiled Lady. When Priscilla is not making purses to support her father, Old Moodie, she performs onstage as the subject of Westervelt's mesmeric powers, hidden behind a many-layered, gauzy white veil. The Veiled Lady is an idea of womanhood as noncorporeal and

6. See Alan and Barbara Lefcowitz, "Some Rents in the Veil: New Light on Priscilla and Zenobia in *The Blithedale Romance*," *Nineteenth-Century Fiction*, 21 (1966), 263–76.

hence spiritual. The idea is carried to an extreme and implicates in its extremity some very base human emotions. Though
she is proclaimed a spiritual being, she is really a possessed
creature, owned and exploited by Westervelt. Her condition
denies her spiritual nature even while pretending to demonstrate it. The particular being in whose service she performs
is a cosmopolitan devil. Like Moodie, another urban figure,
Westervelt lives from the proceeds of his exploitation, but,
because his is a spiritual violation of the woman, his behavior
is much worse than Moodie's. Westervelt caters to prurient
and voyeuristic tastes in an audience that pays to see purity
violated and modesty exhibited. On the one hand, talk of
purity "veils" what is actually taking place; on the other,
purity itself contributes to the prurient excitement of the
display.

The veil, along with references to Priscilla's insubstantial
frame, and metaphors of shadows and melting snows, and contrasts to Zenobia's rich physicality and assertiveness, suggests
that in this spiritual ideal a crude equation has been made between spirit and lack of body. The more body, the less spirit.
To deny the flesh is to deny the emotions flesh arouses, and
hence the normality of sex. The result is an abnormal sex
indeed, in which young, frail, immature girls become objects
of sexual interest while fully sexed adult women are experienced as frightening, corrupt, or repellent. The ideal is diabolic,
for it thoroughly corrupts the natural growth of a strong
human personality. It promises a fulfillment that is in fact an
incompleteness. So Zenobia implies in her "Legend of the
Silvery Veil," which she recites in chapter 12.

Theodore, sneaking into the Veiled Lady's dressing room
for a peek at the hidden lady, is asked for a kiss by the
shrouded figure. The idea repels him. He imagines all kinds
of horrors beneath the evil and refuses indignantly. This failure
to accept the physical aspect of the relation between the sexes
dooms him and the lady to subjection and separation. She

sorrowfully disappears, but not before Theodore has seen her lovely face, the memory of which is to haunt him for the rest of his life, and mock him with his empty and insubstantial existence. Priscilla, then, is both a real person and an image: imprisoned in the image of the Veiled Lady is a girl, or woman, who needs to be rescued, to be made into a being of flesh and blood.

But who will rescue Priscilla? Certainly not Coverdale, who likes her as she is, in all her frailty and vulnerability and in the very insubstantiality of her presence. His imagination is much preoccupied with her feebleness, but, as he admits, he mostly uses her vagueness as the ground for his own fantasies. What she really "is" does not matter to him; he would rather not know. Precisely to the extent that she is unassertive, his imagination can expand. Celebrating the feeble and victimized woman, Coverdale makes no effort to rescue the woman from the image; he locks her more firmly into it. Nor will Hollingsworth allow her out of the prison; he merely wrests the image away from Westervelt's possession. Finally, and perhaps most tragically, Zenobia will not make the effort. As the conclusion to her legend shows, Zenobia, who wants—quite legitimately—to eradicate the image from men's minds, has made the mistake of equating the real human being with its symbolic role. When she throws the veil over Priscilla she plays the role of jailor herself.

Priscilla at Blithedale is the perpetual reminder of ideals that the community has presumably tried to reject. Sensing this, Zenobia attempts to destroy her rival, and in these attempts she shows how much she herself, as a woman, is a victim of the patriarchal system she aspires to overturn. Her strategy of denigrating Priscilla is of course self-defeating, for it summons up all the chivalric impulses of the men, who will fight to the death to preserve Priscilla as a pathetic creature. Increasingly, Zenobia's tactics only define the polarity of pit and pedestal and put Zenobia herself in the pit. Coverdale becomes more and more uncomfortable and hostile as she ridicules his genteel attachments; and as for Hollingsworth, Zenobia's views have never held any attraction for him.

Yet, in this segment of the story, it is less important that Zenobia's strategy fails to engage the affection of the men than that it fails to recognize Priscilla as her sister, which she is, literally. Zenobia thus shows a fatal man-centeredness; the victimized woman in Priscilla, the possible development of Priscilla as a free human being: these issues do not interest her. She is a bad advocate for feminism because she has no sense of sisterhood. Hawthorne points up her frequent cruelties to the young girl, who wants above everything else to be accepted and loved by the older woman. Priscilla goes to Hollingsworth at the end only when Zenobia will not have her. Here is an opportunity wasted, a challenge not responded to. And here is a criticism of Zenobia, not because she is a feminist, but because she is not feminist enough.[7] After all, despite her talent and brilliance, Zenobia as a social creature cannot imagine any function in life other than adhering to some man whose superiority will enhance her own status.

Choosing Hollingsworth as the man she fancies, Zenobia shows that her male ideal is the cultural stereotype of masculinity. There is the shaggy aggressiveness, the scarcely concealed brutality, the obsession with mastery and domination, the sexual coldness (taken as a sign of devotion to "higher" things), the preference for abstractions to human particulars, the lack of sensitivity and subtlety masquerading as forceful

7. The critical treatment of Hawthorne's feminism is very murky, having been mostly carried out by critics who themselves are strongly antifeminist. Hawthorne's dislike for Margaret Fuller has been confused with a general dislike for the feminist movement; but his response to Fuller was a personal reaction that had nothing to do with her views and a good deal to do with his suspicion (perhaps right, perhaps wrong) that she was not sincere in them. Hawthorne's prevailing attitude toward feminist ideas, in all four major romances, is strongly sympathetic.

logic. Hollingsworth is masculine precisely to the extent that he is a human failure. As Jaffrey Pyncheon represents Hawthorne's severely critical embodiment of the patriarchal system, so Hollingsworth is an attack on the patriarchal ideal of manhood. Enslaved by this ideal, Zenobia seriously undervalues herself and has little but contempt for other women. Coverdale is right to be appalled when she weakly acquiesces in Hollingsworth's ferocious diatribe against liberated women: "Her place is at man's side. Her office, that of the Sympathizer, the unreserved, unquestioning Believer. . . . Woman is a monster . . . without man, as her acknowledged principal" (pp. 122–23). "Let man be but manly and godlike," she responds, "and woman is only too ready to become to him what you say" (p. 124).

Later, when Hollingsworth casts her off, she takes refuge in a litany of her feminine imperfections:

A woman—with every fault . . . that a woman ever had, weak, vain, unprincipled, (like most of my sex; for our virtues, when we have any, are merely impulsive and intuitive,) passionate, too, and pursuing my foolish and unattainable ends, by indirect and cunning, though absurdly chosen means, as an hereditary bondslave must—false, moreover, to the whole circle of good, in my reckless truth to the little good I saw before me—but still a woman! A creature, whom only a little change of earthly fortune, a little kinder smile of Him who sent me hither, and one true heart to encourage and direct me, might have made all that a woman can be! [Pp. 217–18]

To perceive Hollingsworth as a "cold, heartless, self-beginning and self-ending piece of mechanism" is evidently not, for Zenobia, to be free of his myths of female nature. So Zenobia, like Coverdale, wants the blessing of male authority.

Her desire to be subject to authority derives not only from her place in the book's scheme as a part of Coverdale. It arises also because, in the modern world in which Zenobia must function as both Eros and Woman, the sole permitted expression is in Romantic Love. After her death, when the cynical Westervelt refuses to be moved by her sentimental tragedy, asserting instead that "it was an idle thing—a foolish thing—for Zenobia to do. . . . She had life's summer all before her, and a hundred varieties of brilliant success!" (pp. 239–40), Coverdale cannot help but partly agree. "It is nonsense, and a miserable wrong—the result, like so many others, of masculine egotism—that the success or failure of a woman's existence should be made to depend wholly on the affections, and on one species of affection; while man has such a multitude of other chances" (p. 241). Zenobia's perversities represent, like the perversities of the wizard Maules, the distortions of Eros in civilized life.

For Coverdale to imagine, then, that his creative energies could rescue him is naive folly. It is he who must rescue them. But to articulate the matter in this way is to realize the impossible situation. This stunted man cannot make himself whole. *The Blithedale Romance* is indeed a criticism of social optimism, but hardly because it warns against the dangers of untrammeled self-expression. It points out, rather, how naive is the assumption that such freedom might ever come to pass in the modern world. The dangers it exposes are of the repressive and punishing forces that will permanently damage the personality if given the opportunity. Such dangers threaten not only the individual personality but society as a whole. Hollingsworth finally becomes his own victim; his repudiation of Zenobia is suicidal. There are no people without passion, and no societies without people. To extinguish passion is to extinguish life. In the civilized man, passion is already more than adequately controlled. It is control itself that needs boundaries.

Thus, although greatly moved by the romantic ideal, Hawthorne in *The Blithedale Romance* expresses no faith in it. But because he is moved by it, he portrays its collapse—a collapse he apparently thinks is inevitable—as a social and personal tragedy. Of course, this collapse is pertinent to the artist. Coverdale's *Blithedale Romance* is the confession of a failed artist, who has abandoned his ideal of writing something strong and true and returned to producing the only sort of art that appears to be possible in his society: genteel art. Having worked through to a conception of imaginative activity that was weighty and significant enough to justify the dedication of a lifetime, Hawthorne now appears to see that the art resulting from such activity is unattainable or forbidden in contemporary America. This was implied, to some extent, in Hester's removal of Pearl to the Old World, where—it was imagined—a more generous society would permit a freer personal development. Coverdale's story shows the American artist in a double bind, prevented on the one hand from developing a serious and worthy art, disparaged on the other for the genteel art he is expected to produce.

Coverdale may be understood as a typical American artist, but it would be a serious mistake to equate him with Hawthorne himself, as so many critics have done.[8] Hawthorne is not Coverdale but his creator, and the imagination that can create such a character and use it as Hawthorne did in *The Blithedale Romance* has clearly transcended the limits that confine the character. Through Coverdale, Hawthorne puts forward an explanation for the prevalence of genteel art in America by demonstrating how one artist of the genteel is produced. The effect of the critical evaluation of the char-

---

8. Mistakes are compounded when, to an identification of Coverdale and Hawthorne, the critics add an interpretation of Coverdale as a cold and heartless observer. From the resulting syllogism (along with the evidence of one fragment of a sentence from "Sights from a Steeple" in which the narrator speculates briefly on the pleasures of being a "spiritual Paul Pry") some critics have constructed an elaborate reading of Hawthorne as an aloof artist filled with guilt by his inability to connect with fellow mortals. This is quite ingenious, but entirely unsupported by the writings or by the biographical facts.

acter is to separate Hawthorne from the kind of art that Coverdale exemplifies.

One may compare Coverdale's literary situation with Hawthorne's as the latter is expressed in the preface to *The Blithedale Romance*. Hawthorne has the problem not of works that he cannot write, but of works that his audience cannot understand. The American audience demands that "beings of the imagination . . . show themselves in the same category as actually living mortals" and thus reveals itself insensitive to the nature of fiction (Hawthorne uses "fiction" interchangeably with "romance" in this preface) and uncomprehending of the artist's purpose. The romancer is not trying to reproduce the texture of the everyday world—such a goal would in fact be inimical to his aims—but to materialize the world of imagination so that all may apprehend it. The romancer's medium is language and his strategy to give his imaginative constructs the appearance of living creatures and involve them in an action that seems lifelike. These figures are not representations of the external, but externalizations of the internal. If the reader misses this point, he misconstrues the nature of romance, judging by the wrong criterion, looking for verisimilitude where his standard should be truth to the heart. The sense of this aesthetic difficulty, Hawthorne writes, "has always pressed very heavily upon him"; he thinks that writers "in the old countries, with which Fiction has long been conversant," are more fortunately situated. It is not that the old countries have handy ruins and traditions for plot-building (which is the point Hawthorne makes in the preface to *The Marble Faun*) but that they provide the artist with sophisticated and sensitive readers. Yet, if the American author's alternatives are to be silent or shallow like Coverdale and expressive but misunderstood like Hawthorne, obviously Hawthorne's is the better situation.

It puts an even better face on the situation if the misunderstood works are selling and giving their author a formidable literary reputation. *The Blithedale Romance*, published on July 14, 1852, was less successful than *The Scarlet Letter* and *The House of the Seven Gables*, but it did not fail, and the reviews make clear that Hawthorne was now considered to be the leading American writer of his day. The critics remarked on Hawthorne's morbid tendencies, but accepted them as an inevitable aspect of his view of life.[9] Hawthorne, however, was less ready to accept his own temperament, and he determined that his next romance, "if possible," would be a more genial affair.[10]

But the candidacy of his friend Franklin Pierce intervened and the romance was not written. When Pierce was nominated for the presidency Hawthorne offered—half hoping to be turned down, but certainly partly with the thought of reward should Pierce be elected—to write his official campaign biography. Pierce accepted the offer. It is difficult to conceive of a genre less suited to Hawthorne's gifts and purposes than this, whose purposes are in the fullest sense of the word superficial. The author cannot invent plot or character or even incident; he may not enter his character's mind or put words in his mouth; he must not speculate on his motives or hint at complexities or subtleties of personality. The whole representation must be rigidly directed toward the goal of creating a public image of the man suitable for the office he hopes to hold. The campaign biography was an early form of public relations; Hawthorne could not possibly take any imaginative interest in, or derive imaginative satisfaction from, such work.

He was not entirely without experience in the mode, however. He had written two partisan sketches of contemporary figures in the late 1830s. One, about Thomas Greene Fessendon,

9. See J. Donald Crowley, ed., *Hawthorne: The Critical Heritage* (New York: Barnes & Noble, 1971), pp. 241–71, for a selection of contemporary reviews of *The Blithedale Romance*.

10. Bridge, p. 131.

a New Hampshire poet of the early nationalist period, appeared in the *American Monthly Magazine* in January 1838. The second, an obituary for his Bowdoin classmate Jonathan Cilley, who had been killed in a political duel, appeared in the *Democratic Review* in September of the same year. The Cilley piece permits us a fascinating view of Hawthorne's ability to twist his own perceptions to suit the public form, when it is contrasted with his journal entries about the same person. After a reunion with Cilley in July 1837, Hawthorne had characterized him privately as "shrewd, crafty, insinuating, with wonderful tact, seizing on each man by his manageable point, and using him for his own purposes, often without the man's suspecting that he is made a tool of. . . . He is really a crafty man. . . . He deceives by truth. And not only is he crafty, but, when occasion demands, bold and fierce as a tiger . . . a daring fellow as well as a sly one."[11]

Such reflections cannot possibly be used for the substance of an obituary sketch to be published in a journal sympathetic to Cilley's politics. So Cilley becomes "endowed with sagacity and tact, yet frank and free in his mode of action, ambitious of good influence, earnest, active, and persevering, with an elasticity and cheerful strength of mind. . . . Mingled with the amiable qualities that were like sunshine to his friends, there were harsher and sterner traits, which fitted him to make head against an adverse world."[12] Even Cilley's appearance has been changed. Hawthorne observed in his journal: "His person in some degree accords with his character—thin, and a thin face, sharp features, sallow, a projecting brow, not very high, deep-set eyes; an insinuating smile and look, when he meets you, or is about to address you. . . . I should think he would do away with this peculiar expression; for it lets out

11. *American Notebooks*, Centenary Edition, Vol. VIII (1972), pp. 61–62.
12. "Jonathan Cilley," Riverside Edition, Vol. XII, pp. 266–67.

more of himself than can be detected in any other way."[13] But in the obituary, Cilley "had an impending brow, deep-set eyes, and a thin and thoughtful countenance, which in his abstracted moments, seemed almost stern; but in intercourse of society it was brightened with a kindly smile, that will live in the recollection of all who knew him."[14]

Because of Hawthorne's long and close friendship with Pierce, whom he had known since their days together at Bowdoin, such hypocrisy would not be demanded of him in the writing of the official biography. And—apart from the possibility of eventual recompense in the form of a political appointment—Hawthorne stood to benefit as a literary man from the enterprise, because it would show that he was a citizen participating actively in his country's affairs, and counterbalance the impression of inwardness that his romances were creating. The campaign biography thus takes its place along with the reissues of early works and the new children's books as part of Hawthorne's effort to broaden his reputation, to define himself as a versatile writer. For the biography he developed an uncharacteristic prose style—unmodulated, unparenthetical, unmetaphorical. This plain style holds close to the subject, not for an instant deviating into the private, fanciful, or speculative; nor does it qualify the simple declaratives of its own utterance.

Hawthorne arranged his material chronologically, including information garnered from several interviews with people who had known Pierce as a younger man. (He made a brief trip to Maine in the summer of 1852 to conduct these interviews.) He also incorporated, as was customary, long segments from Pierce's own speeches. The biography represents Pierce as a man of the people and yet a fit leader. Pierce himself revised the essay in manuscript.[15] As Hawthorne wrote in a

13. *American Notebooks*, p. 62.
14. "Jonathan Cilley," p. 271.
15. See Claude M. Simpson, Jr., "Correction or Corruption: Na-

letter to Bridge, he did not consider the biography a literary production.[16]

In so far as Hawthorne saw an eventual political appointment as the result of doing this friendly favor his motive in undertaking it would be financial security.[17] Hawthorne could now count on making a living from his writing, but the living was small and would clearly require constant exertion. His reputation had far outpaced his earnings. The prospect was not secure, and he was the only breadwinner in a family that had grown to three children. If he were offered a remunerative appointment for the term of Pierce's presidency, he could hope to put financial anxiety out of his life forever. For one who had never, in the twenty-five years he had been trying to support himself by writing, been successful enough to forget about money, this possibility must have been irresistible.

The consulate at Liverpool, because it was the most lucrative of the presidential appointments (and not at all because of a supposed attraction to Europe), came into his mind early. Before the election he had decided to accept this post if it were offered to him. Pierce won the election in November 1852 and did make the offer. Hawthorne determined to sail in the summer of 1853, and planned to complete a romance in the interim. The purchase and remodeling of a home preoccupied him until the spring, however, and did not leave enough time for the writing project. He did turn a new

thaniel Hawthorne and Two Friendly Improvers," *Huntington Library Quarterly*, 36 (1973), 367–86.

16. Bridge, p. 131.

17. I do not mean to denigrate the motive of true friendship here. All the evidence is that Hawthorne was, to his small circle of close friends, deeply loyal and generous. During the Manse period he had edited and seen through the press Horatio Bridge's *Journal of an African Cruiser*, and done it for no benefit at all. In later years, when Pierce was out of favor for his conciliatory attitude toward the South, Hawthorne stood by him even though he himself was much more a partisan of the North.

romance over in his mind, and some critics believe that he actually began one,[18] but more likely he abandoned his plans before committing any of it to paper. What he did compose was the second volume of children's myths. This work, *Tanglewood Tales*, was completed in March 1853 and published in August after his departure for England (July 6, 1853).[19]

These myths, as we have already seen, were like the campaign biography in that they were controlled by a perception of audience expectations. The campaign biography had to suit an ideology of democratic leadership; the myths had to suit a reader's idea of the childish sensibility. This idea was less to be validated in the response of children to the stories (although Hawthorne apparently did test some of the tales on his own children) than in its coincidence with an adult, public stereotype of children's expectations. *Tanglewood Tales* shares the aims and intentions of *A Wonder Book*, but is quite different in format and effect from the earlier work. Hawthorne seems newly aware of the primitive ferocity of the stories and more disturbed by the question of their moral appropriateness for children than he had been in *A Wonder Book*. Moreover, *Tanglewood Tales* lacks the all-important frame of *A Wonder Book*, which makes it a different genre: a collection of stories rather than a framed narrative.

Having moved away from the Berkshire country in the period between the two works, Hawthorne was no longer imaginatively engrossed in the landscape of western Massachusetts, and he recasts the basic narrative situation accordingly. He brings himself into the work as Eustace's editor and presents Eustace in the preface delivering a pile of manuscript to him. The setting is scarcely described; Eustace and Hawthorne engage in literary conversation, and then Eustace also

18. For an account of this mysterious romance, possibly based on an idea supplied to Hawthorne by Melville, see Stewart, pp. 134–36.
19. Centenary, Vol. VI, p. 309.

disappears from the work. The tales do not bear the impress of his personality in their style, nor does Hawthorne present them as transcriptions of oral narrative. Divorced from speaker, setting, and audience, the myths become discrete formal units. The progressive movement provided in *A Wonder Book* by the movement of the frame through the seasons of the year is missing in *Tanglewood Tales*, and one cannot discern a principle of arrangement operating in its stead.

Although Hawthorne used Anthon's *Dictionary* as his source for both volumes, *Tanglewood Tales* embodies a radically changed conception of the Greek versions of the myths. Instead of seeing them as classically cold, Hawthorne now perceives them as "brimming over with everything that is most abhorrent to our Christianized moral-sense . . . hideous . . . melancholy and miserable . . . the sternest forms of grief that ever the world saw."[20] Gone is Greek lucidity, rationality, and seemliness; in its place Hawthorne discerns a literature of suffering and horror. Thus, where Eustace in *A Wonder Book* had faulted the myths for their elegant superiority to human warmth, Hawthorne criticizes them in *Tanglewood Tales* for their unrestrained immersion in the wildest and most woeful extremes of human experience. As the true author, behind his persona, Hawthorne must now admit the essential unfitness of these narratives for children and either relinquish his enterprise or alter not the form but the very substance of the myths: "Was such material the stuff that children's playthings should be made of! How were they to be purified? How was the blessed sunshine to be thrown into them?" (p. 179).

So in these myths Hawthorne found that he could not escape the tendency toward gloom that he had found dispiriting in his own romances. And the word "purified" raises the issue of suppression, which of course is the focus of his three

20. *Tanglewood Tales*, Centenary Edition, Vol. VII (1972), pp. 178–79. Subsequent references are given parenthetically in text.

long romances. In each romance, in a different way, he had worked out the idea of suppressed emotions continuing to exert morbid influences on the seemingly cheerful surface of active life. Dimmesdale's inexpressible guilt, the miasma of unacknowledged crime that wraps about the house of the seven gables, the secret relationships among Zenobia, Priscilla, Hollingsworth, Westervelt, and Moodie—in all three examples we see the idea of the destructive secret. In Hester and Maule Hawthorne created examples of human beings who, in a less repressive society, might be productively creative beings but here turn instead to subversion and perversion. Now in each of these myths for children Hawthorne found a core that had to be suppressed.

The preface to *Tanglewood Tales* justifies its suppressions in a variant of the theory implied in the *Wonder Book* debate between Eustace and Mr. Pringle. This is a theory asserting that the Greek myth is one version of a universal Ur-myth that must be articulated by every age in its own terms. In *A Wonder Book* Eustace insists that the original fables indeed possessed the full life lacking in the cold classical versions. Now in *Tanglewood Tales* he maintains that the originals did not possess the morally objectionable features of their Greek renditions. In order to eliminate the undesirable elements from the myths, he explains to Hawthorne, a narrator need only put himself in sympathy with "the innocent little circle, whose wide-open eyes are fixed so eagerly upon him. Thus the stories (not by any strained effort of the narrator's, but in harmony with their inherent germ) transform themselves, and reassume the shapes they might be supposed to possess in the pure childhood of the world." Proceeding on this theory, Eustace has discovered that the myths' immoralities "seemed to be a parasitical growth, having no essential connection with the original fable" (p. 179).

This phenomenon occurs, Eustace explains, because the original myths were created in the veritable Golden Age, when "Evil had never yet existed; and sorrow, misfortune, crime, were mere shadows." This age is long since over, and "children are now the only representatives of the men and women of that happy era; and therefore it is that we must raise the intellect and fancy to the level of childhood, in order to re-create the original myths" (p. 179). Of course, Hawthorne knew that the concept of the Golden Age was an invalid historical concept. Anthon's *Dictionary* is a scholarly work, describing the myths as products of a slow historical process in which narrative threads and ritual elements combined from the entire Mediterranean region as well as Asia Minor. Moreover, Hawthorne, who had observed his own children very closely and written about them with remarkable precision and honesty in his *American Notebooks*, knew that little people are Rabelaisian rather than pure and spiritual beings.

In fact, Hawthorne makes a point in the preface of attributing this unscholarly and naive theory of the origins of myth and of the race alike to the immaturity and inexperience of Eustace. "I let the youthful author talk, as much and as extravagantly as he pleased, and was glad to see him commencing life with such confidence in himself and his performances. A few years will do all that is necessary toward showing him the truth, in both respects. Meanwhile, it is but right to say, he does really appear to have overcome the moral objections against these fables; although at the expense of such liberties with their structure, as must be left to plead their own excuse, without any help from me" (pp. 179–80). Here Eustace joins the long line of discarded Hawthorne protagonists and personae: Fanshawe, Oberon, the teller of the *Twice-told Tales*, the resident of the Old Manse, Dimmesdale, Holgrave, and Coverdale. In no character yet, except Hester, had he been able to achieve a breadth of vision equivalent to what he himself saw in life. The disagreement between Hawthorne and Eustace, the patronizing tolerance of

Hawthorne's comment on the young man, show Hawthorne's dissatisfaction with "Eustace's" versions of the myths. Eustace was the mediator between content and reader in *A Wonder Book;* by undercutting his authority, Hawthorne undercuts the mood of *Tanglewood Tales*. Once more Hawthorne has pursued a literary intention to a point where its inadequacies overbalance its uses.

The result of this disaffection is a greatly altered tone in the second collection. The delicate lightness and sweetness of *A Wonder Book* gives way to sly parody and broad clowning. The sly parody occurs when Hawthorne's face is turned toward his audience, and he mocks their moral expectations even while satisfying them—for example, when he remarks in the midst of a lengthy description of Europa beguiled by the bull that "the bull had so much intelligence it is really wonderful to think of," or comments, "Well, my stars! Was there ever such a gentle, sweet, pretty, and amiable creature, as this bull, and ever such a nice play-mate for a little girl?" (p. 236). Children will not know what is going on, but surely Hawthorne is winking over their heads at the adult audience. These are dirty jokes, most extraordinary for the author, especially in this context.

The clowning is prominent in the alterations Hawthorne made to Anthon's versions, and can be seen by contrast to *A Wonder Book; Tanglewood Tales* almost begins to seem like a parody of the earlier volume. Without going so far as to assert that Hawthorne chose its six myths deliberately to duplicate elements of the first collection, we may observe close parallels in the stories—parellels that are oddly warped in the narrative process. The mighty Hercules of the *Wonder Book*'s "The Golden Apples" is a foolish blunderer in his adventures among the pygmies in *Tanglewood Tales*, and a buffoon Antaeus replaces the gothic Atlas. The simple but cloying relationship between King Midas and his daughter Marygold is thrown curiously askew when it is repeated with

King Pluto and Proserpina. Making Proserpina (like Europa) a little child, Hawthorne apparently avoids the sexual elements of the story; but the anomalous relationship he substitutes—with the stereotyped father-lover-protector figure of so much Victorian fiction—is fraught (as is the situation of the Veiled Lady) with sexual suggestiveness. The poetic relationship between magic beast and man in the story of Pegasus and Bellerophon and their joint victory over the Chimaera is cruelly parodied in the tale of Europa and the bull, and Cadmus's fruitless quest to find her.

The motif of hospitality and enchanted food and drink is wickedly twisted from the charming magic of the story of Baucis and Philemon, where the pitcher refills itself and the loaf is continually replenished, to the story of Circe, where the hostess is malevolent, the guests gluttonous, and the banquet a study in decadence. An important element in the story of Perseus is the supernatural helper: the cheerful and light-hearted Mercury (called Quicksilver) and his wise, serene sister Minerva offer aid, encouragement, and friendship to the quester. This motif develops ugly undercurrents in the story of Jason, who is helped by the dangerous and equivocal Medea. "If Jason had been capable of fearing anything, he would have been afraid of making this young princess his enemy; for, beautiful as she now looked, she might, the very next instant, become as terrible as the dragon that kept watch over the Golden Fleece" (p. 355).

Concealed or whitewashed sexual relationships run through all these stories, and viewed from the sunny clarity of *A Wonder Book* the second collection is decidedly ambiguous in its effects. In a word, these stories are not innocent; Hawthorne, in showing so obviously where and how he is making the tales morally unobjectionable, continually reminds us of what he is leaving out. In this way the repressed material enters and distorts the stories, precisely as such material does in the long romances. For example, when handling the relationship of Theseus and Ariadne, Hawthorne (or Eustace) remarks that "some low-minded people . . . have the face to say that this royal and honorable maiden did really flee away, under cover of the night, with the young stranger whose life she had preserved. They say, too, that Prince Theseus (who would have died sooner than wrong the meanest creature in the world) ungratefully deserted Ariadne, on a solitary island. . . . But, had the noble Theseus heard these falsehoods, he would have served their slanderous authors as he served the Minotaur!" (p. 210).

As an alternative to this "false" version, Eustace has Ariadne reject Theseus out of duty and love for her father. "Hard as you think his heart is, it would break to lose me. At first, King Minos will be angry; but he will soon forgive his only child, and by-and-by, he will rejoice, I know, that no more youths and maidens must come from Athens, to be devoured by the Minotaur! I have saved you, Theseus, as much for my father's sake as for your own. Farewell! Heaven bless you!" (p. 210). This sequence demonstrates the virtues of the revision by expounding on the wickedness of the original. It also reproduces the process of "improving" a myth by making its most objectionable passages the occasion for noble sentiments. But the gross sentimentality, the false emotions, and the coarse rhetoric together make the sequence a criticism of the process it illustrates. And behind it is the fact, known to all adult perusers of the volume, that the version alleged to be false is true.

We can conclude that the author of the stories in *Tanglewood Tales* is not after all the unsophisticated Eustace but the older, disenchanted Hawthorne. Apparently, the adult problems he thought to escape by retelling classical myths for children returned to him in these very myths—which, after all, are not tales for children. But what caused the change in his apprehension of the myths? Why did elegance in his view give way to sternness, marble coldness to grief? One can only speculate. I would suggest that the gloom of *The Blithedale Romance*, its insights into the tensions between genteel art and significant art, persisted in Hawthorne's mind. Coverdale, knowingly, and Eustace, ignorantly, were artists of the surface. Voices from the depths express themselves in twisted ways or in disguise. Four years later, when he resumed writing again, Hawthorne picked up the same themes just where he had left them.

৩ 7 ৡ

English and Italian Years
1853–1859

During his years as consul in Liverpool, Hawthorne confined his literary activity to writing in his journals. He ultimately wrote some 300,000 words in his *English Notebooks*, the rough equivalent of a thousand pages of typescript. The material is copious but limited in scope when compared with the journals he had kept in the United States from 1835. In the *American Notebooks* he put down ideas for plots and germs for sketches; he and his wife kept a joint journal immediately after their marriage, to celebrate and preserve their first months of extraordinary happiness; when Sophia was away from home, Hawthorne wrote full accounts of his days for her to read when she returned; and he recorded with marvelous precision and humor the activities of his very young children, perhaps for parental delectation in later years. The American journals thus are like a scrapbook, in which items of personal value and interest are laid away without an organizing intention.

In contrast, the *English Notebooks* are much more methodical and much less personal. The writer's intention to build up a backlog of raw material for future treatment is evident everywhere. England is the exclusive subject—England as it might appear to any perceptive observer. Although he knows that any record is limited by the observer, Hawthorne seems to be trying to overcome the limitations of point of view by refraining from subjective commentary. There is little reflection, meditation, fanciful association, or generalization. The work Hawthorne was trying to accomplish in his *English Notebooks* is such as can be achieved today much less laboriously with a camera.

When, years later, Hawthorne turned to these notebooks to construct a series of travel essays, he added a good deal of commentary to the descriptions, but in so doing gave a false impression of his journals to those critics who think he merely mined them for his sketches of England. Comparative generalizations about the differences between the American and English characters or cultures do appear in the notebooks from time to time, but not with such frequency or intensity as to indicate that Hawthorne was collecting material for a study of contrasting manners. Put side by side, the generalizations are often inconsistent, suggesting that Hawthorne had not developed, and was not trying to develop, a system of ideas about British and American national types. His commentary is spontaneous, shifting, and held to a minimum. Hawthorne did not want to restrict his English material to such responses as he might initially make to it. He wanted to keep his options open, to have material that could be used in a variety of ways.

When Randall Stewart edited the notebooks and published them in 1941, he approached them with the assumption that Hawthorne intended them as a statement made by an American about England. He assembled strings of quotations to support the idea that, although Hawthorne dutifully enunciated patriotic and chauvinistic sentiments from time to time, the deeper response to England was a yearning attraction. "England both attracted and repelled," Stewart wrote. It attracted "the imaginative writer, and repelled the American patriot. . . . He was, as we have seen, sensitively responsive to the charms of England's storied and poetical associations; he was also loyal to America's institutions, and, on occasion, indignant toward America's detractors. England, therefore, was an object at once of love and resentment. The psychological result for Hawthorne was an acute mental conflict."[1]

Stewart's approach was much controlled by the paradigmatic example of Henry James, of whom in some sense Hawthorne was made a forerunner—indeed, James himself in his biographical study of Hawthorne claimed the romancer as a literary parent. But the situation is highly overdramatized in Stewart's account. His examples, convincing as they may be by themselves, constitute the entire collection of statements that can be submitted as evidence of Hawthorne's sensitivity to English "storied and poetical associations," and in the context of 300,000 words they make a thin showing. Moreover, some of Hawthorne's very strongest statements of "attachment" occur in the context of a visit to old Boston and imply more an attachment to new Boston than the old country!

Statistically speaking, that is to say, there is no case for Hawthorne's having felt toward England as toward his own home; and, read afresh, the notebooks present a good deal of evidence to the contrary. One looks in vain for an articulation of attraction to, or even awareness of, the density and richness of English life as an interpenetration of past and present. Hawthorne shows very little aesthetic sensitivity to objects, and he approached English architecture for the most part as an element of landscape rather than a symbol of history or an example of aesthetic culture. One finds no Jamesian complaints about a contrasting American bareness, although Hawthorne does delight in the domesticated picturesqueness of English landscape. Landscape and climate seem to have been his chief preoccupations. Not until the very end of his stay, when he spent many successive days at a fine arts exhibition at Manchester, did he show the least responsiveness to paint-

1. *The English Notebooks*, ed. Randall Stewart (reprint; New York: Russell & Russell, 1962), p. xl. Subsequent references are given parenthetically in text.

ing, and the glory of fine interior decoration forever escaped him.

His attitude toward English titles and the appurtenances of aristocracy was much closer to Mark Twain's than Henry James's. He had a democrat's impatience with distinctions based on birth, and he could not understand how an Englishman could feel proud of the existence of classes above him. Americans who went to the consulate obsessed with the belief that they had claim to an English title or an English estate struck him as lunatics, and irritated him beyond words. They were living examples of the madmen who had peopled his early fiction. That Hawthorne should try to make one of their number the hero of an English romance testifies to his underlying hostility to the country—not at all to an attraction.

The *English Notebooks*, I would argue, have very little intrinsic importance; Stewart's assertion that they are "the fullest and richest book ever written by an American in England" (p. v) does not hold up. Basically, the notebooks are not a "book" at all. But the journals are important for their revelations about Hawthorne's attitudes to England as these attitudes bear on the romance that he tried but was unable to write and on the collection of essays that he did succeed in fashioning from the material. Although Hawthorne did see England as a country with a past that persisted symbolically, here and there, in the present, he chiefly perceived England as the most massively actual and materialistic culture he could ever have imagined. Repeatedly, he characterizes the English as a "beef and ale" people, by which he means to suggest their physical substantiality and their lack of imagination.

English life was indeed much denser than American life, but not because the penumbra of associations enriched the actual. On the contrary, English life was richer in the complexity of its actual texture. Hawthorne understood England as a country more industrial, more urban, less wild and primitive, than America. In a word, he saw it as more modern, and his perception might be called directly opposed to the Jamesian view. Castles, nobility, liveried footmen, and crown jewels he dutifully observed but dismissed as irrelevant anachronisms. He made almost no researches into English history. He confined his descriptions to the immediately visible. More than anything else he was fascinated—attracted and repelled—by the street life of the English poor. Influenced perhaps by his readings of Elizabeth Gaskell and Charles Dickens, he walked the Liverpool and London slum districts for hours on end, marveling at the tenacity and vitality of life there, and appalled by its dirt, disease, and promiscuous crowding. His New England conception of character as a private and impenetrable preserve was assaulted everywhere by the display. But he had not developed the literary abilities to handle such scenes.

Hawthorne resigned his consulship as of August 31, 1857, and after the arrival of his successor he left for the continent on January 5, 1858. He had written no literary work except a brief sketch about Samuel Johnson and Uttoxeter, published in 1857. As soon as the family was settled in Rome, Hawthorne began to write a romance set in England. His main character was to be an American tourist; he had not the presumption to try to reproduce the English mind, whose beef-and-aleness in any event was not suited for the central place in romance. The only reference in the *English Notebooks* to the plot of this romance occurs in an entry for April 12, 1855 (p. 107), where, without preface of any sort, Hawthorne wrote, "The original emigrant to America may have carried away with him a family secret, whereby it was in his power . . . to have brought about the ruin of the family. . . . The hero of the Romance comes to England, and finds that, by means of this secret, he still has it in his power to procure the downfall of the family."

This entry is not attached to any incident or setting. It expresses a wish for revenge that will be familiar to any person who has felt at the mercy of a strange and unsympathetic culture, or has been frustrated by a foreign surrounding. All in-experienced visitors to a strange country are apt to feel insignificant, ineffective, and unappreciated, and retaliatory fantasies in such situations are very common. Hawthorne's entry embodies such a fantasy. He did not seem to have any idea what the family secret might be; the idea remains unde-veloped in the entry. Nothing is said of an intention for his hero to claim an English title or an English estate. This is important. The pure germ of the romance originated not in his appreciation of the English, but in his pique that they did not appreciate him.

For the setting of his romance Hawthorne selected scenes from his journal entries,[2] and for the location of the English family an old English house called Smithell's Hall. He first refers to the Hall in an entry dated April 7, 1855, after a dinner party where he met the owners, a couple named Ains-worth. The house had a legend attached to a peculiar reddish-brown indentation in one flagstone on the threshold: this was said to be the print of the bloody footstep of a martyr. The legend interested Hawthorne (p. 106), but he could not have had this place in mind when he noted in his journal the plot line of a family secret because he had not yet visited the Hall, nor does the entry (April 12) refer to a legend.

He visited Smithell's Hall on August 23, 1855, and recorded his visit on the 25th (pp. 193–99). He was impressed by the age of the house and the massiveness of the ancient structure. He admired the medieval dining hall. He paid much attention to the stone and its legend. But when he began to write his romance, he ignored the actual legend, which was tied to English religious history, and invented instead (or tried to invent) a purely gothic, ahistorical legend. He had no use for the owners of Smithell's Hall, who were typical English meat

2. For detailed listings of journal sources, see Edward H. Davidson, *Hawthorne's Last Phase* (New Haven: Yale University Press, 1949), pp. 13–32.

to his perception. "John Bull cannot make himself fine," he wrote of this couple, "whatever he may put on. He is a rough animal, and incapable of high-polish; and his female is well adapted to him" (p. 197).

The journal entries provided very little material for a romance, and it might be predicted from them that he would have difficulty if he tried to write one. But he had evidently committed himself to writing something about England, and as a writer of romances he would inevitably turn his gifts to what ought to have been a promising subject. To the end of his life he remained unwilling to admit that he could not make a romance out of England. Of course, when he sat down to begin it in Italy he could not foresee that it would come to be the great albatross of his last years. Still, from the beginning it did not have much drawing power. His mind slipped away from it. Italian impressions flooded in on him. He worked on the romance during April and May 1857. But in April he had seen a copy of the *Faun* of Praxiteles,[3] in May his English romance developed an Italianate villain, in June he wrote nothing on it, and in July he began *The Marble Faun*. Italy struck his imagination in a wholly different way from England and released powers that England inhibited.

The fragments of the unfinished English romance were published after Hawthorne's death as *The Ancestral Footstep*. In format the work is different from anything extant of earlier date. It is a series of dated journal entries in which the romance is partly written, partly summarized, partly discussed, partly speculated upon. As his son-in-law George Parsons Lathrop wrote in an introductory note to the fragments, "It would not be safe to conclude, from the large amount of preliminary writing . . . that Hawthorne always adopted this laborious mode of making several drafts of a book. On the contrary, it is understood that his habit was to mature a design

3. *The Marble Faun*, pp. xx–xxi.

so thoroughly in his mind before attempting to give it actual existence on paper that but little rewriting was needed."[4] Actually, the brevity of incubation time and rapidity of composition of the four major romances argue more for Hawthorne's maturing his design as he went along than before sitting down to compose. But the point is that he was little prone to false steps, and the procedures used for *The Ancestral Footstep* argue for a contrasting lack of imaginative certainty about his direction.

In the course of his work on *The Ancestral Footstep* Hawthorne went back to the beginning twice, so that, in effect, the story is told three times in different versions. New starts were necessitated by the introduction of new material for which there had been no preparation. The second version gives space to the relationship between hero (Middleton) and heroine (Alice) as well as to the latter's character. Neither of these elements was more than touched on in the first telling. At the end of the second version, however, Hawthorne found himself with an unsuitably developed antagonist, and so he went back to try again. Now he produced an Italianate villain who so modified his original design that he needed yet a fourth version.

Those aspects of the story that remain constant through the three tellings, or are not in conflict with other aspects, probably represent the fixed part of Hawthorne's plan. The hero is an American named Middleton, vacationing in England. He gets the idea of trying to locate his ancestral family; the founder of his family is known to have emigrated from England under mysterious circumstances that have become lost in legend. The American's half-serious explorations set in motion a chain of dire events in his English family, events precipitated by the discovery that Middleton himself, and not the present incumbent, is the rightful heir to title and property.

4. *The Ancestral Footstep*, Riverside Edition, Vol. XI, pp. 435–36. Further references are given parenthetically in text.

The chain of events in the present would repeat the events of the past that had forced the ancestor to leave England. Aghast at the evil that his fooling with the past has inadvertently caused, Middleton "resigns all the claims which he might now assert, and returns, arm in arm with Alice. . . . The estate takes a passage into the female line, and the old name becomes extinct, nor does Middleton seek to continue it by resuming it in place of the one long ago assumed by his ancestor. Thus he and his wife become the Adam and Eve of a new epoch, and the fitting missionaries of a new social faith, of which there must be continual hints through the book" (p. 490).

The chief intention behind this romance, one can plainly see, is to criticize the false attachment to England that leads so many Americans astray, as Hawthorne had himself seen at Liverpool. Far from embodying a yearning attraction to England, the romance satirizes that attraction in the person of its deluded protagonist. At the same time, Hawthorne must avoid making his hero so deluded that he will be unfit for his final role as the American Adam. He must walk a delicate line between making him overly deluded, on the one hand, and admirable to the point that his delusion will not show, on the other. The romance is a story of enlightenment, in which the hero sees the error of his ways and rectifies his behavior. But he cannot be too far gone in his error.

What Hawthorne tried to do at first, then, was to touch very lightly on Middleton's obsession and to make the evil events happen in such a way that the protagonist could not possibly be held responsible for them. Middleton is to learn his lesson without having become deeply implicated in the story. But the natural result of a complex development is to implicate the hero in the action. Hawthorne's "solution" to his plotting dilemma was to eliminate the adversary as soon as he appeared on the scene. Middleton is wandering around the grounds of his ancestral home; the incumbent squire does not know who Middleton is but is enraged at his trespassing. He waves his gun about in a wild, threatening way and accidentally shoots himself dead with it. This representation of the necessary evil event keeps Middleton uninvolved to be sure, but it also terminates the story. And Hawthorne wanted more from his four years in England than one short moralized fiction. The solution threw the baby out with the bath water, so he tried again.

He started on a second version that would permit a much greater expansion of the squire's character as well as a relationship between Middleton and the squire. As he worked on his English character, he created, in Davidson's words, "a very commonplace landowner,"[5] the texture of whose life afforded no aperture for the insertion of a gothic catastrophe. In fact, his bluff heartiness casts Middleton in a morally ambiguous light. Middleton himself "sometimes regretted that he had not listened to those forebodings which had warned him back on the eve of his enterprise," but he has become "careless of the result in respect to its good or evil" (pp. 487–88).

It would not do, as I have said above, to make Middleton so deluded that he would seem (like so many of Hawthorne's protagonists in the early stories of this mode) either criminal or insane, so Hawthorne had to try again. In his third version, he makes Middleton's motives entirely pure. The American "felt as if he were the original emigrant who, long resident on a foreign shore, had now returned, with a heart brimful of tenderness, to revisit the scenes of his youth, and renew his tender relations with those who shared his own blood" (p. 493). The "wild American character" (p. 451) has become innocent, and the English squire has taken on Middleton's fanaticism. English squires, however, are made fanatics in a gothic scheme with great difficulty, so Hawthorne hit on the plan of making him a recently repatriated Englishman who had been raised in Italy and who brings with him a full complement of Italian characteristics. This was a solution of sorts,

5. Davidson, p. 23.

but it did not appear to satisfy Hawthorne, for after the third try he put the romance aside to write *The Marble Faun*, which came from his pen with characteristic fluency.

Clearly, something in the English material was wrong for Hawthorne. The dilemma was that, from the vantage point of his current concerns, its "meaning" was either false or trivial. The purpose of *The Ancestral Footstep* was to make a statement about the necessity for Americans to overcome their self-indulgent and unhealthy attachments to England. America represents a clean break with the past and the founding of a new social order. To try to reverse the course of history is retrogressive and psychologically destructive. But none of the three major romances allows the possibility of either a radical break with the past or the rapid establishment of a new social order. *The House of the Seven Gables* shows that the radical hero is far more likely to be absorbed into the old system than to begin afresh. *The Blithedale Romance* demonstrates how, even without social pressures, the socialized psyche would reconstruct the old order. In *The Scarlet Letter* there is no past, properly speaking, but the views of the old patriarchs are incorporated in the social institutions that repress the young. Whether we know it or not, and whether we like it or not, the past exists in the forms of the present. Proof that Hawthorne still felt in 1858 as he had in the early years of the decade exists in *The Marble Faun*, which takes up the theme of the guilt incurred by the radical hero when he overthrows the old order; it is probably the most deeply anguished of all four of these "radical romances."

The Ancestral Footstep is based on the assumption that a clean break not only is possible, but has already occurred. Middleton has already been severed from England by the action of his ancestor. His return is willful and gratuitous. He has alternatives denied to the protagonists of the other romances: he can choose to attach himself to his past or not; obviously, then, he is not attached to it at the moment.

Throughout the text of *The Ancestral Footstep* run images of a broken thread, a sundered chain, and two unjoined electric wires. When the break is repaired, the current will begin to flow. But in the major romances the thread is not broken—it *cannot* be broken. The situation is precisely the reverse of that in *The Ancestral Footstep*.

If Hawthorne felt, as he was writing *The Ancestral Footstep*, that the past was still continuing to influence the present—and the evidence of *The Marble Faun* is that he did—then he was basing his English romance on an assumption he did not believe. If he thought that the past had actually ceased to affect the present, then he was presenting as his hero one of those lunatics who peopled his early stories. He felt little sympathy for this protagonist, but his design required sympathy. The surface praise for Middleton, ambiguous as it is, is undercut still further by the metaphors in which Middleton's actions are described. Middleton "remembered to have heard or read, how that once an old pit had been dug open, in which were found the remains of persons that, as the shuddering bystanders traditionally remembered, had died of an ancient pestilence; and out of that old grave had come a new plague, that slew the far-off progeny of those who had first died by it. Might not some fatal treasure like this, in a moral view, be brought to light by the secret into which he had so strangely been drawn?" (p. 442). This image attributes to the past the same baneful influence that is attributed to it in Hawthorne's other mature romances; whether that force shall be felt or not is, however, a matter of choice. But any character who persists, as Middleton does, in his behavior after having perceived this truth, is a dangerous fool. Try as he does, Hawthorne cannot keep Middleton from becoming an obsessed monomaniac, acute enough to realize what he is doing but powerless to stop himself. As he articulates this theme, Hawthorne sounds like Governor Randolph chastizing old Esther Dudley in 1839 (see pp. 76–77): "The moral, if any moral were to be gathered from these petty and wretched circumstances, was, 'Let the past alone; do not seek to renew it; press on to higher and better things,—at all events, to other things; and be assured that the right way can never be that which leads you back to the identical shapes that you long ago left behind. Onward, onward, onward' " (pp. 488–89).

Since Hawthorne was reviving a plot design that he had long ago left behind, this apostrophe might have been meant for himself. The English material seemed to shape itself into the form of outmoded concerns. The use of such words as "petty" and "wretched" above suggests Hawthorne's acute discomfort with what he was doing. His difficulty is plain to see. If the English past is really sundered from the American present, then it is not the "past" in the sense in which it had engaged his powers in his long romances. It is a purely gratuitous past, the product of a sentimental and self-indulgent fancy. The true past continues, whether we will or not, to live in the present. England than cannot be used as the basis for the sort of romance Hawthorne had most recently been writing, and therefore, Hawthorne's work reflects his frustrated sense of the triviality of this enterprise. He was no longer interested in his old themes, and England gave him no symbols for his new interests.

But Italy gave him what England did not. In Rome as well as in the Italian hill towns Hawthorne saw a persisting antiquity that visually dominated all impressions of modern Italian life. Rome was the house of the seven gables writ large: everywhere in the city people carried forward their lives within the shapes bequeathed to them by an ancestry stretching back to the beginning of time. Rome was thus to Hawthorne, as England had not been, the tangible realization of a profoundly held idea, and it struck him with the shock of recognition that enabled him, in *The Marble Faun*, to assimilate it entirely into his own vision. As he wrote in the first chapter of this last completed romance, in Rome there is "a vague sense of ponderous remembrances; a perception of such weight and density in a by-gone life, of which this spot was the centre, that the present moment is pressed down or crowded out, and our individual affairs and interests are but half as real, here, as elsewhere. . . . Side by side with the massiveness of the Roman Past, all matters, that we handle or dream of, now-a-days, look evanescent and visionary alike."[6]

To be sure, the real existence of a city that so palpably represented Hawthorne's deepest belief was not an altogether happy matter for one who experienced the pressures exerted by the past as restrictive, distorting, and unhealthy. But Hawthorne also discovered in Rome the realization of his own counterstatement: in antique and Renaissance art he found evidence of another kind of imaginative reality—the creative and artistic forces that resist the enormous pressures of history. And so he opens *The Marble Faun* in the sculpture gallery of the Capitol, where antique statues stand "still shining in the undiminished majesty and beauty of their ideal life" (p. 5).

The Marble Faun is by far the most complex and ambitious of Hawthorne's mature romances. It records the distorting effect of repressive institutions on human life. It attempts to discover the origins of reverence for the authoritarian within the psyche. It postulates art as the expression of an erotic counterforce to civilization, and chronicles the struggle between them. It carries its investigation of all these concerns beyond the bounds of the earlier romances and comes to conclusions even more anguished. It is especially forceful in its articulation of the dilemma of the modern artist. Like *The House of the Seven Gables* and *The Blithedale Romance*, and also *The Scarlet Letter* in part, *The Marble Faun* is the story of a failed artist. But the implication of *The Blithedale Romance*—that artists fail because society will not permit strong

6. *The Marble Faun*, p. 6. Subsequent references are given parenthetically in text.

art to exist—is much more the explicit subject of *The Marble Faun*.

Kenyon is greatly superior to Coverdale in the vigor and scope of his talent. He is a truly promising American artist. His failure results directly from his acceptance of the social view (represented by Hilda) that great art is inferior to genteel art, because it is too crude, coarse, and unmannerly for a polished and improved civilization. Classical and Renaissance art is great because it is not civilized art or, at least, is much less civilized than modern art. But modern civilization is an indisputable improvement over civilizations of the past, and therefore has no place for these less civil productions. Kenyon's tragedy is that he accepts this popular rationale without believing it, because he cannot live without the love and approval of one who embodies this belief herself.

Hester, we remember, found herself stigmatized in a society that refused to recognize the private and personal emotions which, when realized in action, must be labeled sins. Hester thought herself the only person like herself in the world, and hardly dared to credit her intuitions that all around her people were living in their emotions much as she did. Granted the existence beneath the orderly social surface of the turbulent private life, would society be better or worse if it developed a language through which this life might be permissibly expressed? Or was society founded precisely on the suppression of the private? For the Puritan elders it certainly was; preoccupied, in *The Scarlet Letter*, with establishing a lasting settlement in the wilderness, they saw no possibility of survival unless individual need was suppressed and individual force channeled into socially sanctioned forms. Yet *The Scarlet Letter* concludes on a note of qualified historical optimism. Gradually, as necessity pressed less and less on the community, it might relax to include a fuller expression in public life of the private, the various, the individual. As evidence for this hope, Hawthorne suggested the Old World, which had evolved to a condition of far greater tolerance of individual differences.

The House of the Seven Gables also expresses a qualified optimism. If the community had expanded to receive Hester, Holgrave contracted in order to be received into the community; yet even in his reduced state he was a clearly better figure of authority than Pyncheon. *The Blithedale Romance*, however, offers a bleak view, because, although society was apparently permitting a great range of personal expression, it was actually allowing a set of conventional pleasures that served to pacify rather than liberate. *The Marble Faun* likewise has no suggestion of a true historical progress toward individualism. It is suggested that the modern age is more repressive than earlier times, and that the modern age justifies its own repressions by labeling them social refinements and advances. Modern society is built on the foundation of a great hypocrisy about human nature, and it offers its hypocrisy as a virtue. Is such a civilization really an advance? Each artist must answer this question as he can. If he feels it to be real progress, he must regard great art as an expression of the childhood of the race and define his own genteel productions as superior. If he feels classical art to be manifestly greater than anything attainable by the contemporary artist, he must see his own civilization as a decline and accept an irrevocable sense of separation from the complacent contemporary culture. At the end of *The Marble Faun* Kenyon finds himself unable to sustain the degree of social criticism and isolation that goes with acknowledging the greatness of art of the past. He abandons his position, and Hawthorne finds it a tragedy for modern art.

The Marble Faun is designed as a sequence of parallels and contrasts between two couples. Kenyon and Hilda are modern Americans who represent socialized beings. The obscure, ancient origins of Donatello and Miriam link them to the beginning of human history. Although it is clearly impossible that any presocial beings should actually exist in the present, Hawthorne comes as close as he can to the idea of such a being in Donatello. Newly arrived from the country, Donatello is certainly not civilized at the story's outset. Through his attachment to Miriam, however, he is initiated into the civilized human condition. This story is only a segment of the romance, for it is contained within the larger story of Kenyon's comprehension of, and response to, Donatello's fate.

Ultimately, all the events of the romance fall into place as aspects of Kenyon's experience. According to how he makes use of his experience, he will become a great artist or he will not. At first open and responsive to the lessons he is learning, he panics and draws back when he discovers that the value system implied in Donatello's history is incompatible with Hilda's values. If he accepts Donatello, he must lose Hilda. Like Hawthorne's other protagonists under pressure, Kenyon is too socialized a man to endure long without the iron framework of familiar institutions. With some regret, but more relief, he leaves his intellectual wanderings to come home to Hilda. Donatello and Miriam are safely stowed behind their labels as penitent sinners; there, like Hester behind her *A*, they represent no further threat to the values of the group.

"Did Adam fall, that we might ultimately rise to a far loftier Paradise than his?"

"Oh, hush!" cried Hilda, shrinking from him with an expression of horrour [*sic*] which wounded the poor, speculative sculptor to the soul. "This is terrible; and I could weep for you, if you indeed believe it. Do not you perceive what a mockery your creed makes, not only of all religious sentiment, but of moral law, and how it annuls and obliterates whatever precepts of Heaven are written deepest within us? You have shocked me beyond words!"

"Forgive me, Hilda!" exclaimed the sculptor, startled by her agitation; "I never did believe it! But the mind wanders wild and wide; and, so lonely as I live and work, I have neither pole-star above, nor light of cottage-windows here below, to bring me home. . . . Oh, Hilda, guide me home!" [Pp. 460–61]

The romance falls into three parts of roughly equal length. The first, which runs through chapter 19, introduces all the characters, themes, and symbols, and closes with the chief event of the story: Donatello's murder of Miriam's phantom persecutor. The second section chronicles Donatello's inner struggle after the event, his growth, maturation, and eventual reconciliation with Miriam in chapter 35. At the same time, and more importantly, this section shows Kenyon's role in Donatello's development—his support and guidance—which implicates him in Donatello's story. For much of the section Donatello is in a severe mental depression, given over to guilt and self-loathing. But Kenyon intuitively perceives the murder as an inevitable rite of passage and even an act of heroism (p. 384). He quite deliberately guides the despairing hero back to the light, and arranges for Miriam to meet them in Perugia. At this reunion, under the benign eye of the statue of Pope Julian, the story of Donatello and Miriam comes to a logical, and a happy, ending. It is at least possible that chapter 35 was originally designed to conclude the romance. The chapter has a heavy oratorical rhetoric like the last scaffold scene in *The Scarlet Letter* and the conclusion to *The House of the Seven Gables*, and at thirty-five chapters *The Marble Faun* was already the longest work Hawthorne had written. With Miriam and Donatello brought together, and Kenyon hastening off to Rome and Hilda, the reader might anticipate a second happy union and close the book contented.

But in the last third of the romance Hawthorne in a sense begins again, following Kenyon back to Rome and through his mental crisis as he now suffers the consequences of his sympathetic participation in Donatello's "crime." Hilda disappears, and Kenyon cannot live without her. Like Dimmesdale returned from the forest, Kenyon finds the clarity of his moral vision dissipated in the context of civilization. The issue that connects Donatello's act to Kenyon's is what has been identified repeatedly in the criticism as the "fortunate fall." Miltonic (and Dantean) echoes abound in *The Marble Faun*, but the issue is really just like that in *The Scarlet Letter*. A certain act is stigmatized by society as a crime. It is experienced psychologically as a sin—that is, it produces guilt. But is it really a sin in an absolute sense? Without a divinity present to make his commandments clearly known, and with society claiming, but by no means demonstrating, divine sanction for its judgments, the question remains open. Each "sinner" must work the problem out in solitude and suffering.

Now it might appear that a murder would belong to the small category of acts clearly and absolutely evil, so that Donatello would be unquestionably a sinful man. But the penumbra of allusions surrounding his act prevents one from coming to this conclusion. The persecutor comes to life in the catacombs when the friends are touring them, and he thereafter follows Miriam about like a vengeful ghost. Posing as her model, he is a maniac and a specter of evil; her thralldom is horrifying. Because the model is characterized as a living phantom, his murder does not strike one as the taking of a life. Donatello's act is assimilated into the heroic tradition wherein innocent maidens are rescued from monsters, ogres, and demons. In *A Wonder Book* and *Tanglewood Tales* Hawthorne presented five examples of heroic monster-slayers: Jason, Theseus, Perseus, Hercules, and Bellerophon. He knew that such slayers are never criminals, always heroes. Guido's painting of the archangel Michael as slayer of the monster Satan carries the pagan tradition into a Christian context; and when he invents a drawing of the painting in which Satan has the model's face, Hawthorne puts Donatello into the tradition as well.

Many of the monsters who devour innocent youths and maidens in classic myths are associated with evil, tyrannical kings like Minos. With the Cenci allusions—especially as these are filtered through the Shelley play—Hawthorne also makes such an association. Cenci was certainly a tyrannical persecutor of the young and he flourished (in Shelley's representation) because he was protected by the Pope, a politically corrupt figure. The Pope supported Cenci because he was a member of the ruling class; he aimed to make sure that those who had power kept it. By identifying radical libertarianism with youth and repressive despotism with age, Shelley had made both a political and a psychological statement.

The Marble Faun echoes Shelley's meanings. By making the model a Capuchin monk Hawthorne links him to the Roman power structure and turns his murder into a crime against the state. The power structure, associated with the great weight and age of Rome (the model is persistently identified with each antique sight in the city), becomes a symbol of the "fathers" in the sense of elders. The idea of patriarchy is of course embodied in priestly nomenclature. To the elders are opposed the passion and spontaneity of the young Miriam and Donatello, their sheer wish to live, to love, to express themselves. The wish, and the behavior it occasions, are harmless in themselves but, forbidden by society, involve defiance of the rules.

Self-expressive behavior, then, is not evil in an absolute sense. It is defined that way by a power structure that sees such behavior as a threat. If in fact such behavior really threatens the power structure we do not know; of course, it becomes threatening in the circumstances, because it defies authority. Thus, the authorities create the situation that threatens them. Despite the move across the ocean and into an entirely different symbolic vocabulary, the symbol system is precisely the same in *The Marble Faun* as in *The Scarlet Letter*. The Puritan and Catholic oligarchies are one and the same.

Miriam plays much the same role in regard to Donatello that Hester did for Dimmesdale. She is, in fact, much less developed as an independent character, and is much more a functional figure in relation to others, than Hester was. She is another representative of passion, creativity, and spontaneity, also like Zenobia although less flawed. She is supposed to be the most beautiful woman in the world. As a woman she stands for the full idea of womanhood that must be accepted if man is to do her justice and grow to his own fullest expression. Like Hester in the forest, or Zenobia at the outset of *The Blithedale Romance*, she suggests a richer and more generous humanity than that permitted under the sterile patriarchy (in the case of a Catholic hierarchy, the sterility is more than metaphorical). And she may also stand for an alienated part of the masculine psyche—aspects of tenderness and passion that the male has repressed and needs to recover to be a whole person. For although there is a certain appeal in Donatello as a faun, there is also something contemptible about him. The many animal allusions state plainly that he is not quite human. He is a case of arrested development, a curiosity. His feelings for Miriam are the agency by which he is transformed from monstrously overgrown child to adult.

Familiar as we are by now with Hawthorne's meanings in the romances of the 1850s, we do not have to ask why society considers this transformation evil and why it defines the precipitating act a crime. But we do have to ask why Donatello, who is not a socialized man like Coverdale and Dimmesdale, feels guilty after he has committed the deed. Both Coverdale and Dimmesdale start as social products and cannot break through in any sustained way to a condition of inner freedom. But Donatello has passed his life outside society. He should be able, if anyone can, to escape the recoil into guilt. But because Miriam is deeply bound up in the social order, Donatello is implicated in society through his feelings for her. The model materializes as a consequence of Donatello's growing passion for Miriam; he is the symbol of the guilt that shadows sexuality. Thus, the crux of Donatello's deed is not murder but sex.

The fall of man, in Judeo-Christian tradition, has of course long been associated with the awakening of human sexuality. After the murder Miriam and Donatello spend the night together, and we may assume that they become lovers. Then it turns out that the model is only "apparently" dead; his corpse bleeds in their presence the next morning, and thereafter he assumes a greater reality, as punishing agent in Donatello's mind, than he ever possessed when he simply followed Miriam about. For Hawthorne in *The Marble Faun* the human being—or more precisely the human male, since the female, as we shall see, has a different development—is not adult unless his life has sexual expression. But sexual expression in the modern world is necessarily accompanied by the profound ambivalence that modern culture feels toward sex. Guilt, therefore, is an aspect of adulthood in modern society.

Guiltless sex, which once existed—the testimony of antique sculpture is clear on this point, and the Monte Beni males have been enjoying a promiscuous existence for centuries—is no longer attainable; to avoid guilt one must avoid sex, in which case one exists as an incomplete or puerile human being. The fall of man, then, lies in the event that makes him perceive sex as shameful. Once sex is perceived in this way, man can be expected to create his own repressive social institutions. Because he wishes to punish himself, and to suppress his offending sexuality, he invents the patriarchy. But what has taken place in human history to charge the sex act with this dire import?

At first glance, the text might appear to support an Oedipal interpretation like that constructed by Freud in *Moses and Monotheism*. The youth kills his father in order to possess the mother, and then feels a guilt that is nothing more than the fear of being punished. Because he is a primitive being, the young man believes that the dead have the power to avenge themselves, and therefore the fact that he has killed the enemy augments rather than relieves his anxiety. Some sort of incest motif is certainly implied in the layer of Cenci allusions, and in the initial relationship of Donatello to Miriam, which is so patently that of a small boy to his mother. Yet the explanation works only partially, for it does not explain the transition from guilt-free early social structures to the guilt-ridden organization of modern society.

Once the patriarchal society has been constructed—however that comes about—the sex act becomes even more guilt-ridden because it is now hedged round with social prohibitions. Most important, sex means a surrender to female power that, however temporary, and while perfectly natural in a matriarchy, is abhorrent in a patriarchy and indeed a threat to it. Every sexual act in modern times represents, for the male, the momentary triumph of the archaic and outlawed power of the female. Donatello's story, then, embodies that crucial—and, so far as I can see, unexplained—moment in history when sex (either in fact or in fancy understood as the union with the mother) ceased to be a joy for the male and became instead a horror. That moment is the fall of man, and there is no returning to the innocent ages preceding it. The question for modern man is whether he will be able to transcend that fall or will forever remain its victim.

Donatello's first impulse is to get as far away from Miriam, whom he now sees as the instigator, as he possibly can. But in returning to prepatriarchal Monte Beni he actually enters her kingdom. Her presence is felt all around the grounds, whose fertility and subtropical sunshine are associated with her. She even has a shrine in the manor, where, it seems, "the sun was magically imprisoned, and must always shine" (p. 279). To escape, Donatello climbs the ancient, masculine tower which reaches away from nature and earth but symbolizes neither enlightenment nor freedom. It is a cold, dark, cheerless monument to death. The dynamics of Donatello's guilt, as it pushes him toward a punitive authoritarian superstructure as well as patriarchal celibacy, are seen in his new, obsessive Catholicism. He decides to become a monk. Thereby he will repudiate his sexuality and take on the role (the model, too, was a monk) of Miriam's oppressor instead of her liberator.

And yet, even at the height of his alienation from Miriam, Donatello repeats his crime. At the top of his tower a green plant grows, existing mysteriously in an ambience that would appear to offer it absolutely no support. Kenyon, the teacher and guide, asks Donatello what lesson he can draw from the little shrub. " 'It teaches me nothing,' said the simple Donatello, stooping over the plant, and perplexing himself with a minute scrutiny. 'But here was a worm that would have killed it; an ugly creature, which I will fling over the battlements' " (p. 259). Miriam, like the plant, is life. If it is a crime to defend her, it is suicide to deny her.

While Donatello struggles in this morass, Kenyon enters his story as the apparent embodiment of an enlightened, liberal view. Kenyon came to Rome naively believing that Victorian "ideal" art was the culmination of artistic progress through the centuries. At home in America he had industriously and profitably turned out a series of busts of public men of the day. But in the presence of classical art the true artist in him emerges; he recognizes its greatness and is inspired by it. He also knows at least on an intuitive level that he cannot achieve this greatness himself simply by imitation. He must re-create classical goals by modern means of expression. He cannot, for example, sculpture nude figures as the Greeks did, because modern people differ from ancient Greeks in their perception of the body. Now although classical art is superior for precisely those qualities that genteel art congratulates itself on having surpassed, Kenyon at first thinks he can succeed in his aim. His conviction that modern times are compatible with great art parallels his belief that Donatello can be reconciled to Miriam within the precincts of the patriarchy.

It looks at first as though Kenyon's optimism is justified. His Cleopatra actually succeeds as he wants it to. Remaining within the limits of decorum (the statue, for example, is fully and magnificently clothed), it still celebrates the anarchic eroticism of the queen. When he begins work on the bust of Donatello, he advances beyond simple eroticism into more complex and timely ideas. He perceives, and represents, beauty and virtue in the very qualities of Donatello that have separated him from the faun he earlier was: in suffering, in self-knowledge, in self-consciousness. The bust is Kenyon's formulation of the "fortunate fall." The fall begins a process through which man grows—or can grow—beyond the pretty simplicity of childhood into a rich and complex awareness of his life in history and time.

Of course, if the man does not grow, but remains paralyzed by his guilt, there is no fortune in the fall. That is why Kenyon is at such trouble to bring out in the real Donatello what he has put into his sculpture. He is continually exhorting him, through the second third of the book, to leave off his slothful remorse and his self-indulgent penitences (much like Dimmesdale's) and go about the business of becoming a man. It is he who persuades Donatello to leave Monte Beni at last, and he directs Miriam to meet them beneath the Pope's statue in Perugia. The couple is reunited there under the apparent blessing of papal authority symbolized in the statue of Pope Julian.

To end at this point must have been a temptation to Hawthorne, for it is a conclusion in accord with Kenyon's optimism and Hawthorne's hopes for the future of art. But he must have felt that its sanguine character was unjustified, for the last third of The Marble Faun utterly undoes it. The statue of Pope Julian is not a real ruler, but an artist's dream of one; it corresponds to the truth of the heart's craving but to no actual pontiff. Donatello's fall will be interpreted as a crime, and no art but genteel art will be permissible in modern times.

When Kenyon returns to Rome he arrives just in time to observe Hilda on her knees at the confessional, and, although his Yankee soul is dismayed, he has too much respect for

Hilda to argue with her at length. Indeed, he is afraid to risk her displeasure. The myth that we have been following in Donatello's case is exclusively masculine. Woman's situation is necessarily quite different. The advent of the patriarchy means a radical change in the way woman is perceived. The idea of woman as a self disappears, and she is viewed only in terms of her relation to man. She is repressed as a means of controlling the male. So far as a woman is sexually attractive she inspires fear and persecution.

Under the relentless pressure of persecution, the generous and loving nature of a beautiful woman like Miriam undergoes evident violent distortion. She is driven to the verge of madness; in the supposed privacy of the Coliseum at night she vents a depthless despair. At times she is totally abject, as when she kneels in broad daylight before her persecutor. At other times she hates men. She creates a powerful series of bitterly misandrous sketches representing the great female killers of history, including Jael and Judith. But we see how inessential this warping is by observing how rapidly she is transformed when liberated by Donatello.

Hilda, however, is a wholly different case, a deliberate contrast to Miriam. Like Priscilla, she is a social product who has internalized social rules and restrictions. But Priscilla represents woman as man's servant while Hilda represents her as his chaste ideal, his inward monitor. The incident at St. Peter's implies no new development in her character—she has always worshiped the fathers. She did, however, mistakenly think that the Old Masters, the Renaissance artists whom she so reverently copied (while bowdlerizing their work), were the proper authority. She misunderstood them, because she was innocent. The great achievement of Renaissance art in Hawthorne's interpretation here is the way in which it succeeds in celebrating Eros within the forms of an antierotic culture. Pretending to paint the Virgin, the Renaissance master in fact painted his mistress. Hilda's special talent as a copyist is called the spiritualizing of such paintings. She selects a small detail (here is the miniaturizing impulse again, which Hawthorne always associates with genteel art) and reproduces it in a chaster, more ideal redaction. That is, she makes the painter's mistress truly into the Virgin. Obviously, she misses the point of the painting. But the culture is delighted with her sort of work, for through it the unsocial energies of these unmistakably great paintings can be assimilated into the social matrix.

However, Hilda loses her naive talent when she witnesses the murder, and gains an unhappy enlightenment. She now has the same opportunity that the murder gives Donatello, to grow beyond her narrow reach into a fuller humanity. But she cannot do this, and she resolutely determines to keep an innocence that in fact she no longer has. Her conflict is expressed as a polarity between concepts of art-mothers and church fathers. Miriam offers her, as she offers Donatello, an example, but it is rejected with fear and loathing. (Observe the contrast between Miriam's original, honest, and very feminine art—dealing with women's subjects from a woman's point of view—and Hilda's exclusive devotion to male painters.) Hilda's despairing progress toward the confessional is impeded not, as she believes, by her Puritanism (in the symbol system of *The Marble Faun* Catholicism and Puritanism are identical), but by the restraining spirit of her mother, whose presence she feels "weeping to behold her ensnared by these gaudy superstitions" (p. 391).

Hilda bemoans her motherless plight throughout the romance, and it is certain that a mother might have stood as buffer between the girl and the exclusive influence of the fathers. But as a result of the latter influence, Hilda repeatedly rejects all images of maternity that are presented to her. No mother is good enough for her. Miriam, called her older sister (p. 207), is a case in point; and Hawthorne treats the subject in art imagery as he follows Hilda's quest, in chapter

38, for a satisfactory picture of the Virgin. Although Hilda says she is looking for a mother, in fact she is looking for a virgin, and since mothers are not virgins, she must reject each image. "She never found just the Virgin Mother she needed," Hawthorne comments (p. 348). The symbolism of tower, dove, and shrine implies Hilda's devotion to the idea of chastity. But her devotion is founded on fear. Under stress she reveals that her true motive is less a conviction of the beauty of chastity than her desire to be good and obedient: "I am a poor, lonely girl, whom God has set here in an evil world, and given her only a white robe, and bid her wear it back to Him, as white as when she put it on" (p. 208). And, she continues (for she is here casting off Miriam), "Your powerful magnetism would be too much for me. The pure, white atmosphere, in which I try to discern what things are good and true, would be discoloured." In another part of the romance a portrait is made of her, which shows Hilda "gazing, with sad and earnest horrour, at a blood-spot which she seemed just then to have discovered on her white robe" (p. 330). The menstrual and defloration imagery betrays Hilda's intense sexual anxiety.

Hilda then is deeply implicated in the sexual morbidity underlying the structure of guilt, remorse, misery, inhibition, repression, and hypocrisy that is the social atmosphere of *The Marble Faun*. Her dedication to the Virgin shows her longing to escape sexuality, as does her rejection of the sexual nature of her own mother. She would like to think herself the product of a virgin birth, miraculously free of the curse of a sexual nature. Her meditations on the portrait of Beatrice Cenci show her need to believe that one can remain sinless in a fallen world. In her words with Miriam she envisions herself as a child of the father, not of the mother; her ideals are based on an intransigent refusal to know the facts of life. But of course she does know them, so her refusal is hypocritical. Yet she honestly believes that her hypocrisy is a high moral attitude, and the culture supports her belief. To deny the existence of evil is a kind of good.

After the murder, Hilda's ability to deny evil is sorely tested. It turns out that she can deny evil in herself only by imputing it to others. She is driven by anxiety and fear to expose her friends as a means of absolving herself. Using the confessional for this purpose, she patently perverts the intentions of that ritual, which require the penitent to confess one's own sins. Instead, she confesses the sins of others and fiercely insists that she is blameless. Her psychological structure is too rigid and fragile to permit the incorporation of an idea of fault or error in herself. Tattling rather than confessing, she exemplifies the way in which socialized people act as cultural police. She delivers up Miriam and Donatello to the authorities.

And so does Kenyon. The last third of the romance explores his mental collapse and recovery as he loses and regains Hilda. When he explains to her something of the new insights that Donatello's story has given him, she disappears. Miriam and Donatello, now a composite figure, return; they can no longer coexist with Hilda. Kenyon must choose between them. Miriam and Donatello offer him the promise of great artistic achievement. He cannot accept it if Hilda is the price, and she is. He rejects the couple and they give themselves up to the authorities in exchange for Hilda, who returns when they are arrested. Thus Hawthorne shows that neither of his young Americans can rise to the complex lessons that Europe is offering them.

Hawthorne takes an entirely different approach to Miriam and Donatello in this last section of the book; they seem much less real, more remote and fanciful. In effect, the story of the characters Miriam and Donatello has come to an end, and the two figures in the last third of the romance are aspects of Kenyon's drama, phantoms in his consciousness. They are the beautiful man and woman he has created out of his artistic and erotic energies. Now he has to give them up.

In a strangely mythic and magic episode on the campagna, this significant exchange takes place. The scene of their meeting is a sunken spot in the fields, at once underground and in the sun, in the country away from Rome and yet within the enclosure of a Roman ruin. A magic animal leads Kenyon to this sacred spot, where he unearths and assembles the fragments of an exquisite antique Venus. The goddess of love and mother of Eros, she is a symbol of the matriarchy and an example of the greatest art. The order in which Kenyon puts together the pieces of this shattered work—torso, arms, head—represents the progressive embodiment of the fundamental erotic force, an epitome of the artistic process of creation. The Venus is a work that Kenyon discovers, that he digs up, that he re-creates.

As Kenyon completes his work he is joined by Miriam and Donatello, who inform him that they had discovered the statue and left it for him to put together. They are like Surveyor Pue and Hester in the Custom House, the source and symbol of Hawthorne's artistry. But Kenyon is not Hawthorne. He rationalizes his disaffection by explaining that the statue is cold marble, while his lost Hilda is life. But all the rhetoric of the romance contradicts him. As Frederick Crews has expressed it, Hawthorne "seems to be saying that Kenyon's human love is supplanting his cold aesthetic taste. . . . Yet when we reflect that vapid Hilda is here dethroning a supple and lovely Venus, the surface meaning becomes exactly reversed."[7] The "surface meaning" is no more than Kenyon's uneasy defense. Victim of his age's malaise, he chooses the virgin over Venus, a choice resulting from the same panic that drove Hilda into the church.

Yet Kenyon's fear is absolutely justified—this is Hawthorne's most bitter perception—for without Hilda he will certainly go mad. He cannot survive without her. He has already endured

7. Crews, *The Sins of the Fathers*, p. 239.

a period of protracted mental depression. He has already
ceased to be an artist. "Ah, Miriam, I cannot respond to
you," he says crossly. "Imagination and the love of art have
both died out of me" (p. 427). He does not have the stamina
to be the artist he wanted to be. The carnival scene shows him
at lowest ebb, and Hilda is restored to him in the nick of time.
The carnival scene recalls moments in Hawthorne's fiction
stretching all the way back to "My Kinsman, Major Molineux."
Dimmesdale's return from the forest; the phantasmagoric
chapter woven about the corpse of Pyncheon; the bitter
pageant of repudiation at Blithedale—each romance has had
such a climactic scene, but the Roman Carnival is the most
grotesque of all. The psyche in a state of anarchic turbulence
throws up into the light of consciousness a host of horrible
fears and fantasies symbolized by a succession of grotesque,
partly sexual, dream figures. If Kenyon sinks into this swamp,
he is lost forever.

At the close of this scene, Miriam and Donatello take a
formal farewell of their friend. "Donatello here extended his
hand, (not that which was clasping Miriam's,) and she, too,
put her free one into the sculptor's left; so that they were a
linked circle of three, with many reminiscences and forebodings flashing through their hearts. Kenyon knew intuitively that these once familiar friends were parting with
him, now. 'Farewell!' they all three said, in the same breath"
(p. 448). Soon after, Kenyon hears that they have been arrested, and "just as the last words were spoken, he was hit
by . . . a single rosebud, so fresh that it seemed that moment
gathered" (p. 451). This dewy messenger signifies the end of
Kenyon's feverish season in purgatory. Hilda is back; he is
safe. At the same moment he is also hit by a cauliflower, a
gratuitous expression of the author's disgust that yet another
surrogate has been unable to survive social pressure.

Whether or not Kenyon will actually give up art in his
American future, he will certainly produce no more feline

Cleopatras or broodingly beautiful fauns. In his Roman weeks before Hilda's disappearance, the nature of his art was already beginning to change; while his artisans were at work turning the Cleopatra into marble, he modeled "a beautiful little statue of Maidenhood, gathering a snow-drop" (p. 375). The energy and vigor of his monumental productions are shrinking into the delicate, miniaturing craftsmanship of the genteel artist. Kenyon will emerge from his ordeal another artist of the beautiful. He is already becoming impatient and disenchanted with his Cleopatra: "I should like," he tells Hilda, "to hit poor Cleopatra a bitter blow on her Egyptian nose, with this mallet" (p. 378). The act of consigning Miriam and Donatello to the lifelong status of sinners represents just such a bitter blow to the values of art, as it defaces and discolors the image of "the beautiful man, the beautiful woman" (p. 323), which the romance had so lovingly developed.

Kenyon rejects these two figures; but does not Hawthorne also? We can, of course, dismiss the contention of some critics that Hawthorne is creating a dichotomy between life and art, rejecting art in favor of life; because, as we have seen through all the major romances, art and life stand together and are rejected together in favor of inhibition and security. But it is Hawthorne's act as author that permits Miriam and Donatello to vanish from the sunlight of the romance, and he who gives Hilda the last, horrified criticism of the theory of the fortunate fall. Is Hawthorne himself thus retreating from the bold position he had staked out?

In a sense, he most certainly is. But I am inclined to think that the gesture represents not so much timidity as realism. Hawthorne concluded that society would not permit such a pair to exist uncensured or knowingly entertain an art that celebrated them. The dark finale represents his clear-sighted estimate of their chances for survival. Ultimately, society is to blame for making serious artistry so psychologically strenuous. Hester had won the right to take her letter off, and when she refused to do so society slowly came around to accept her. Hawthorne's view of individual force and social flexibility seems more cautious in *The Marble Faun.*

On the other hand, the authorial treatment of Hilda certainly suggests a divided loyalty. She is narrow, she is merciless, she is finally inhuman, but Hawthorne nowhere summons the rhetoric to condemn her. Miriam makes a few complaints about her, but is sternly rebuked by Kenyon; and Hawthorne permits Kenyon to have the last word. Hilda is the culture's most cherished stereotype; the author who would openly attack her certainly runs a terrible professional risk. But Hawthorne's attitude toward Hilda is less duplicitous than genuinely ambivalent. Great art is unquestionably the product of human imperfection; if it were possible for mankind to advance into the serene atmosphere of moral perfection, then perhaps art might be a small sacrifice. The question revolves around the place of an ideal of perfection in a situation where perfection is unattainable. Is such an ideal, unattainable though it is, useful because it spurs men on to better things? Or is it not only useless but pernicious because it keeps men from recognizing the reality of their condition and from progressing within that reality? But even if the ideal is pernicious in practice, might it still not be beautiful in itself? Such questions keep Hawthorne from making the final judgment on Hilda that the narrative presses upon him.

The Marble Faun is Hawthorne's gloomiest work. It is also the most technically complex and the most difficult to understand. But Hawthorne was not trying duplicitously to conceal his meanings in a labyrinth of obscurities. He was giving them the kind of expression he felt that they required, as articulations of fantasy. He wished greatly to be understood, but he knew the chances were against him. In his preface he wistfully addresses "that one congenial friend—more comprehensive of his purposes, more appreciative of his success, more indulgent of his short-comings . . . to whom he implicitly makes his appeal, whenever he is conscious of having done his best" (p. 1). It is necessary for a professional writer to believe that someone understands what he is doing.

But the reader response to *The Marble Faun*, when it was published in February 1860, was not such as to encourage him in that belief. The public approached the work as Hilda did the paintings of the Renaissance, selecting here and there a detail and rhapsodizing over its beauty, delicacy, and spirituality. No one grasped the overall design. Even so sympathetic a critic as the Englishman Henry Chorley, whose sensitive and favorable reviews in the *Athenaeum* had been central to the development of Hawthorne's British reputation, complained about the obscurity of events in the romance. Where had Hilda been during her absence from Rome? What was Miriam's ancestry, and the crime with which she had been innocently associated? What finally happened to Donatello? These requests for clarification indicated a failure to take the events as they were intended, as symbolic expressions of a psychological drama.

Hawthorne knew his duty as a professional, and in March 1860 he proposed to write an explanatory postscript for the second edition. The piece he produced, however, clarifies almost nothing and is a subtle joke on his readers' obtuseness. Hawthorne appears in his own person as the author engaged in conversation with Hilda and Kenyon, who answer his questions about what really happened in the romance. Of course, it was because they mistook the characters for real people that readers wanted the kind of information they asked for; so now Hawthorne presents Kenyon and Hilda as his readers thought them to be—as actual people—and by getting answers from them he pretends that the events of the romance actually occurred. He blurs the line between imagination and actuality exactly as his readers blurred it. Yet acceding to his readers' wishes to make these characters real, he does so "reluctantly . . . because the necessity makes him sensible that he can have succeeded but imperfectly, at best, in throwing about this Romance the kind of atmosphere essential to the effect at which he aimed. He designed the story and the characters to bear, of course, a certain relation to human nature and human life, but still to be so artfully and airily removed from our mundane sphere, that some laws and proprieties of their own should be implicitly and insensibly acknowledged" (p. 463). In other words, the questions his readers asked meant that *The Marble Faun* had not been understood, and if it was successful it succeeded with people who were largely unaware of what Hawthorne had been doing. If he had been understood, would he still have been successful? Hawthorne was never to know the answer to this question.

Here was an ironic culmination to his career as a romancer, for *The Marble Faun* was the last work he completed. Over the decade his reputation had risen until he was now the most celebrated living American author; but that celebration indicated no comprehension of his purposes. The purport of *The Marble Faun* was that great or serious art was no longer possible. Hawthorne's career in its major phase suggests an ironic modification of that dictum: such art was possible but would not be understood. Having come to this perception about himself, Hawthorne might reasonably have ceased to write, and *The Marble Faun* has a valedictory air about it. As a professional, of course, he had to keep on. Yet one of the several reasons for his failure to complete another romance might be that in *The Marble Faun* he said farewell to the concept of serious art that had sustained him since *The Scarlet Letter.*

⊰ 8 ⊱

The Last Phase
1860–1864

In May 1859 the Hawthorne family left Italy and returned to England. They remained a year while Hawthorne rewrote *The Marble Faun* and saw it through British publication (thus ensuring the British copyright). Late in June 1860 they arrived back in the United States and settled down at the Wayside in Concord, the home they had bought shortly before Hawthorne received his consular appointment. Hawthorne began to write a romance—a second version of his English story—almost immediately, but could not complete it to his satisfaction. Subsequently, he started but could not finish two other romances. He did, however, work up a series of essays deriving from the *English Notebooks*. Most of these were published in the *Atlantic* as he wrote them, and the whole collection appeared in September 1863, entitled *Our Old Home*. At about this time Hawthorne became seriously ill. He refused to see a doctor until his sickness was far advanced, and he died during the night of May 18, 1864, while on a recuperative journey with Franklin Pierce.[1]

Trying to account for Hawthorne's difficulties with the

1. The doctor, Oliver Wendell Holmes, saw that Hawthorne was fatally ill. See Stewart, *Nathaniel Hawthorne*, p. 237, and Arlin Turner, "Hawthorne's Final Illness and Death: Additional Reports," *ESQ*, 19 (1973), 124–27. The illness was never diagnosed, but the symptoms suggest some sort of gastrointestinal cancer.

uncompleted romances, many critics have hypothesized a general loss of artistic powers in these years, caused perhaps by physical or mental collapse. They ignore *The Ancestral Footstep*, which, initiated before *The Marble Faun*, testifies to Hawthorne's difficulty with the English material in and for itself. Pursuing the idea of a collapse in the years after 1860, critics have discounted the evidence of achievement in *Our Old Home* by arguing incorrectly that it is nothing more than a composite of notebook entries. The descriptions in these essays derive, to be sure, from the notebooks, but in most cases they are assembled from many different passages and require considerable expertise to unify. Moreover, to each essay Hawthorne adds a running layer of general reflection and commentary that the notebooks did not have; this layer, which gives *Our Old Home* its focus and character, is the product of the late years. The mind behind it is sharp and clear, and the style of the essays—as all critics have admitted—is as good as Hawthorne's best. And the length of the work (more than three hundred printed pages), along with the several hundred thousand words of drafted romances, argues against the idea of flagging energy.

Until he became physically debilitated, I would argue, Hawthorne's problems were with the romances and with the romances alone. Individual passages in the various drafts display the highest craftsmanship, but there is no coherence. In none of the many fragments of the three incomplete works do we find the tightly knit subterranean symbol system that unites surface events into a meaningful action. Hawthorne had lost not his powers but his purpose. The stories move forward in a fitful and indecisive way. They have no direction.

There are several theoretical explanations for the disintegration of the productive synthesis of the 1850s. We recall, for one, the pessimistic conclusion of *The Marble Faun:* although there was a job for the artist well worth his doing, he was not to be permitted to do it. As far back as *The Story Teller,*

Hawthorne had shown the writer in uneasy tension between fruitless alienation and trivial sociality. After many years, he had circled back to something like the same polarity. A second explanation lies in his stubborn but understandable unwillingness to jettison the English romance. We have seen why it was an unpromising subject for him; but, in quest of some literary return from those four years, he threw away the better part of his imaginative energies during another four.

Finally, we cannot ignore what Hawthorne himself thought to be the chief explanation, and may very well have been so: the enormous effect of the Civil War. All Hawthorne's literary work derives from the conviction that the imaginative world is more real than the actual—that, if properly perceived, the actual manifests the controlling drives of imagination that inform and shape it. But war, as it disrupts and dislocates so many lives, is the great counterstatement of the actual. Like the avalanche in "The Ambitious Guest," it makes a mockery of the inner life. It cuts the romancer's ground out from under him; it urges him to keep silent.

And perhaps Hawthorne would have preferred to keep silent. But the English venture had not been as remunerative as he had hoped, and the expenses of additional years in Europe had mounted; once again Hawthorne felt financially pressed. So he tried. Not until the preface to *Our Old Home* did he acknowledge that he was finished: "These and other sketches . . . were intended for the . . . exterior adornment, of a work of fiction. . . . It has been utterly thrown aside, and will never now be accomplished. The Present, the Immediate, the Actual, has proved too potent for me. It takes away not only my scanty faculty, but even my desire for imaginative composition, and leaves me sadly content to scatter a thousand peaceful fantasies upon the hurricane that is sweeping us all along with it."[2]

2. *Our Old Home*, Centenary Edition, Vol. V (1970), pp. 3–4. Subsequent references are given parenthetically in text.

The first of the unfinished romances was *Dr. Grimshawe's Secret*, which, according to Davidson, he worked on until early in 1861.[3] The romance survives in seven preliminary studies (one a transcript in Julian Hawthorne's hand), a complete draft, and a revision of about a quarter of the draft. All but one of the seven studies retrace ground covered in *The Ancestral Footstep* and re-create, without solving them, Hawthorne's earlier problems. An American (he has various names, but is most often called Etherege) goes to England, seeks out his English lineage, finds that he is the heir to the title and estate enjoyed by the English branch of his family, and precipitates a catastrophe among his English relatives. Distressed at his unintentional mischief-making, he returns to America with the heroine.

As we recall, Hawthorne thought of the Americans who came to the consulate requesting aid in pressing English claims, as twice-deluded fools. Their claims were never valid, but simply represented the projections of a wish that, in itself, Hawthorne found reprehensible. To have selected a character like them as the hero of a romance involved him inevitably in acute problems of authorial attitude. The character kept changing shape in response to Hawthorne's ambivalence. It was impossible for Hawthorne to give his sympathy to one who willfully elected to attach himself to an institution; and try as he might, he could not feel the English past as a valid presence in the American psyche.

In the course of his work on *Dr. Grimshawe's Secret* Hawthorne arrived at two major modifications of the scheme in *The Ancestral Footstep*. He developed, at great length, a justification for Etherege's behavior; and he made his claim invalid. Etherege's search for his English ancestry is explained by the circumstances of his childhood in Salem. There, as the orphan

3. Edward H. Davidson, *Hawthorne's Last Phase*, p. 30. This is the authoritative work on the unfinished romances.

boy Ned, he is raised by a kindly but eccentric doctor who fills his mind with tempting ideas about his home across the ocean in England. The draft begins with an expansion of these childhood experiences to constitute a considerable segment of the romance, with a corresponding shrinkage of the English section.[4] The doctor is responsible for influencing the young boy so that the search for his lost home becomes an overriding purpose. Middleton's whim grows into Etherege's obsession.

Hawthorne's decision to make the claim invalid came farther along in the draft, and it necessitated a recasting of the doctor's character. For if Ned's claim was false, then the doctor who led him to believe that it was true had to be seriously deluded himself, or evil. Hawthorne revised to make the doctor an evil character, driven by a desire to revenge himself, for unspecified reasons, on this English family. We know he is evil by the fact that he conducts mysterious experiments with spiders. He teaches young Ned to think himself an English heir and thus trains him as the instrument of his own revenge. The alteration, complex as it is, has the effect of making Etherege more sympathetic by making him less responsible for basically misguided behavior. Shaped by the doctor, he is under the control of events from the past—not a fancied English past, but the real past of his own childhood.

This is the only example in all Hawthorne's writings of a work dealing with the formative influence of childhood experience. Hawthorne goes beyond the gothic ministrations of the doctor to sketch out a receptive personality in the young orphan, who lacks the secure identity that most children get from their parents—especially (Hawthorne writes) from the love and faith of a mother. Ned needs a definition of himself,

4. *Dr. Grimshawe's Secret*, ed. Edward H. Davidson (Cambridge, Mass.: Harvard University Press, 1954). Davidson's edition includes the preliminary studies, the complete draft, and the revision, along with all Hawthorne's marginalia.

and the doctor provides one. Later in life he becomes a successful lawyer and statesman, but an unassuaged basic insecurity remains. Etherege is unable to identify his accomplishments with himself. Within, he remains a homeless boy. The English claim thus answers to a psychological need.

Hawthorne's conclusion to *Dr. Grimshawe's Secret* symbolizes his dual skepticism about the search for English identity: the search is bound to end in frustration, and it is based on a false set of values. The first of these points is implicit in Etherege's discovery that he is not the true heir after all. The true heir is a saintly old pensioner living in a nearby hospital; and the pensioner has known of his claim all along, but had no interest in pressing it. The pensioner rightly saw such a claim as trivial. This point is soon grasped by Etherege and encapsulated in a grotesque gothic sequence: a coffin supposed to contain the documents establishing Etherege's claim is opened, and is found to hold nothing but a mass of golden ringlets, the hair of a long-deceased beauty. This unpleasing image mocks the chivalric fantasies that keep the American infatuation with Britain alive.

These shocking events are supposed to have the effect of jolting Etherege back into the real world. He should now be free to accept himself for what he is: a self-made American. Hawthorne has certainly steered an indirect course, but he has brought his romance into port. But it is the port of a new social faith, and of an American Adam, in which Hawthorne believed no more than he believed in the American attachment to the English past. He has evaded one dilemma only to encounter another. Despite all the complex alterations of the plot of *The Ancestral Footstep*, *Dr. Grimshawe's Secret* has solved none of its problems. And the revision of the draft appears to be only an expansion, which would ultimately have greatly lengthened the work but left all its inconsistencies intact.

Hawthorne may have been unable to make anything of his

English material, but he did have the acuity to see that he was in trouble, and he abandoned the project early in 1861. For some six months he did no writing. The Wayside was being remodeled, and he had no place to work. The outbreak of the Civil War meant for him, as for so many other Americans, a major psychological reassessment. Hawthorne was in no sense a bellicose personality, and he could not bring himself to believe in war as a good thing under even the most extreme kinds of provocation. He had little interest himself in American Blacks, and hence in the slavery question. On the other hand, he had a good deal of sympathy for a people—any people—who defended their own beliefs, and he was sure that the South was defending its own beliefs. He was a Democrat, and the war president was a Republican.

Nevertheless, and with all these qualifications, he was a sincere supporter of the northern side. But his sincere support was a good deal less than the total commitment considered appropriate in a time of actual hostilities. He knew this and recognized an alienation in his failure to feel as deeply, and as easily, as his neighbors did in this crisis. His tendency toward reserve increased; he withdrew into his private world even at a time when the war was making a mockery of private worlds. When he began working again in the fall of 1861, he portioned his time between *Septimius Felton*, a new romance that reflected some of the issues preoccupying him, and the English essays, which he was writing simply for money. His projected English romance had not materialized; he needed to support himself; he could no longer write short fictions. Essays seemed the answer. In the spring of 1862 he went to Washington, and reported on his visit in the article "Chiefly about War Matters," published in the *Atlantic* in July 1862. As his work on *Septimius* slowed down, work on the essays gathered speed. After he ceased work on *Septimius*, he added six English essays between January and June to the six he had already written, so that he had a group of twelve to publish (with a dedicatory letter to Franklin Pierce) as *Our Old Home*.

The composition of *Septimius Felton* followed a course like that of *Dr. Grimshawe's Secret*. Hawthorne wrote several preliminary studies and then a complete draft. Well into the draft, he changed the narrative in ways that required recasting some of the earlier scenes; consequently, he began a second draft. In rewriting, he seems to have become bogged down in rhetorical elaboration and found it increasingly difficult to keep the story moving. Midway through the action in the second draft, he gave up the romance.

The changes that Hawthorne made in *Dr. Grimshawe's Secret* improved it because they better reflected Hawthorne's own critical opinion of the American mania for establishing English lineages. But in *Septimius Felton* his alterations wrecked a promising romance. For one thing, he introduced into his story some of the unworkable material from the English romance: an emigrated ancestor, a bloody footstep, an American claim on an English estate. None of this matter was germane, and it brought with it those same tired problems Hawthorne had twice been unable to surmount. For another, he altered the relationship between hero and heroine from sweethearts to siblings, and thus eliminated a fascinating psychological study of two people who did not love each other and were not really suited to each other, but had become engaged in a moment of psychological stress. Chronicling their growing disaffection and uneasiness, Hawthorne had been at his very best; but since he could not see any way to disengage them, he changed them into brother and sister and sacrificed some splendid writing.

Septimius Felton takes place at the time of the outbreak of the American Revolution, giving Hawthorne the occasion to work in ideas that he was turning over about war and its relation to the individual and the community. The protagonist is a young man who wishes to discover the elixir of life. As the work exists, with all its contradictions, in a completed draft (which was first published in 1884, in the Riverside Edition of Hawthorne's works), it is much more like a Hawthorne short story of the 1830s than a romance of the 1850s. In its world, the human community represents the richest expression of human fulfillment and happiness, and discontent and desire for change are aberrations. The male protagonist has reverted from the oversocial person of Hawthorne's major works, struggling to assert himself against institutional repression, to the earlier antisocial being who perversely dissociates himself from the human community. The heroine too is a return from the passionate stimulus to change of the later works to the social mediator and reconciler. The drift in the English romances toward Hawthorne's earlier formulations has been solidified in *Septimius Felton*.

Septimius is like the heroes of "The Birth-mark," "The Minister's Black Veil," "The Man of Adamant," and "Egotism" because his search for perfection stems from his inability to see that perfection already exists in the here and now. And this inability is the sign of his emotional inadequacy, his cold heart that cannot respond with relish and delight to earthly things. His search for the elixir is an alienating activity that further separates him from his fellows, and like Ethan Brand he defends himself against their efforts to re-engage him in social existence.

But this return to an earlier imaginative synthesis is accompanied by a passionate affirmation of real life that is rarely found in the early fiction, which tended to express the positive values of community in conventional and superficial language, and had very little to say at all about the sensuous pleasures of existence. Perhaps, although he was not yet seriously ill, Hawthorne felt himself to be aging, and became newly aware of the value of a world he might not enjoy much longer; but more probably his sense of life's preciousness resulted directly from the threat to life and continuity presented by the war. The war might also account for a restored sense of the value of the community. The contrast between Septimius, puttering about in his study seeking the elixir, and his friend Robert Hagburn, who goes off to war at the first call, is clearly in Hagburn's favor, and Hawthorne gives him some of the most moving words of appreciation and affirmation that he had ever written:

> In hot blood, and for a good cause, who cares for death? And yet I love life; none better, while it lasts, and I love it in all its looks and turns and surprises,—there is so much to be got out of it, in spite of all that people say. Youth is sweet, with its fiery enterprise, and I suppose mature manhood will be just as much so, though in a calmer way, and age, quieter still, will have its own merits,—the thing is only to do with life what we ought, and what is suited to each of its stages; do all, enjoy,—and I suppose these two rules amount to the same thing. Only catch real earnest hold of life, not play with it, and not defer one part of it for the sake of another, then each part of life will do for us what was intended.[5]

A second difference between it and the earlier fiction of this type is Hawthorne's willingness to let Septimius's activity stand as a criticism of the romantic artist. Since it was Hawthorne's intention in the earlier works to distinguish the artist—the persona who was telling the story—from the variously obsessed protagonists, he had carefully pointed out how, even though they were all victimized by wayward imaginations, their imaginative aberrations did not implicate the imaginative activity of the artist. But Septimius, who alternates between pacing around a grave and trying, in his study, to decipher the text of an ancient, mysterious document, comes across as a maker of romances.

Since the tone of *Septimius Felton* is so critical of Septimius, it can only be that this is not a romance, but an antiromance. If so, it means that Hawthorne no longer completely identifies

5. *Septimius Felton*, Riverside Edition, Vol. XI, p. 390. Subsequent references are given parenthetically in text.

himself as an artist with the romance form; that he is secure enough in his own voice to contemplate breaking out of the mold in which every single one of his fictions had been cast. Although it replicates the structure of his earlier fictions, *Septimius Felton* lacks entirely the elements of defensiveness and self-display that had characterized the narrator's voice in the moralized fiction. It is a return, and yet an advance. In its preliminary draft, it promised to be the best thing of its kind that Hawthorne had done.

The delusion Hawthorne invented for Septimius is probably the richest in implications of the many obsessions he had bestowed on his alienated protagonists. Septimius wants to live forever because he loves life; he has failed to comprehend that life produces its beauty through growth, and hence through decay—he does not understand that death is the mother of beauty. Septimius perceives that human life is too short for any person to accomplish a lasting improvement in the world, and since he sincerely wishes to do good for mankind, he believes that to ensure a longer life span must be the first step. Again, he has made a mistake. He imagines that change is to be brought about by individuals, but Hawthorne points out (using the war as an example) that change can be brought about only through the united efforts of a whole community. Indeed, as one "legend' incorporated into the body of *Septimius Felton* demonstrates, the prolongation of individual life is precisely a lack of change.

The incorporated legend concerns an Indian Sachem in remote times who did possess the elixir of life. In an aside (the draft has considerable marginalia and interlinear commentary by the author) Hawthorne wrote, "Make this legend grotesque, and express the weariness of the tribe at the intolerable control the undying one had on them; his always bringing up precepts from his own experience, never consenting to anything new, and so impeding progress; his habits hardening into him, his ascribing to himself all wisdom, and depriving everybody of his right to successive command; his endless talk, and dwelling on the past, so that the world could not bear him" (pp. 318–19). Behind the apparent altruism of Septimius's quest is the same benighted egotism that, as Hawthorne had expressed it in earlier fiction, characterizes all deviation from social normality. To wish to live forever is greedily to pre-empt the lives of one's descendants, who have the same right to the earth as oneself.

Finally, as Septimius discovers, the elixir itself will not enable a man to live forever, but must be accompanied by rules of conduct whose import is the total suppression of passionate feelings, as "the causes which almost invariably wear away this poor short life of men, years and years before even the shattered constitutions that they received from their forefathers need compel them to die" (p. 342). Among these rules, as Septimius deciphers them from his antique manu- script, are the following: "Keep thy heart at seventy throbs in a minute; all more than that wears life away too quickly"; "run not; leap not"; "on the whole, shun woman, for she is apt to be a disturbing influence. If thou love her, all is over, and thy whole past and remaining labor and pains will be in vain"; "do not any act manifestly evil; it may grow upon thee, and corrode thee in after-years. Do not any foolish good act; it may change thy wise habits"; "read not great poets; they stir up thy heart" (pp. 339–42). The point is clear: the pro- longed life is death-in-life.

As Septimius withdraws into his obsession and becomes in- creasingly estranged from those around him, Hawthorne em- bodies, as he has so often before, the fantasies of his protag- onist in characters who materialize in the narrative. First, a pale, melancholy girl appears by the side of a grave that is the focal point of much of Septimius's brooding. This girl, Sibyl, is designed as a *femme fatale* (a most unusual figure in Haw- thorne's writings) to replace his sweetheart Rose (not yet changed into his sister) and thus symbolize the overcoming of a healthy earthly love by an infatuation with the morbid and unwholesome. Next, on the same spot appears a Dr. Portsoaken from England, who despite his comic name is a satanic figure. He is a learned scientist who offers Septimius knowledge of the elixir at the cost of involvement in evil.

The two converse in Faustian rhetoric: " 'Sir, I am with you,' said Doctor Portsoaken, 'I will tell you what I know, in the sure belief (for I will be frank with you) that it will add to the amount of dangerous folly now in your mind, and help you on the way to ruin. Take your choice, therefore, whether to know me further or not.' 'I neither shrink nor fear,—neither hope much,' said Septimius, quietly. 'Anything that you can communicate—if anything you can—I shall fearlessly receive' " (p. 304). The materialization of fantasy figures symbolizes Septimius's growing absorption within his own mental constructs. Hawthorne has made a literary representation of the idea of living in one's dreams.

Sibyl and Portsoaken have emerged from the grave of a young English soldier, Norton, whom Septimius had killed on the first day of the war, early in the narrative. This deed, however, was a private rather than a public act, for Septimius did not kill out of patriotism, but because the handsome young Englishman had stolen a kiss from Rose. Rose had not much minded. Norton was a marvelous physical being, well suited for earthly pleasure. Perhaps Septimius chose his withdrawn mode of life not in order to exercise his mental superiority, but from a sense of physical inadequacy. Frankly jealous of the other, he shoots him. Norton takes a long time to die, and his last words convey brotherly love for Septimius, a love of life, and a willingness to die. He gives Septimius all his possessions, asks Septimius to bury him, and designates the spot. Among his papers Septimius finds one containing the "recipe" for the elixir of life, and another intimating that he and Norton belong to the same family tree.

Septimius is not at all surprised to discover the formula in this odd fashion—he seems almost to have anticipated it. Clearly, then, Norton too is a figure in Septimius's symbolic world. Perhaps Septimius, in killing Norton, is killing off a part of himself—the simpler, earthier, joyful, world-involved self who must be transcended in order to undertake the spiritual quest that Septimius contemplates. The event can be read as the protagonist's surpassing his earthbound self, but it can also be reversed to show that the man who dedicates himself to an alienating mission is a sort of suicide. From the grave of his unrealized earthly self emerges Sibyl to supplant Rose, Dr. Portsoaken to supply forbidden knowledge, and finally a beautiful crimson flower, the last ingredient necessary for the elixir. But when Septimius makes an experiment by adding this flower to his Aunt Keziah's tea, she dies a horrible, painful death. So, like Aylmer and the others, Septimius becomes an inadvertent criminal.

Introducing Sibyl and Dr. Portsoaken into the narrative, both of whom are English, Hawthorne resuscitates material from his dead English romance. Sibyl narrates a legend of the bloody footstep—the same footstep that decorated the ancestral mansion in *The Ancestral Footstep* and *Dr. Grimshawe's Secret*—which connects it to the motif of the elixir of life. One of Hawthorne's minor technical problems with the English romances was his inability to invent a legend for the footstep that would make it a meaningful symbol; in *Septimius Felton* he provides an apt legend, but the footstep itself is an entirely superfluous device, as is the whole English subplot, which increasingly dominates the last half of the draft. Dr. Portsoaken becomes another version of Dr. Grimshawe, trying to persuade Septimius to use Norton's paper to press his claim to the English title. Perhaps Hawthorne meant to associate a foolish search for the elixir of life with the foolish search for an English connection, but the identification of these two motifs is farfetched and requires excessive rhetorical elaboration for its basically minor place in the story. Septimius himself is completely indifferent to the title and impatient with any advice from Dr. Portsoaken that does not relate directly to the elixir. Still, Hawthorne did not take the obvious step of excising this overgrowth from his manuscript.

He did, however, as the English material threatened to choke out his main action, bring the draft to a rapid conclusion. Septimius concocts the elixir, and prepares to drink it with Sibyl on the day of Rose's marriage (Hawthorne has now made Rose a half-sister) to Robert Hagburn. Thus a human marriage and a diabolic one would be celebrated at the same moment. At the last moment, however, Sibyl has a change of heart. An evil person, she had tampered with the elixir so that Septimius brewed in fact a deadly poison; but in a crisis of conscience and love, Sibyl drinks the potion herself and destroys the flask. She dies and leaves Septimius a solitary failure.

This event saves Hawthorne the difficulty of dealing with the problems that would follow if Septimius actually had succeeded in brewing the magic drink. The ideas Hawthorne was pursuing in his narrative have little pertinence to the question of whether or not Septimius would in fact achieve his aim. Septimius was wrong to wish for immortal life, not because it was impious, but because his wish embodied a radical disjunction between him and other human beings. There would be no point in "punishing" him by making the drink fatal—he was already punished, by his defective character, by his thralldom to fantasy, by his separation from all that makes life pleasurable. On the other hand, if Septimius concocted and drank the potion, Hawthorne would have a deathless man on his hands, with no idea what to do with him. So he arranged that Septimius would never drink the potion, and thus avoided the question of whether such a drink could actually be brewed by having the potion contaminated from the beginning.

After Sibyl's death Septimius disappears, and it is suggested that after all he has gone to England and claimed his estate. Within the value system of the story, this act must mean Septimius's total corruption, his decline from misguided spiritualism into gross materialism. Yet Hawthorne is so quick and vague in his ending that his intentions are not certain. Either he lost interest, or he saw that revision was required and was not concerned to perfect a draft that must be entirely rewritten. In his revision, he altered the early passages to make Rose a half-sister from the beginning—sacrificing, as I have suggested, some of the best psychological passages in the work. And he brought the English material into the story earlier, thereby increasingly warping *Septimius Felton* into a third version of the English romance. At about the midpoint of the action, he dropped the revision and abandoned *Septimius Felton* altogether.

Norton's legacy to Septimius had expanded in the course of the draft from a sheet of foolscap to a thick manuscript, written in a mixture of Latin and Old English interspersed with a mystic writing; and these recurring, unintelligible passages seemed to contain the heart of the document: "What was discoverable was quaint, curious, but thwarting and perplexing, because it seemed to imply some very great purpose, only to be brought out by what was hidden" (p. 298). As Septimius struggles day and night to bring out the hidden meaning of his manuscript, the war goes on around him. If Hawthorne is here deliberately satirizing the arcane activity of the romancer who turns away from great events of the day to shape a meaning from his fantasies, he was not always able so humorously to accept the disparagement of his life work that the war implied.

His article, "Chiefly about War Matters," by a "Peaceable Man," was composed while he was at work on the first draft of *Septimius Felton,* and is an attempt to belittle the war, to treat it as lightly, so to speak, as it had treated him. Hawthorne sets forth his personal pique at the beginning of the essay: "The general heart-quake of the country long ago knocked at my cottage-door, and compelled me, reluctantly, to suspend the contemplation of certain fantasies, to which, according to my harmless custom, I was endeavoring to give a sufficiently life-like aspect to admit of their figuring in a romance. . . . It seemed, at first, a pity that I should be debarred from such unsubstantial business as I had contrived for myself, since nothing more genuine was to be substituted for it."[6] The war deprived Hawthorne of his profession and of his respect for it simultaneously; "Chiefly about War Matters" was intended as lighthearted revenge.

But it can hardly be imagined that such an intention could succeed, or that, if it succeeded, it could be acceptable to the inflamed emotions of the audience. The editor of the *Atlantic* asked him to remove several paragraphs pertaining to Washington officials that seemed to lack the appropriately respectful spirit. Hawthorne made the deletions, but put in sardonic footnotes to indicate where cuts had been made and to deplore (mockingly) his failure to strike the right tone. Had he engaged in a serious consideration of the war, however, he would have written an essay even less publicly acceptable than "Chiefly about War Matters." Hawthorne hated the war not merely for selfish reasons, but on principle.

He had always been, as he labeled himself in this essay, a peaceable man. As far back as the sketches in 1830 of William Pepperell and Sir William Phips he had made it clear that he had no respect for martial exploits or soldier heroes. He saw war as waste and corruption: the waste of life and material, the corruption of morals. Even the bloodshed of the American Revolution, though unavoidable, was unfortunate. The Civil War, he was persuaded, might have been avoided. The North could not possibly care what went on in the South—human sympathy did not stretch so far. No theoretical evil—for so he

6. "Chiefly about War Matters," in Riverside Edition, Vol. XII, p. 299.

regarded slavery—could outweigh the certain horrors of a war. The South could not be faulted for objecting to northern interference in her affairs, nor for fighting against an invader of her territory: "In the vast extent of our country,—too vast by far to be taken into one small human heart,—we inevitably limit to our own State, or, at farthest, to our own section, that sentiment of physical love for the soil. . . . If a man loves his own State, therefore, and is content to be ruined with her, let us shoot him, if we can," he wrote scornfully (p. 315). In contrast to the heartfelt involvement of the South, northerners seemed to him engaged in an impulsive and theoretical struggle (p. 317).

A person with such leanings living as Hawthorne did in a stronghold of prowar and pronorthern sentiment would have done well to refrain from commentary on the subject. Hawthorne knew this well, and the article is marked by continual and embarrassed shifts of tone and stance. He begins one paragraph, for example, with a passage of conventional praise for war as an occupation for young men, a celebration of military heroism: young men "now make it their daily business to ride a horse and handle a sword, instead of lounging listlessly through the duties, occupations, pleasures—all tedious alike—to which the artificial state of society limits a peaceful generation. . . . The enervating effects of centuries of civilization vanish at once, and leave these young men to enjoy a life of hardship, and the exhilarating sense of danger." War sounds like an improvement over Blithedale Farm, salvation for a generation of Coverdales. But in midsentence the tone changes: these young men are "to kill men blamelessly, or to be killed gloriously,—and to be happy in following out their native instincts of destruction." "Heaven forgive me," he concludes weakly, "for seeming to jest upon such a subject!—only, it is so odd, when we measure our advances from barbarism, and find ourselves just here!" (pp. 320–21).

A reader today will not respond with the sense of outrage

that might have been expected from a New Englander of Hawthorne's own time; yet the essay seems hard and tasteless even now. Still, "Chiefly about War Matters" represents a brave little attempt to speak back to the war whose great voice was drowning out the sounds of his own work and threatening retrospectively to make a mockery of his entire career and his hard-won expression of the significance of imaginative activity. To assert his private sensibility and pit its force against the national calamity was, of course, a futile and absurd gesture. Even as he composed "Chiefly about War Matters" he abandoned *Septimius Felton*. But he could not, even had he wished to, abandon writing altogether, because he needed money and had no other means of earning it. So he rapidly completed six English essays and prepared a volume for the press. The essays reflect his contracted sense of the power of imagination—not in their own imaginative short-comings, but as the unifying motif of the volume. England—as one might have expected from reading the notebooks—emerges as a great symbolic expression of the Actual, before which the imagination has no recourse but retreat.

Hawthorne began to write the essays as a side occupation, and the first three ("Some of the Haunts of Burns," "Near Oxford," and "A Pilgrimage of Old Boston") drew on the journals in a relatively straightforward fashion. As the pieces became a more central literary concern, he began to build them from numerous passages scattered throughout the journals, so that each final product represented a complex process of interweaving. The essay called "A London Suburb," for example, the seventh in order of composition, draws on eleven widely separated journal entries; the ninth ("Outside Glimpses of English Poverty") uses thirteen different sources; and the tenth ("Civic Banquets") employs fifteen. As he made the essays more complex redactions of original notebook material, he mingled with them a coherent commentary that has no source in the journals. This commentary clearly reflects the issues that were involving him in 1862 and 1863. Even when a particular essay contains a relatively small proportion of such newly written matter, the latter has great importance because it provides interpretation and meaning for the scenes described. Hawthorne began to write his English essays as a simple copying exercise, but when imaginative writing failed him they became more the vehicle for his artistic energies. By the end, the journals became merely the base for constructions expressing his last phase.

The scenes in *Our Old Home* exist in a tension between the poles of the actual and the imaginary. On the one hand is England as it actually is, on the other, the dream of England that the imagination had created long ago. As the two are brought into juxtaposition by the experience of visiting the real sites that have so long been real to the fantasy, the imaginative vision fades before the stronger impression of an inferior reality. Actual and imaginary do not interpenetrate. One or the other triumphs, and victory almost always goes to the actual.

On a very few occasions the actual surpasses the dream, but only when the actual is itself the realization of someone else's dream, as for example in the Gothic cathedral, to which Hawthorne returns over and over again. Leamington Spa is a town that has grown from a "magic well" whose "fiction . . . is so far a reality that out of its magical depths have gushed trees, groves, gardens, mansions, streets, and churches"; Blenheim Palace is nearly entirely "the embodied thought of a human mind" (pp. 43, 169). In such experiences the imagination recognizes itself in the actual and rushes to embrace it; on most occasions the imagination withdraws in order to protect itself from being destroyed by something inferior.

As an example of this destruction we may note Hawthorne's chronicle of old Warwick Castle near Stratford:

The sight of that long series of historic rooms, full of such splendors and rarities as a great English family necessarily gathers about itself . . . is well-worth the money, or ten times as much, if indeed the value of the spectacle could be reckoned in money's worth. But after the attendant has hurried you from end to end of the edifice, repeating a guide-book by rote, and exorcising each successive hall of its poetic glamour and witchcraft by the mere tone in which he talks about it, you will make the doleful discovery that Warwick Castle has ceased to be a dream. It is better, methinks, to linger on the bridge, gazing. . . . [The towers] will have all the more reality for you, as stalwart relics of immemorial times, if you are reverent enough to leave them in the intangible sanctity of a poetic vision. [Pp. 67–68]

Observe the fragility of imagination, and Hawthorne's protective attitude toward it. Imaginative visions no longer powerfully affect the superficial surface of actual life, as in the romances of the 1850s. Now such visions must be scrupulously, even religiously, preserved from the contaminating influences of a powerful actuality.

Dozens of such passages could be culled from *Our Old Home*, and in the essay called "Lichfield and Uttoxeter" the confrontation of precious, long-imagined scenes with actuality is the entire point of the essay. The piece is a romance about Hawthorne's pilgrimage in the footsteps of Samuel Johnson with the intention of actualizing a long-cherished vision. But the episode turns out to be an ironic joke.[7] To his amused distress, Hawthorne discovers that Johnson's penance, if it really occurred in front of the church as history has it, took place on "merely a street of ordinary width," while "the picturesque arrangement and full impressiveness of the story absolutely require that Johnson shall not have done his penance in a corner, ever so little retired, but shall have been the

7. In 1857 Hawthorne had worked up a brief sketch on this topic, which was published in both England and America, in *The Keepsake* and *Harper's* respectively. The essay in *Our Old Home* is drawn from this sketch, with further material from the journals interpolated and with an extensive additional commentary. The Centenary Edition reprints the text of the 1857 piece, pp. 481–85.

very nucleus of the crowd—the midmost man of the market-place—a central image of Memory and Remorse, contrasting with, and overpowering the sultry materialism around him." In fact, the sultry materialism is overpowering the central image of Hawthorne's vision, so on grounds of imaginative necessity he declares "that the true site of Dr. Johnson's penance was in the middle of the market-place" (pp. 133–34).

Hawthorne's error was to expect that the meaning he gave to events would actually be found symbolized in them:

A sensible man had better not let himself be betrayed into these attempts to realize the things which he has dreamed about, and which, when they cease to be purely ideal in his mind, will have lost the truest of their truth, the loftiest and profoundest part of their power over his sympathies. Facts, as we really find them, whatever poetry they may involve, are covered with a stony ex-crescence of prose, resembling the crust on a beautiful sea-shell, and they never show their most delicate and divinest colors, until we shall have dissolved away their grosser actualities by steeping them long in a powerful menstruum of thought. And, seeking to actualize them again, we do but renew the crust.   [Pp. 135–36]

Hawthorne concludes his contrast between actual and imaginary by opposing himself, the man of imagination, to the inhabitants of Uttoxeter, who are completely unaware of the most important event in their town's history: "Just think of the absurd little town, knowing nothing of the only memorable incident which ever happened within its boundaries since the old Britons built it, this sad and lovely story, which consecrates the spot (for I found it holy to my contemplation, again, as soon as it lay behind me) in the heart of a stranger from three thousand miles over the sea! It but confirms what I have been saying, that sublime and beautiful facts are best understood when etherealized by distance" (p. 138).[8]

8. This conclusion is quite different from the ending of the 1857 sketch, in which Hawthorne attributed the overpowering of the ideal by the actual to the weakness of his own imaginative conception.

This essay permits us to generalize about the coherent view of the actual and imaginary presented in *Our Old Home*. Because the actual is material, it lacks meaning and has no relation to human needs and desires. Actualities are given meaning and brought into relation with feelings by the act of the imagination, which re-creates the actual in conformity with human pressures. The actual itself, lacking the human dimension, is basically empty even though it may be dense and crowded with events: it is empty of meaning. But this empty actual is much stronger, because of its power over the senses, than the rich imagination, which is apprehended more weakly. Consequently, when the two come into contact, imagination is overpowered. The job of the romances has been to impart such vividness to the creatures of imagination as to make them strike with something of the same strength as sensory impressions.

The assumption here of an absolute disjunction between the actual and the imaginary—the removal of all human meaning from the actual (unless, as noted above, the actual object is the embodiment of imagination, as in a work of art) and the insistence that the imagination can maintain its visions only in the absence of the actual—is much more extreme than anything we can find in Hawthorne's earlier writings, although it is closer to the writing before *The Scarlet Letter* than to the major romances. In different ways, the work of Hawthorne's earlier and major phases depended on some certainty of an area of overlap between the two spheres. And, of course, that work derived from a certainty that ideality, though differently

---

"I cannot help envying those happier tourists," he had written, "who can time and tune themselves so accurately, that their raptures . . . are sure to gush up just on the very spot, and precisely at the right moment!" (p. 485). This ironic comment looks all the way back to *The Story Teller* and the failure of Hawthorne's imagination in the presence of touristic set-pieces; but the motif of his own inadequacy is dropped in *Our Old Home*, and the inadequacy is generalized to pertain to the imaginative faculty itself.

apprehended from actuality, was no less real—his motive was to make the ideality seem as real to his readers as it did to him. But now he posits an unbridgeable gap. On one side is imagination, which is vastly superior to actuality; on the other is actuality, vastly stronger than the world of the ideal. Rather than attempt to project his imaginative visions on the actual, or to disclose their subterranean control over the "real," the poet's business is to protect his fantasies from the influx of the actual.

In discerning the reality of Uttoxeter enshrined in the heart of "a stranger from three thousand miles over the sea," Hawthorne picks up a second motif in *Our Old Home:* the idea that the American, who lives in an emptier environment, is the true man of imagination, while the Englishman, who lives enmeshed in the dense texture of the actual, is an unimaginative person. He observes in "Up the Thames" that the English, having lived in a traditional society all their lives, have lost the power to respond to it imaginatively: "These matters are too familiar, too real, and too hopelessly built in amongst and mixed up with the common objects and affairs of life, to be easily susceptible of imaginative coloring in their minds; and even their poets and romancers feel it a toil, and almost a delusion, to extract poetic material out of what seems embodied poetry itself to an American. An Englishman cares nothing about the Tower, which to us is a haunted castle in dream-land" (p. 253).

The deprived American, who lives in the plain sunlight of an austere environment, compensates by developing imaginative responses to other places, another world, which those who live in rich surroundings will never be motivated to achieve. Surfeited by experience, the Englishman leaves his imagination undeveloped.[9] The view of imagination as a compensatory activity is common among New England writers. But the

9. See Terence Martin's fine article on the need for atmospheric

American makes a bad mistake if he thinks that the country in his imagination is "England." It is not a real country, but the country of Imagination itself. The lesson for the American tourist is that he must protect his precious faculty by withdrawing from a suggestive actuality.

From this view, what is the function of the romancer? The romancer has no time to create; he is far too busy defending the vulnerable borders of his dream territory from the inroads of rough actuality. The strong artist of the 1850s has receded into the nerveless figure of Owen Warland. The imagination has neither pertinence nor effect. The view of imagination in *Our Old Home* expresses a profound defeat, which might be attributed to the events of the Civil War or to the inevitable aftermath of the pessimism of *The Marble Faun.* Yet we need not leave Hawthorne on this somber note, for in *Our Old Home* there is a stirring in the ashes, a suggestion that he would after all, if he had time, work through to yet another useful formulation of his role.

Except for the decade of the major romances, Hawthorne's career developed as a series of tentative solutions to the question of the social significance of the artist. Regularly, he worked within a conception that satisfied for a little while but then was abandoned for another, slightly different formulation. During the major decade, he found a position that released his greatest burst of creativity: the idea of the artist as chronicler of the hidden life and representer of repressed but necessary emotions. That synthesis reached its final expression in *The Marble Faun,* where Hawthorne concluded that such a role, vital though it is for the survival of the human being, was simply not possible for an artist in a genteel culture. The return to America, the effect of the war, the fruitless commitment to making a romance out of his English experience all prevented Hawthorne from moving on to another for-

---

thinness in Hawthorne's work: "Hawthorne's Public Decade and the Values of Home," *American Literature,* 46 (1974), 141–52.

mulation of art in society. Now in *Our Old Home*, which was the work he could write about English society, and which seemed to turn away from the imagination as a useful faculty even while sanctifying its visions, he says good-bye to romance as a mode of authorship and appears ready to break into a new synthesis. Dissatisfaction with the romance mode was also evident in the satirical allusions of *Septimius Felton*. Especially in the last essays written for the collection, *Our Old Home* develops a quite remarkable realism.

The essay entitled "Outside Glimpses of English Poverty" escapes altogether from the categories of actual and ideal; it is a merciless description of the miserable conditions of the English poor, a description pervaded simultaneously by Hawthorne's revulsion from the hopelessness of their existence and by his strong sense of his own implication (and of all comfortable people's) in their distress. At the conclusion of his essay he contrasts the luxurious wedding of a wealthy pair with the mass marriage ceremony of a horde of poor couples. "Is, or is not, the system wrong," he asks, "that gives one married pair so immense a superfluity of luxurious home, and shuts out a million others from any home whatever? One day or another, safe as they deem themselves, and safe as the hereditary temper of the people really tends to make them, the gentlemen of England will be compelled to face this question" (p. 309). Hawthorne experiments here—not unsuccessfully—with the voice of the socially aware Victorian narrator.

In 1860 Hawthorne wrote to Fields: "My own individual taste is for quite another class of works than those which I myself am able to write. If I were to meet with such books as mine, by another writer, I don't believe I should be able to get through them. Have you ever read the novels of Anthony Trollope? They precisely suit my taste; solid and substantial . . . and just as real as if some giant had hewn a great lump out of the earth and put it under a glass case, with all its inhabitants going about their daily business."[10] Toward the end of his life, in the last essay he wrote for *Our Old Home*, Hawthorne transcended the defeatist synthesis of most of the volume and made a start at Trollope's kind of writing. This new start can be felt in the author's voice throughout all the essays, even those not Trollopean or Dickensian in subject matter, for it is at once a public and relaxed voice. Hawthorne speaks without self-consciousness in his character as well-known author and public functionary. The person who talks in *Our Old Home* is not a romantic poet but a Victorian sage.

A developing realism is also displayed in what little Hawthorne accomplished on his last work, *The Dolliver Romance*. Despite the valedictory to imaginative writing in the dedication of *Our Old Home* (which, addressed to Franklin Pierce, involved Hawthorne in one last political wrangle), Hawthorne was after all a professional, who would die with his pen in hand. Within a few months of the publication of *Our Old Home*, and probably knowing himself to be a dying man by this time, Hawthorne began another story about the elixir of life. As with the other unfinished romances, he began by drafting a number of preliminary studies, and then turned to the work itself. He had finished only three chapters at his death. The studies show a quite different orientation toward the subject from that in *Septimius Felton*. Instead of having a young man looking for the elixir, *The Dolliver Romance* centers on an old man who possesses it. The point is thus no longer the perverse folly of one who insists on seeking immortality, but the practical question of what an old person should do with his life.

The studies suggest that Hawthorne meant to have his hero stay alive for the sake of others, especially for his great-granddaughter Pansie, whose guardian he is. His altruism would be contrasted with selfish and sensuous motives for

10. Quoted in the "Historical Commentary" to Centenary *Mosses from an Old Manse*, p. 536.

immortality on the part of an antagonist. But the drafted chapters immediately drift away from the announced plan of the studies, and their living center is the description of the aging protagonist in his experiences of failing health and advancing age. Hawthorne is creating a realistic character (and not a parody of one, such as Hepzibah in *The House of the Seven Gables*), an old, sick man:

Patient as he seemed, he still retained an inward consciousness that these stiffened shoulders, these quailing knees, this cloudiness of sight and brain, this confused forgetfulness of men and affairs, were troublesome accidents that did not really belong to him. He possibly cherished a half-recognized idea that they might pass away. Youth, however eclipsed for a season, is undoubtedly the proper, permanent, and genuine condition of man; and if we look closely into this dreary delusion of growing old, we shall find that it never absolutely succeeds in laying hold of our innermost convictions. A sombre garment, woven of life's unrealities, has muffled us from our true self, but within it smiles the young man whom we knew.[11]

This meditation and others like it, in which the psychology of the old man is projected with both sympathy and objectivity, comprises the heart of the fragment of *The Dolliver Romance*. There is no way of knowing whether, with more time, he would have recast his plot into a realistic mode to suit his new interests. But it is a sign of continuing vitality that he made a beginning at a radical reformulation of his role as artist. All his life Hawthorne had sought to establish a tie between himself as a romancer and the public; he had questioned many aspects of the complex relationship of writer to audience, but he had never questioned the equation of the writer with the romance form. That equation seemed given. At the end, however, nothing was given except Hawthorne's determination to live and to die an author. Even romance could be left behind.

11. *The Dolliver Romance*, Riverside Edition, Vol. XI, pp. 30–31.

Index

Adams, Richard P., 30n
Adkins, Nelson F., 25, 30n, 39n, 40n, 42
American Monthly Magazine, 39-40, 40n, 205
Anthon, Charles: *A Classical Dictionary*, 173, 209, 211, 212
Arabian Nights, The, 16n
Athenaeum, 249
Atlantic, 251, 267

Bell, Michael Davitt, 80n
Bell, Millicent, 163n
Bridge, Horatio, 20, 22, 23, 153, 154n, 179, 180, 181, 184, 204n; *Journal of an African Cruiser*, 207n
Bunyan, John, 16; *The Pilgrim's Progress*, 100, 101
Byron, George Gordon (Lord), 17

Chandler, Elizabeth Lathrop, 30n
Channing, Ellery, 113
Charvat, William, 11, 12, 17n, 21n, 27, 27n, 124n, 152n, 153n
Chorley, Henry, 249
Clark, C. E. Frazer, Jr., 11, 82n, 86n
Colacurcio, Michael J., 88n, 92n
Coleridge, Samuel Taylor, 10, 58n
Cooper, James Fenimore, 17
Crews, Frederick C., 9-10, 110n, 245
Crowley, J. Donald, 11, 12, 69, 70n, 71n, 114n, 115n, 204n
Cummins, Maria Susanna: *The Lamplighter*, 19

Dante Alighieri, 234
Davidson, Edward H., 221n, 225, 254, 255n
Democratic Review, 101, 172, 205
Dickens, Charles, 220
Doubleday, Neal Frank, 11, 16n, 33n, 69n, 80-81
Duyckinck, Evert, 98, 115n, 172

Edgeworth, Richard L., *Memoirs*, 16n
Emerson, Ralph Waldo, 121, 147

Fielding, Henry: *Amelia*, 16n; *Tom Jones*, 16n
Fields, James T., 152, 153, 173, 174, 276
Fogle, Richard Harter, 9
Fossum, Robert H., 37n
Franklin, Benjamin, 18
Freud, Sigmund: *Moses and Monotheism*, 237
Fuller, Margaret, 199n

Gaskell, Elizabeth, 220
Gilkes, Lillian B., 40n
Godwin, William, 16n; *Caleb Williams*, 16n; *Mandeville*, 16n; *St. Leon*, 16n
Goodrich, Samuel G., 39
Graham's Monthly Magazine, 179n
Gross, Seymour L., 32n, 37n, 41n

Harper's, 271n

279

The Shape of Hawthorne's Career

Designed by R. E. Rosenbaum.
Composed by York Composition Company, Inc.,
in 11 point linotype Janson, 2 points leaded,
with display lines in Weiss.
Printed letterpress from type by York Composition Company
on Warren's Number 66 text, 50 pound basis.
Bound by John H. Dekker & Sons, Inc.
in Columbia book cloth
and stamped in All Purpose foil.

Library of Congress Cataloging in Publication Data
Baym, Nina.
  The shape of Hawthorne's career.

  Includes index.
  1. Hawthorne, Nathaniel, 1804–1864—Criticism and interpretation. I. Title.
PS1888.B3   813'.3   75-36994
ISBN 0-8014-0996-9